Table Tennis Tactics for Thinkers

By Larry Hodges
TableTennisCoaching.com
U.S. Table Tennis Hall of Famer and National Coach
©2013, v01-02-15

On the Cover:
My fellow MDTTC coach Cheng Yinghua, 2000 Olympian,
2-time U.S. Open and 4-time USA Nationals Men's Champion,
and former member of the Chinese and USA National Teams
Photo by John Oros

Table Tennis Tactics for Thinkers

TABLE OF CONTENTS

Introduction		3
Chapter One	Tactical Thinking	6
Chapter Two	Strategic Thinking	13
Chapter Three	Your Tactical Game	24
Chapter Four	All About Spin	39
Chapter Five	Beginning Tactics	52
Chapter Six	Conventional Tactics	59
Chapter Seven	Tactical Examples	72
Chapter Eight	Service Tactics	84
Chapter Nine	Receive Tactics	110
Chapter Ten	Rallying Tactics	125
Chapter Eleven	Different Grips	137
Chapter Twelve	Pushing	142
Chapter Thirteen	Loopers	149
Chapter Fourteen	Blockers, Counter-Drivers, and Hitters	160
Chapter Fifteen	Choppers	177
Chapter Sixteen	Fishers and Lobbers	187
Chapter Seventeen	Non-Inverted Surfaces	193
Chapter Eighteen	Hardbat Tactics	203
Chapter Nineteen	Doubles Tactics	215
Chapter Twenty	Tournament Tactics	223
Chapter Twenty-One	Coaching Tournament Matches	227
Afterword	Tactical and Strategic Thinking Revisited	231
Glossary	Table Tennis Terminology	232
Appendix	Recommended Reading	237
About the Author		238
Index		240

Larry Hodges

INTRODUCTION

Table tennis has been called chess at lightning speed. There are hundreds of books on chess tactics. Why aren't there more books devoted to table tennis tactics?

Future U.S. Table Tennis Hall of Famers John Tannehill and Dell Sweeris play chess at the 1968 U.S. Open. Photo by Mal Anderson

The purpose of this book isn't to just tell you how to play tactically against various styles, though we'll do that, but to get you thinking both tactically and strategically. What's the difference? I'll go over that. The goal is to make the most out of whatever table tennis skills you have so you can be world champion, beat the guy next door, or somewhere in between.

This book is for anyone who wants to make the most of his game, especially those who like to think. It is for all ages and levels, including:

- **Beginners**, who should focus on developing their game strategically so they can later have the tactical weapons needed to win;
- **Intermediate players**, who can execute many of the shots the best players do, and need to find ways to both maximize their tactical performance with the tools they have, and to strategically develop new weapons;
- **Advanced players**, who can use this book to develop—or further develop—the habit of thinking tactically and strategically so as to maximize their performance.

There are three ways you should use this book. First and most important, read it through, and develop the habit of tactical and strategic thinking. They are your friends. (I almost called this book "Table Tennis Tactics and Strategic Development," since strategic thinking is so much a part of it.)

Second, learn and understand the general tactics that you and your playing style should use against various playing styles. When I say playing

Table Tennis Tactics for Thinkers

styles here, that includes not only different styles of play, but also different grips and surfaces.

Third, it's a reference for when you are trying to figure out the specific tactics needed to beat a specific player. Once you've analyzed the player in question, go to the appropriate section or sections and understand the tactical ways to overcome that player.

There's a lot to digest here, so perhaps take it in chunks. Take notes or use a highlighter. Think about how each item may affect your game. Most important, don't memorize - *understand*.

There are some redundancies in the book, with some techniques discussed in multiple chapters. This is unavoidable since there are overlaps between the chapters. For example, pushing short is discussed in both the chapters on Receive and on Pushing. I don't want readers to have to constantly jump around in the book, and it doesn't hurt to hear something twice.

Most of this book is new, but some of it comes from past coaching articles I've written. (And some of the Tips of the Week that I put up on TableTennisCoaching.com came from this book as I was writing it.) And speaking of table tennis past, does having twenty-one chapters bring back some table tennis nostalgia?

Want to know more about the Olympic Sport of Table Tennis? In the U.S., visit USA Table Tennis at www.usatt.org, and learn about the hundreds of tournaments, clubs, and coaches throughout the country, including my club, the Maryland Table Tennis Center, where I've been coaching since it opened in 1992. Elsewhere, visit the International Table Tennis Federation at www.ittf.com, and see their directory for other countries.

You might also want to visit my table tennis website and daily blog, which goes up every morning, Mon-Fri, at TableTennisCoaching.com. I started the blog in Jan., 2011, and hopefully it'll still be there and going strong when you read this book. There you'll also find a huge number of articles, videos, and just about anything else that has to do with table tennis. (And you'll love the Fun & Games section, which links to all things involving table tennis humor—videos, pictures, games, etc.) You can also find info there on my other books on table tennis, all sold at LarryHodgesBooks.com:

- *Instructor's Guide to Table Tennis* (1989)
- *Table Tennis: Steps to Success* (1993, revised 2006, 28,000 copies sold)
- *Table Tennis Tales & Techniques* (2009)
- *Professional Table Tennis Coaches Handbook* (2009, updated 2013)
- *Table Tennis Tips* (2014)

I've adopted two conventions for this book. First, it is written as if the reader is right-handed. Lefties should reverse. My apologies, but this makes explaining things a lot easier. Second, I'm using "he" to describe players. I'm not going to write "he or she" and "him or her" a zillion times, nor s/he, or write everything in the plural so I can clumsily use "they" every time.

You are not expected to memorize this book, or to learn every tactical intricacy on its pages. There's something more important than that, and that is to get in the habit of thinking tactically and strategically. And so at the end of this book, in the Afterword, I will have one question for you: Did I make you think?

Glossary

Table tennis is full of colorful terms that some might not be familiar with. "Heavy no-spin"? "Half-long" and "Tweeny" serves? "Reverse Pendulum serves"? "Fishing"? "Banana" and "Strawberry" flips? Throughout this book, if you find a term you are not familiar with, go to the glossary at the back. Better still, why not browse it now, and familiarize yourself with any terms you might not know?

Editorial Board

I'd like to thank the following "Super Seven" coaches and players who reviewed, edited, proofed, and critiqued this book. Their insights and comments greatly added to the book as well as causing many long, sleepless nights as I pondered their notes.

- **Scott Gordon**, USATT Certified Coach and former chair USATT Hardbat Committee
- **Chris Grace**
- **Stephanie Hughes**
- **Richard McAfee,** USATT Coaching Chair, 2009-2013
- **John Olsen**, ITTF Certified Coach
- **Dennis Taylor**, former chair of USATT High Performance Committee
- **Kevin Walton**

And now it is time for you to enter into another dimension, a dimension not only of speed and spin, but of mind. A journey into a wondrous land of thought. It is a thing we call . . . table tennis tactics.

CHAPTER ONE
Tactical Thinking

Tactics isn't about finding complex strategies to defeat an opponent. Tactics is about sifting through all the zillions of possible tactics and finding a few simple ones that work.

In simpler terms, the purpose of tactics is to mess up your opponent.

You do this by messing up his game, and by forcing your game on his. More specifically, tactics is finding ways to get your strengths into play while avoiding your opponent's, and going after the opponent's weaknesses while not letting him go after yours. It's figuring out how you win and lose points.

Hopefully I'm giving good tactical advice to USA National Cadet Team Members Jonathan Ou and Tong Tong Gong at the Junior Team Competition at the 2011 USA Nationals.
Photo by Bruce Liu

To do this, you have to know both your game and your opponent's. While you might go into a match not knowing much about your opponent (though ideally you would have scouted him out in advance), you should know all about your game. How well do you know your game?

If you couldn't write a book about your game, either you don't know your game, or you have no game. (We'll get back to this shortly.)

Table tennis is a game of utter complexity and utter simplicity. If you get too caught up in the myriad of complex strategies available, you'll be lost in a sea of uncertainty. Think KISS—"Keep It Simple, Stupid." Most matches are tactically won on at most two or three tactical things, not the zillions that are possible. It's finding those two or three out of the zillions that's key. On the other hand, if your thinking is too simple, you aren't maximizing your play.

There's no conflict here. Much of tactics involves simplifying things so the game becomes simple and easy. If you use tactics that force your opponent into predictable returns that feed into your strengths, you've won the tactical battle and made the game simple and easy. In this book we'll cover the tactical and strategic ways of doing this, as well as the tactical frame of mind that makes tactical play come naturally. (We'll talk about the difference between "strategic" and "tactical" thinking soon—an important distinction.)

The primary purpose of this book is to help you think tactically and strategically, not just as an occasional thing, but as a habit. The more you do it, the more habitual it becomes, and the more you'll gain from it in terms of maximizing your game. Some of it might seem overwhelming to beginning and perhaps intermediate players, but with experience it'll all make sense.

Tactical thinking is a habit. I know some brilliant people who do not think at the table, and some not-so-brilliant ones who know exactly what they are doing out there. Which do you choose to be? It's a choice.

A comprehensive book on table tennis tactics would run about a zillion pages. If you look at just the membership of, say, USA Table Tennis, that's about 8000 members, or 8000 times 8000 tactical match-ups, or about 64 million tactical plans. Even if you narrow it down to 100 styles, that's 10,000 match-ups. Ten major styles? We're still talking 100 chapters. Instead of trying to be foolishly comprehensive, I'll cover each style's tactical strengths and weaknesses. I'll try to give you a feel for what's needed to both play with and against these styles, so you can figure out what you, with your style, need to do. You don't learn tactical thinking by just being told what to do; you develop it by thinking about it and applying it in match situations. It takes practice.

You shouldn't have to memorize everything. Tactical thinking is a habit you should develop, and the first step is to *understand* why certain tactics work.

We will cover the major points you should know about the major styles, and some of the subtle ones. Rather than tell you everything, the goal here is to give you a good starting point, and help you get into a tactical state of mind so you can come up with a good tactical plan for your matches—for that is the $64 million dollar question you have to answer every time you compete.

There are chapters on the various grips, surfaces, strokes, and playing styles. These chapters mostly cover it from both the point of view of the ones using these attributes, and the ones playing against them. So the chapter on loopers is both about what a looper wants to do, and what you want to do against a looper.

Tactics is not an exact science. Everyone's different, and when there are two on the table (or four in doubles), the complexities magnify. *Tactics are not rigid rules, just guidelines.* Repeat that three times.

For example, one of the basic rules of playing a chopper is to attack the middle, where choppers are weakest. I strongly urge you to learn to do this. And yet, when I play a chopper, I only occasionally go after the middle, even though I'm probably stronger against that style than any other. Why? Because for me, and my particular game, I have a deceptive forehand

Table Tennis Tactics for Thinkers

that fools choppers into going the wrong way. And so I focus on wide angles, and watch as choppers break the wrong way. But that's just me. (I'll talk more about this and choppers later on.) I'm not the only one with a unique way of playing a style. Jan-Ove Waldner, arguably the greatest player ever, also ate up choppers, and much of his tactics involved sidespin looping. Few other players near his level play choppers that way, but it worked for Waldner. (And yes, I did just mention my tactics in the same paragraph as Waldner's—author's privilege.)

Tactics are meaningless if you can't execute the shots necessary. So a book on tactics is not a substitute for coaching and practice. Develop your game, and do so strategically—there's a whole chapter here on that, "Strategic Thinking."

This is not a book about sports psychology, a related topic. Given a choice between a player with average tactics who is "in the zone" (i.e. playing very well) or a player with great tactics who is not "in the zone" (i.e. not playing very well), take the one in the zone every time. However, good tactics will allow you to win matches you might otherwise lose when you are not playing very well, as well as keeping opponents uncomfortable so they do not get into the zone. And if you have good tactics when you *are* in the zone . . . the sky's the limit!

The Myth of Thinking Too Much

I mentioned above you don't want to get caught up in the myriad of complex tactics available. Many players are accused of "thinking too much." The real problem is in knowing *when* to think. (You *can* think too much if you try too many complicated tactics; remember KISS and keep it simple. This is covered later in the section on "Common Tactical Thinking Problems," under "Don't overdo the tactics: Choose the best few.")

The rule is simple. In a match, you think between games and between points. When the point is about to play, you stop thinking consciously. You blank your mind out and just let go. It is thinking during the point that causes a person to freeze up with uncertainty, often labeled as choking. Once the point begins, the conscious you is not controlling play; it is your subconscious that takes over.

One important item, however—between points you should keep your thinking relatively simple since you need to be able to clear your mind for the next point, and it's not easy doing that if you are having deep thoughts between each point. If you find yourself furiously thinking about tactics, then you've gone too far, and probably can't clear your mind when it's time to play a point. Tactical thinking should be very objective and unemotional. In fact, once you know what you are doing in a match, you don't need to think too much, just focus on executing your tactics and making adjustments. Be ready to rethink your tactics when necessary.

Think about what actually happens when you play. Suppose your opponent gives you a backspin. Do you consciously say to yourself, "Ah, the ball has backspin. I must aim up to return it." Hopefully not! Instead, after facing backspins for a while—and probably messing up at the start, and telling yourself you need to aim up against backspin—your subconscious gets the message, and it becomes habit. The same is true of tactics. To quote 2003 World Men's Singles Champion Werner Schlager (from his book *Tips from a World Champion*): "The faster you play the more important subconscious tactical decisions become."

How can you play tactics during the point if you aren't thinking during the point? The answer is if you spend enough time thinking about tactics, it will get absorbed by your subconscious, and tactics will become mostly reflexive. If you decide you need to loop a deep serve, you don't wait until you see a deep serve, and tell yourself, "Ah, a deep serve. I should loop it." Instead, remind yourself regularly of what you need to do, the subconscious will get the message, and you'll do it automatically. It becomes ingrained.

What does this mean? It means that a major part of tactics is developing reflexive tactics to cover basic situations.

Thinking too much is not a problem. It's thinking at the wrong time, such as an inability to turn off the thinking and clear the mind as the point begins, that is the problem. If frozen by indecision, then that's a *lack* of thinking. Make a tactical decision and be decisive.

Of course, some experienced players will protest that this entire book is an example of over-thinking, that tactics are simple—you find what works and do it. (And there's a certain truth to that.) This type of player probably plays pretty good but relatively basic tactics; however, he has been doing it so long it is instinctive—and he doesn't even realize it. Because he's now mostly relying on his instincts to play good tactics, he may no longer be thinking tactically, and so will have trouble playing *great* tactics. (There will also be a small number of compulsive non-thinking types who simply cannot comprehend the vast array of tactics available, but let's not worry about them; let's just take them down at the table.)

Strategic Versus Tactical Thinking

What's the difference? Strategic thinking is how you develop your game. Tactical thinking is how you use what you already have to win. Strategic thinking is long-term planning while tactical thinking is short-term, usually confined to a specific match. (These are the general definitions, and they are what I will use in this book though they are not

Table Tennis Tactics for Thinkers

universal.)

For example, a strategic thinker with a good loop might think about what types of serves will set up his loop, and develop those serves in practice sessions. A tactical thinker might think about what serves he should use to set up his loop in a match against a given opponent. Strategic thinking takes place during the developmental stage of your game—which never ends as long as you are still practicing. Tactical thinking takes place while preparing for and playing a specific match.

Suppose you have a weak forehand attack against backspin. When an opponent pushes heavy to your forehand, you have to tactically choose whether to use your weak forehand attack (perhaps using good ball placement to make up for the weakness of the attack), or whether to just push it back. Tactically, these may be your only options. Strategically, you should note this weakness in your game and go practice your forehand attack against backspin so next time you aren't so limited tactically.

It is the strategic thinking that leads to developing the tools needed for tactical play. But it works both ways—it is tactical thinking that makes you aware of what parts of your game need development, which leads to strategic thinking. Call it the Circle Of Strategy & Tactics, or COST.

Many years ago there were two juniors at my club. Both started out together, and by age twelve were getting pretty good. One mostly won by pushing and blocking, a winning tactic, while the other mostly attacked, using tactics to allow himself to do so. When they played in tournaments, the pusher/blocker won over and over. Then one tournament match the pusher/blocker tried to win by attacking, and lost. After the match his father yelled at him, and over the next year his father made him play tactically, both in practice and tournaments, relying on his pushing and blocking to win. The other junior continued to attack, even though he kept losing to the pusher/blocker. Then, predictably, about a year later the attacker began winning, and soon his level was much higher. This was a classic case of strategic thinking (the attacker) versus tactical thinking (the pusher/blocker). You need both.

There are also countless cases of strategic thinkers who never learn to play tactically, and so never win at the level they should win. You need to learn both strategic and tactical thinking. It's a balance. From a mental and tactical standpoint, you should develop the mindset that you should win, and expect to win, against players at your level, and even those above. Playing matches strategically too often (and thereby not thinking tactically) may affect this winning mindset. So find a balance.

As you read these pages, think about how each topic relates to your own game—which is both tactical and strategic thinking.

Find Out What Works

Ultimately, this is all tactics is about. No matter what someone tells you, or what this or some other book or article says, the correct tactics for winning are whatever works. (Within the rules and spirit of the game. Cheating and bad sportsmanship are not options.) The wrong tactics are the ones that don't work. *Never forget this!*

And yet, you don't always want to play tactically. Note the story of the two juniors I wrote about above, who approached the game very differently. The slightly better one played to win now, while the second one played the way he hoped someday to win, and in the end, became the far better player by playing strategically. This *doesn't* mean you don't play tactically. If you strategically decide to attack, then choose the appropriate tactics that allow you to do so. That's what our rising junior attacker did, and after a year of this, he could serve short and attack consistently, and could also loop his pushing-and-blocking opponent's serve. He had developed his game both strategically *and* tactically.

How Much Better Will Tactics Make Me?

This is a good question, but there are two answers. In the short term, good tactics instead of average tactics might improve a player something like 100 USATT ratings points, perhaps a bit less at higher levels, somewhat more at lower levels. (Roughly speaking, this means you will now play even with a player who normally beats you five out of six times.) But tactical thinking leads to strategic thinking which leads to major improvement in the long run. Without this type of thinking most players get stuck and stop improving.

Your Book on Table Tennis

Your Table Tennis Game
By You

Earlier I wrote, "If you couldn't write a book about your game, either you don't know your game, or you have no game." I meant that literally. This doesn't mean you have to actually write this book. Such a book would most likely have an audience of one, though a few of your tournament opponents might be interested. But that one primary reader—you—is the most important person to your table tennis game. So start thinking about that

Table Tennis Tactics for Thinkers

book.

     Many long-time players could actually write this book, but have never really thought about it. At first they might think it's silly, but when they start thinking about all the things they've learned as they've developed their games—serves, receives, strokes, footwork, drills to improve, equipment, tournament play, tactics for their game, tactics against all the many styles and players they've learned to play against, the mental game—they start to realize just how much they could write about. Even if you haven't played that long you should be able to write at least a short book, perhaps a manual. Start thinking about your game, and the pages will practically write themselves.

     While you don't have to actually write this book, I urge you to take notes for it. During my first few years I kept a notebook. On all the right-hand pages, I kept running notes on my own game—mostly strategic notes on what parts of my game needed improvement and how to improve it. On the left-hand page, I kept notes on opponents—generally a page for every major opponent I played (or watched, if I thought I'd be playing them), with detailed tactical notes. These notes should give you a clear idea on what you need to work on to develop your game.

CHAPTER TWO
Strategic Thinking

Strategic thinking is how you develop the tools you will use tactically. If you don't have the proper tools, you can't get the job done. It's like driving a nail with a screwdriver—you are using the wrong tool.

There are two main ways strategic development can go wrong.

ITTF Coaching Seminar in Maryland, USA, where 14 coaches learned to think strategically.
Photo by Shaobo "Bob" Zhu

First, and most commonly, a player simply doesn't develop certain techniques, and so they aren't there when they are needed. For example, suppose your opponent likes to serve short backspin and loop, and he has a tremendous loop against any deep ball. If you push long or flip, the ball goes long, and he attacks, and he dominates the point. But his serve is a simple backspin serve, and all you have to do is push it short. Except, gosh darn it, you don't know how to push short. You forgot to add that to your toolbox when you were developing your game! And so you do not have the necessary tool for this match.

Often a player experiments with a new tactical tool, but because he's not comfortable using it at first, he stops using it and so never develops it. If you are in that position, force yourself to use and develop the needed tools, even if it means taking a few beatings at the table in practice matches at first—remember, they are called *practice* matches for a reason. *Much of strategic development is doing what's uncomfortable to make it comfortable.* For example, when you first work on pushing short, you'll make lots of mistakes—you'll pop the ball up or go into the net. But if you stick with it, you'll gain that control, and then you'll be tactically ready to face that looper who likes deep balls—all because you thought (and played) strategically.

Second, a player may have mismatched tools, like the nail and screwdriver above. Suppose you have a nice forehand loop against backspin, but all your best serves are topspin. You aren't going to get very many backspin returns off your serve.

In both cases, you have a strategic problem which leads to tactical problems. So how do you develop your game strategically? By developing a successful playing style.

Table Tennis Tactics for Thinkers

Playing Style

When you start out, you need to develop the fundamentals. As you develop your shots, your playing style will gradually emerge. Some players have a firm idea on how they want to play almost from the start—hitter, looper, blocker, chopper, etc. Others aren't sure at first, often for years, as they develop their game. And styles often change. I was an all-out hitter my first few years, and then switched gradually to all-around, with equal emphasis between looping, hitting, blocking, and a little bit of just about everything else.

Style comes from two things: what the player does well, and what the player wants to do. They are not always the same, but they usually have a large overlap as players tend to get better at the things they want to do (because they use them more), and they tend to want to do the things that they do well, since that leads to winning. So most often players naturally develop a style based on these two factors. Others may want to play a specific style, perhaps because they saw a top player play that way. They may simply want to be a chopper or lobber because of the spectacular points they play. Or they may have developed a blocking style, but then decided they wanted to play like most world-class players and become a looper. (That's a primary reason why I switched from all-out hitting to more looping.)

I regularly advise players on how to develop their games, with two things in mind. First, they should develop an over-powering strength (or strengths), something that will dominate at whatever level they are at, and develop a style around those strengths. This also means strategically developing the tactical tools that allow them to use their strengths. Second, they should develop all aspects of the game they will use since having strengths do not help if opponents can simply play into their weaknesses. So I try to lead them into a style that will win for them. But that style also has to match what they want to do. There's no point telling someone to be a looper if he hates looping, like one of my students.

Once you have begun developing a style, you should continue to develop that style *strategically*. Watch players with similar styles, learn what they do and *why* (this is important—don't be afraid to ask the player). Incorporate into your game whatever you think will work for you.

Since rallies begin with serve and receive, this means developing serves and receives that work for your style. This is probably the most under-utilized, under-thought, and under-developed part of most players' games.

For example, if you have a nice loop against backspin, it might not be to your advantage to push too many short serves back long, since this gives the opponent a chance to loop and so lowers the chance of a backspin return you can loop. It also might not be to your advantage to flip, which gets you into a topspin rally, and again takes away your loop against backspin. Instead, a player like this might develop a short push, which increases the chances that the opponent will push it back long to you, giving you that backspin ball to loop. Similarly, short backspin serves will often give you long push returns to loop. And if you serve topspin, you are unlikely to get a backspin return from most players. (This doesn't mean you don't vary in these other receives and serves, just remember they are variations to the shots that should be more central to your game. For example, a sudden long push receive against some players will often result in a push return to set up your loop.)

If you are a hitter or counter-hitter who likes to get into fast, bang-bang topspin rallies, you might want to serve and receive more with topspin. Or you might serve short backspin and follow with a slow, steady loop to get into those topspin rallies.

Find the unique aspects of your style that give opponents trouble and focus on winning with those shots. Germany's Timo Boll, the #1 European as I write this, forehand loops with a somewhat unorthodox forehand grip. This gives him one of the best inside-out loops in the world (his lefty loops usually break to his left), and he uses this to great effect. Much of his

Timo Boll of Germany
Photo by Diego Schaaf

game is used to set up this shot, which is a primary reason he's often the only European who can challenge the Chinese. At the same time, if a shot is too unorthodox, consider whether the benefits of the shot outweigh the negatives, since the very fact that it is unorthodox means it likely has problems, or it would become "orthodox." (Sometimes the unorthodox becomes orthodox, such as reverse penhold backhands or attacking short serves to the forehand with the backhand.)

Another thing to think about when developing your style is how your serves and receives affect it, and vice versa. Your style should dictate what types of serves and receives you use. At the same time, your style may develop *because* of your serve and receive. For example, if you develop a serve that players keep popping up, you might develop a nice smash, and you are well on your way to becoming a hitter—all because of the serve y

Table Tennis Tactics for Thinkers

developed. Or if you have a nice backspin serve, you'll get a lot of backspin returns, and so you might develop a nice loop, and you are well on your way to becoming a looper—all because of the serve you developed. Or if you are good at attacking serves, you might develop an all-out attacking style as a result. So while you should develop serve and receive to match your style, sometimes your style comes from the serve and receive.

Ultimately, you should develop a personal style that's all your own, and really know your style. (Remember that part about being able to write a book on your game?) Keep adding strategic aspects to your game, both to address your current game, but just as importantly, where your game is going.

Your "B" Game

What if you've diligently developed a style of play, but play someone who happens to be good against that style? Perhaps the opponent does something that completely stops you from doing what you do best. Or perhaps your best shot is simply not working that day. What then?

Most players develop both an "A" style, and a "B" style when in trouble. (It's usually referred to as their "A" game and "B" game.) For example, a looper might play someone who serves and receives short serves short while attacking deep serves. The looper may not be able to find many balls to loop—and when he does, suppose the opponent is a very good blocker as well. What to do? If he only has his "A" looping game, the looper has a serious problem. But if he can switch to, say, a steady counter-hitting game, serving and receiving with topspin to get into fast exchanges, he might be able to win that way.

To use a personal example, my "A" game involves lots of forehand attack, especially when I'm serving. Sometimes I play an opponent who is just too quick and consistent, and who places balls at wide angles, for me to keep using the forehand. So I switch to a steady counter-hitting game, especially on the opponent's serve, my "B" game. If that doesn't work, I'll even bring in my "C" game, and drop back and chop, fish, and lob. (Note that my forehand-attacking "A" game is really two games as well—sometimes I focus on forehand looping, other times on forehand hitting.)

Another classic example would be Cheng Yinghua, a fellow coach at the Maryland Table Tennis Center. During his prime years (11 years on Chinese National Team, then 2-time U.S. Open and 4-time

Cheng Yinghua
Photo by John Oros

16

U.S. National Men's Champion) he essentially had three games: two-winged looping, all-out forehand looping, and a straight blocking game. At his prime he'd mostly two-wing loop (his primary "A" game), mix in all-out forehand looping (sort of a secondary "A" game), and fall back on blocking (his "B" game) when in trouble. After he came to the U.S. and got older, he became more of a blocker, and his looping game became his "B" game—which he'd often pull out at the end of a close match as a surprise.

More Strategic Development: How to Move Up a Level

What does it mean to move up a level in table tennis? I'd define two players to be on different levels if it would be a major upset if one defeated the other. Another way of looking at it would be to say that if the stronger player plays his normal level, he would win nearly every time, though he might get challenged occasionally.

Based on this, I'd say that a level in table tennis (using the USATT rating system) ranges from about 300 points at the lower levels (under 1000) to about 100 points at the higher levels (over 2500). For most USATT players, a level would be about 200 points.

How can you move up a level? By improving all major aspects of your game, because one weak link in your game is like a weak link in a chain.

You could work hard, dramatically improve one aspect of your game, and hope to move up a level. But it's not that simple. Suppose you develop a really nice forehand loop. With this weapon, you would think that your level would go up dramatically. And sure enough, you will do better against players around your own level.

But when you play players a level higher, their level is far enough ahead of yours that they'll simply do something to disarm your new weapon. They may serve or push short, push very heavy, throw spinny or fast serves at you, use ball placement, block well, force backhand exchanges, play quick shots, or simply attack first to take your weapon (in this case your forehand loop) away.

Often, stronger players will seem to win as a result of one of their strengths, when in fact they are winning by exploiting a weakness of yours that allows them to use their strength. A strength in your game can

Table Tennis Tactics for Thinkers

compensate for a weakness, but only to a certain extent. A stronger player will simply go after your weaknesses.

The lesson is that to move up a level, you need to strategically improve your game overall, not just one aspect. A player who is a level stronger than you rarely defeats you with one aspect of his game; he does so by using the overall level of his game.

There are, of course, players who have improved all but one aspect of their game, and, by improving that one final aspect, suddenly go up the coveted level. But they do so not just by developing that final aspect, but by having developed the other aspects as well.

So how do you go about moving your game up a level? You have to be able to strategically match the higher-level players on **five key things**:

Five Things Needed to Move Up a Level

1. Returning your opponents' serves as well as they return yours.

2. Either rally as fast as your opponents do, or force your opponents to rally at your pace (by slowing the pace down with pushes, slow loops, controlled drives, etc.). Rallying at their pace can also mean reacting to their pace (i.e. blocking or chopping), because "pace" means both speed and quickness.

3. Reacting to your opponents' rallying spins (loops, pushes, chops, lobs, spins returned by long pips, etc.) as well as they react to yours.

4. Ending the point (i.e. smashing or loop killing) as well as your opponents do. This can also mean stopping them from ending the point effectively or consistently by not giving them easy shots, or it can mean a series of strong shots that win the point.

5. And finally, possessing at least one strength that threatens your opponents as much as their strengths threaten you. It could be your serve or receive, or something you do in rallies, often a shot that ends the point. If your strength is a rallying shot, you also have to have ways to get that strength into play, either with serve or receive, or some other rallying shot.

You may have noted that tactics is not one of the five "keys." This is because tactics is part of all five. Stronger/weaker tactics simply make you stronger/weaker in each key. The same is true of physical fitness, which is part of all or most of the five keys.

If you can do some (but not all) of the above five keys, your performance in matches will go up some, perhaps even half a level, but not a full level. Developing a single "overpowering" strength won't raise your level as much as you'd think, as opponents a level higher will beat you on the less developed parts of your game. Even players at your "previous" level will still often beat you by exploiting these weaknesses. But . . . if you work to improve all five of these keys, you may find yourself going up dramatically.

What's stronger, a chain with four powerful links and one weak one, or a chain with five pretty strong ones?

Specifics on Strategic Development

Most of this chapter has been on general or even theoretical strategic development. Let's get down to specifics.

No two players play the same, so there are no rules on how you must play. Some readers of this might play such an outlandish style that very little they read here or elsewhere specifically applies to them—other than the type of thinking they should employ in developing this outlandish style. But there are a number of things the large majority of players should focus on to strategically develop their games. Many of the details come later in this book, but here's a short list.

Serve: Learn a wide variety of serves. Develop short serves that opponents have difficulty attacking, and that allow you to serve and attack. Also develop deep serves as variations that may give opponents trouble. (Some even develop their games around deep serves, though that's difficult at the higher levels.) The goal is to develop serves that set up whatever it is you do best.

Receive: Focus on receives that get you either into neutral rallies, or (better still) rallies that you can dominate. Be consistently aggressive against deep serves. Learn control, placement, and consistency against short serves.

Rallies: Develop an overpowering strength (or strengths), and develop your serves, receives, and other shots to set up this strength. It might be your forehand or backhand loop or smash. It might be your blocking or chopping. It might be your overall consistency. But you must have *something* that scares your opponents.

Footwork: Learn to move to the ball—develop positional footwork. Learn to move and cover much of the table with your best shot or shots, which is often the forehand.

Tactics: Learn to think tactically so as to best use the tools you have.

Table Tennis Tactics for Thinkers

Coaching Against Yourself

One thing that will help in your strategic development is to imagine coaching someone against yourself. What would you tell them? Now imagine coaching yourself to fix up the very weaknesses that you would coach an opponent to tactically use against you. The top authority on your game should be you, so listen to yourself; you are a wise and knowledgeable coach! (If not, then some tactical and strategic thinking can change that.) Learn to mentally coach both sides of a match, yours and the opponent, both tactically and strategically. It's a great exercise in developing your game in both ways.

Play Both Weaker and Stronger Players

Many players who want to improve make the mistake of trying to play only stronger players. The result is the opponent controls play, and all the player can do is react to the stronger player's shots, or go for wild shots. A player may develop some shots this way, but it'll be hard to strategically develop new shots or to learn how to use them in a game situation.

If you are trying to improve you need to both try out new shots that you are developing and to try out new combinations and strategies. If you do this against a stronger player, you probably won't do so well, and you'll probably stop doing it. You won't have any way of knowing if the new shot, combination or strategy may work since the stronger player may win the point simply by being a stronger player against something you are just trying out and are not yet comfortable with.

Instead, strategically try out new things against players who are weaker than you. Develop them against these players, in an environment where you can control play a little more (since you are the stronger player), and where you can see if the new things might work. Don't worry about winning or losing—this is practice—as you will undoubtedly lose sometimes when trying out something new, even against a weaker player. (Imagine how bad you'd lose in this case against a stronger player!) When your new techniques begin to work against a weaker player, then it's time to try them out against your peers and stronger players.

Example: suppose you want to develop your loop against backspin. The best way to do this is to serve backspin, and loop the pushed return. A stronger player may flip the serve, push short, quick push to a corner, or push extremely heavy—and you won't be able to develop the shot very well. A weaker player would be more likely to give you a ball that you can loop, which is what you need until the shot is more developed. You need to both develop the shot and your instincts on when to use it, how to follow it up, etc. When you can do it against a weaker player, then it's time to try it out against tougher competition.

Larry Hodges

Learn From Your Losses

The quickest way to learn how to beat a stronger player is by losing to him while understanding why you lost. This way you know what to work on so as to increase your chances of winning next time, or at some time in the future—it involves strategic and tactical thinking. It's a continuous learning process, and players who improve rapidly are constantly learning.

For example, if your opponent keeps beating you by attacking your wide forehand, and you aren't able to move to cover it, then the problem isn't your forehand defense—it's your inability to move to cover it. So don't spend the next few months working just on forehand blocking or counterlooping. Think strategically and do footwork drills where you practice covering that wide forehand against attacks. Think tactically and develop tactics so that you don't give that opponent an angle into your wide forehand. It's all these bits and pieces learned here and there that add up to a savvy player.

One of the interesting things one learns when talking to top players is that they say they are still learning. Some make it a goal to learn something new each time they play. Do you?

Strategic or Tactical Play?

Sometimes you have to choose between playing strategically or tactically. For example, during the writing of this book I coached Tong Tong Gong at the USA Nationals in December, 2011, which included the trials for the National Cadet Team.

I also coached him the previous year, at the 2010 Cadet Trials, when he was 13. He went in seeded

Two-time USA National Cadet Team Member Tong Tong Gong glares icicles as he and I discuss tactics between games.
Photo by Bruce Liu

#9. To make the team, he had to finish in the top four. With strong backhand play (both hitting and looping) but a relatively weak forehand, he pulled off four upsets in a row to grab the #4 spot.

Strategically, he needed a better forehand. So over the next year his focus was on forehand play and

Two-time USA National Cadet Team Member Tong Tong Gong glares icicles as he and I discuss tactics between games.
Photo by Bruce Liu

Table Tennis Tactics for Thinkers

forehand footwork. (Most of his training was with top coaches and players Cheng Yinghua, Jack Huang, Jeffrey Zeng Xun, and Han Xiao, some of the best players in the U.S., whose level of play can push players like Tong Tong at a higher level than I can, alas.) We knew he was never going to be an all-out forehand attacker, but by playing that way, he developed his forehand far faster. As could be expected, the more he played forehand, the better it got—but it also meant that he was using less backhand, his strength, and his tournament results showed this. It was a depressing year for him as he lost many matches he might have won by playing more backhand. He was bigger, stronger, and had a more powerful forehand, and it seemed he should have been much better than before—yet his results were only marginally better than a year before.

Going into the 2011 Nationals and cadet trials, the last year he'd be eligible for the cadets, he was seeded #10, one spot *lower* than the previous year. (He's actually gone up slightly in rating, but the depth of the competition had improved.) His forehand was now pretty good, and he could even control the table with it. The problem was that he was now playing his pretty good forehand more and more, and so he was using his strong backhand less and less. It was a five-day tournament, and the Cadet Trials were on days four and five. Playing in other events the first three days, he lost over and over, often in close matches where, under pressure, his forehand let him down. Since he was focusing on his forehand, his backhand play also suffered. All the forehand play had been great strategically. However, tactically he was losing matches because of it, and he was about to play the most important matches he would play that year.

The night before the Cadet Trials I told him it was time to unleash his backhand. (I probably should have told him to do this before the Nationals.) And so for the Cadet Trials he switched to a more two-winged attack. This brought his backhand into play more often, and since he was now focusing on it equally with his forehand, his backhand was once again very strong. Since he no longer was running about so much trying to loop forehands from all over the court, in fast rallies he only had to cover the forehand side with his forehand. Because of that, his forehand loop went up a level. Players who went that way paid for it, as Tong Tong would often forehand counterloop off the bounce, usually with a hooking loop to the wide forehand (i.e. with sidespin so the ball broke left). If they went to his backhand, he was even stronger. And when there was a weak ball to any part of the table, he could now quickly move into position to forehand rip it.

This time he pulled off five upsets (including beating the #1 seed, deuce in the fifth), and made the team, finishing in the #3 position. Tactically, he played brilliantly. Strategically, he's going to continue to develop his two-winged attack, focusing on turning his pretty-good forehand into a powerful one, and turning his powerful backhand into a devastating one. (On a side note, doesn't he have the perfect name for our sport—yes, Tong Tong Gong *can* play ping-pong!)

Use It or Lose It!

When a player finds that a part of his game is not working as well as he'd like (either because he is getting older or slower, or because it simply wasn't a strong shot to start with), the tendency is to use the shot less and less. Result? The shot gets even weaker.

The classic case is an aging player who finds that his footwork is not as fast as before, or his loop not as strong. He begins to play a more passive game, with less footwork and less looping, and thinks it will help his game. However, all this does is start a downward spiral. By moving and looping less, the player's footwork and loop get worse—and so the player uses them even less! And so the player's level drops even more. This is exactly what I've faced for years, and my response has been to stubbornly (and strategically) keep moving about, trying to keep up with the much faster kids, and the result is my footwork is still pretty fast for my age (almost 53 at this writing). There's also the side problem that when an aging player plays more passively, the game becomes less physical, he gets less of a physical workout, and so the game becomes less of a health benefit.

Tactically, it might be best to stop using a shot that isn't as effective as before. Strategically, this may be the worst thing you can do. Find a balance.

The moral: *Use It or Lose It!*

Table Tennis Tactics for Thinkers

CHAPTER THREE
Your Tactical Game

Chapter one was on Tactical Thinking. Now we're going to apply your tactical thinking to your tactical game.

What is tactical thinking? Tactical thinking is how you figure out the best way to use what you have to win. Pretty simple, right?

The goal of tactics is to mess up your opponent. That's all there is to it.

Tactical thinking is a habit. Many highly intelligent people are not good tactical players because they never developed the habit. And I've seen some not-too-bright people who were good tactical players because, yes, they spent a lot of time watching and observing, and learned what to do to maximize their games—and so became very good tactical players.

My fellow MDTTC Coach Jack Huang coaching USA #1 Under 12 Girl and National Cadet Team Member Crystal Wang.

Tactical thinking takes place in six settings: Between tournaments, before matches, after matches, between games, between points, and during practice. The one time you *don't* think is during points—that's when you let your subconscious take over and do what it has been trained to do. Let's go over each of these.

Between tournaments

When I say "between tournaments," you should read "between important events." This may be league matches or even practice matches. I'm just using "tournaments" for short.

Between tournaments is where you tactically and strategically think about your game and how best to use it. Don't just think; figure out what parts of your game need further development and what new parts you should add, and actively develop those aspects. A good tactician still needs as many weapons as possible; he doesn't want to get stuck with a knife at a gun fight.

For example, suppose you have a nice loop against backspin. Against some players, you can serve and loop over and over. But then you play a stronger player who you think you might be able to compete with—

but unlike the weaker players you were playing, he's looping your serve, which you now realize is going long. (A short serve would, given the chance, bounce twice on the other side of the table, making it difficult or impossible for the opponent to loop.) What do you do? Start working on shorter serves, of course. Then, when you play those stronger players, you'll have that short serve in your arsenal.

This is not always as simple as it seems. Continuing on the example of long versus short serves, some players develop very spinny and deceptive serves that work over and over against their peers. Then they find that if they overuse them, stronger players can attack them effectively because they are going deep. It might be difficult to learn to do these same serves short, and so you'd have to learn a whole new type of short serves. You'd still have your spinny and deceptive long serves as a variation, but if you don't develop short serves as well, you'll probably spend the rest of your table tennis life beating the same players while losing to the stronger ones who can attack that deep serve. Many fall into this trap. Do you?

Between tournaments is also where you spend your practice matches experimenting on various tactics to see what works. More on this later.

Before matches

Do you know your opponent? If not, have you scouted him out? Try to see him play so you have a good idea of what you are up against. Ask others who have played or watched him play, and see if they have suggestions. You want to go into the match with a good idea of what the opponent can do, and a good idea of what you want to do. This way you'll start off with an advantage, and may even win the first game while your opponent is still trying to figure out what to do against you.

Everyone has a different "checklist" of things to look for in an opponent before a match. See the "Watch" listing coming up shortly in the "Developing Your Tactical Thinking" section for a listing of possible things you should watch for, and pick out the ones you think might be important for you.

After matches

What happened in the last match? You should analyze both what worked and what didn't. What serves were effective? What serves gave the opponent fits as long as they weren't over-used? What type of set-up did each serve give you? What type of receives worked? Was it best to play control or aggressive receives? Where did you want to place your returns? Were there specific receives that took the server out of his game, or was it best to vary things to throw him off? What rallying tactics worked? These are some of the things you should be thinking about after a match. Remember

Table Tennis Tactics for Thinkers

these things or you'll have to start from scratch the next time you play that player. You might write them down. And remember that whatever worked or didn't work in that match is not just for that player—the same things should work or not work against some other players. As you find what does and does not work against various styles, you develop your tactical game.

Between games

This is where you analyze what happened in the last game, and figure out what, if anything, you need to change tactically in the next game. You want to have a clear idea in your head of what worked—what serves, receives, and rally shots. Serve and receive are particularly important here, as you have more control over them. This is especially true of the serve, where you have 100% control. At the lower levels, players can't do too much tactically on the receive because they simply do not yet have the control. As they improve, they gain this control, and receive gains in importance. At the intermediate and advanced levels, it's important between games to settle on perhaps two or three serves that you have confidence in, one or two receives, and a general idea of what type of rallies you want.

Between points

This is where you plan out the next point, especially if you are serving. When I say "plan out," it has to be a very flexible plan, since you don't know what the opponent is going to do.

If you are serving, you must decide what serve to use. Generally go with the serve that will maximize your scoring the point. That sounds obvious, right? But sometimes you want to hold back on a serve that might force a miss or set you up for a strong follow-up because if you over-use it, the opponent will get used to it. Also, if you use it too much in a game you win easily (or lose badly), you've wasted the serve, and the opponent is now more used to it.

You also have to decide whether to go with a "trick" serve (where you try to score with the serve outright, or at least get an easy setup) or a more standard third-ball serve (where the opponent is less likely to miss outright or pop the ball up, but is very likely to give you a ball to attack.) Trick serves work best at the lower levels; as you advance, they are also the serves that are often easiest for opponents to attack, putting you on the defensive. So you may want to focus more on third-ball serves, and use the trick serves as a variation.

Beware—between points is where some players fall into the trap of "overthinking." Keep your thinking simple between points. Too much thinking here will make it difficult to clear your mind for the next point. Which should be the last thing you do between points.

During points

Don't think. Just before the point begins, blank your mind out, and just play. If you've been thinking tactically, and made it a habit, your subconscious, which controls your actual play, will get the message. Remember what Werner Schlager said: "The faster you play the more important subconscious tactical decisions become." While there might be some conscious thinking during a slow rally (such as when smashing lobs or pushing), you should limit that as much as possible. Trust your subconscious, i.e. your instincts.

You should also avoid conscious thinking when returning serves. You may seem to have a lot of time against a slow incoming serve, but you don't have time to consciously recognize the spin, speed, direction, and dept of the serve, note the positioning of your opponent, and then decide what shot you should respond with. It has to be instinctive, i.e. subconscious.

During Practice

This is where you think strategically about what you learned during matches (and thinking about them afterwards), and practice what is needed to give you the tools needed for tactical play. Be very specific in figuring out what you need to work on. I remember watching a player lose a match because he kept making weak pushes off the opponent's serve, giving the opponent easy forehand loops. Afterwards, the player focused on working on his own forehand loop in the belief that he wanted his loop to be as good as his opponent's—not a bad strategic goal—but of course the real problem was he was giving the opponent easy loops.

DEVELOPING YOUR TACTICAL THINKING

There are four parts to developing your tactical game. *WEAR them!*

- **W**atch
- **E**xperiment
- **A**nalyze
- **R**emember

Watch

You should make a habit of watching and studying both top players and peers.

You should watch top players to learn. They have been doing this for years, probably decades, and there's a reason they are top players. Not all of them are great tacticians, but all of them have, at minimum, developed lots of effective tactics. What do they do to maximize their game, and what can you learn from this?

Table Tennis Tactics for Thinkers

You watch peers both to learn from them—everyone has something you can learn from, even if it's learning what *not* to do—and to learn how to beat them. What do they do to maximize their game, and what can you learn from this? The more they play like you, style-wise, the more you can learn. But be careful—if they are peers, then by definition they are not as good as the top players you should also be watching. This is especially true of their techniques (which is outside the focus of this book—see TableTennisCoaching.com for info and links on technical development). However, many lower-level players are very good tacticians, and you can learn from them, as long as you understand what they are doing.

When watching others play, learn to recognize what they are trying to do. For example, a looper is looking for chances to loop—how does he go about doing it? How does a hitter find chances to hit? How does a blocker find ways to rush his opponent and force him into errors? How does a chopper force an opponent into seemingly easy mistakes? The more you understand what they are trying to do, the more you can mess up what they are trying to do while avoiding messing up yourself.

What should you be watching for when you watch other players? Here's a breakdown of some things to watch for. You don't need to memorize this, just watch for the most important parts for you. The more you think about these things, the stronger and more automatic your responses to them will be. Note that these are also the things you should be watching for when tactically scouting out an opponent (before and during a match), though (important!) you'd want to simplify it to just a few things.

- **Serves**
    - What is the server trying to do?
    - What serves do they use?
    - What motions?
    - Are they short or long?
    - How spinny?
    - What type of placement?
    - What types of spin?
    - Are they deceptive, and why?
    - How long and fast are the deep serves?
    - Are the short serves very short (easier to flip, drop short, or quick-push at an angle) or is the second bounce (given the chance) near the end line?
    - Are the short serves low?
    - What "trick" serves do they have that you have to watch for?
    - How are each of these serves returned effectively by others?
    - Are there any mannerisms that give away what type of serve it is?

- **Receive**
    - How do they return short backspin serves—do they push long, push short, flip, or mix these up?
    - How do they return short sidespin and topspin serves?
    - How do they return deep backspin serves?
    - How do they return deep sidespin or topspin serves, including ones that break away or toward them?
    - How do they return fast and deep serves?
    - Do they receive long serves with both forehand and backhand, or do they favor one side?
    - How do they return long serves to the wide corners, including breaking sidespin serves?
    - How do they return long serves to their playing elbow?
    - Where do they place their returns?
    - How quickly can you tell what type and placement of return they are doing?
    - How effective are these receives?
    - What serves give them trouble?
    - What serves do they give predictable returns that you might like?
    - What serves do they return effectively, either with strong returns or variation?

- **Rallies**
    - Are they loopers, blockers, counter-drivers, hitters, choppers, fishers, lobbers, or some variation or combination of these?
    - What type of rallies do they prefer?
    - How do they attack?
    - How do they defend or counter-attack?
    - Do they attack mostly with one wing or both?
    - What distance from the table do they prefer?
    - Are they more spin- or speed- or control-oriented?
    - How do they handle balls to the corners?
    - How do they handle balls at their playing elbow?
    - How do they place their shots?
    - What type of rally shots do they do that you are comfortable against?
    - What type of rally shots would you prefer to avoid against this player?

Experiment

It's not enough just to watch. You have to go out there and try out the things you saw. Did you see a serve that you might like to try? Then get

Table Tennis Tactics for Thinkers

a bucket of balls and go practice it. Then test out these new serves in practice games. Keep expanding your repertoire of serves as you never know when you'll find someone who can't handle one of them. Perfect your primary serves while developing alternate ones, and see which ones work for you. Focus on developing serves that set you up to do whatever you do best, or whatever you hope to learn to do well.

Do you want to improve your receive? Find someone who can serve to you over and over so you can experiment and practice your receive. (This is probably the most under-practiced aspect of the game.) Then play practice games where you practice receiving the way stronger players receive. For example, rather than predictably pushing backspin serves back long to a server waiting to loop, try pushing short or flipping. Or perhaps just improve your long push by making it quicker and fast, longer, wider, lower, with heavy or deceptive spin, and with deceptive placement. (Deceptive placement comes by aiming one way and then at the last second changing directions.)

Do you want to improve how you rally? Yep, go practice. But keep pushing yourself to do stronger or more effective shots. Remember what your shots look like to your opponent, and experiment to find ways to make things as difficult for him as possible. For example, many players don't think about where they place their attacks, which normally should go the wide corners or the opponent's playing elbow. Once you've mastered that skill, go to the next level—learn to both hide your direction and to change it at the last second. Or learn to change pace. Or to add different spins to the ball. Or wider angles. The key is to take what you've seen others do, as well as your own experiences and imagination, and experiment.

Analyze

After you have experimented, it's time to analyze strategically. What works for you? Even more important, what will work for you in the future, with practice? Are there certain tactics that you feel you could incorporate into your game? Are there shots you now realize you need to develop so you can use them tactically? This is where you think both tactically—what works now—and strategically—what will work later.

Here's an example. There are players out there with fantastic attacks and great footwork, but because they have never developed their games strategically, they haven't developed the serves, receives, and rally shots to set up their attack. And so they are continually handicapped and lose to players with seemingly weaker shots. Then there are players who do not have the attacking skills and footwork of others, but because they have developed their game strategically, they have serves, receives, and rally shots that set up their attack, and so they beat seemingly stronger attackers.

The example given here can be used for just about any aspect of the game. So think strategically in developing both your tactics and the techniques needed for those tactics.

It's important to remember that tactics are a two-way street. While you want to focus on tactics you can force on an opponent, your opponents might have differing ideas. So think strategically both about your game and what different opponents might do, and develop your strategic game appropriately, so that you will have the right tactics available no matter what your opponent does.

Your service game should be the most strategic and tactical part of your game. This is the one shot where you have complete choice and control over what you do. What type of serves will give you the best tactical options for your game as it develops?

Sometimes think outside the box. For example, if you are better serving sidespin-topspin and looping the expected topspin returns, then this might seem to be the strategic and tactical serves to focus on. But then you'll get little practice looping against backspin, which might be a weakness. In that case, perhaps serve more backspin to develop that part of your game, and then you'll have both weapons. Then, when you play someone who aggressively attacks your short sidespin-topspin serves, you'll be ready to switch to or mix in backspin serves, where they might not be so aggressive.

Remember

It doesn't help to figure things out if you forget them. Over and over I've seen players unlearn things as fast as they learn them. Since they are focused on the learning part, they often don't even realize how much they are forgetting.

Keep a notebook. For example, you might get a steno notebook—they are about 6" wide, 9" tall. From the front, keep notes on your game each time you play. From the back, keep notes on opponents. This might be old-fashioned these days, so feel free to use whatever smart phone or smart pad device works for you. The key is that you keep these notes, both on yourself and on opponents, that they are easily accessed, and that you actually access them regularly.

This doesn't have to be a lifelong thing. I kept notes the first ten years or so I played, but then remembering things about my game and opponents became so automatic I stopped. (As a coach, who coaches many players with many different styles against many opponents with an equally large number of styles, keeping notes is important. While I no longer keep notes on my game, I do for players I coach.)

Table Tennis Tactics for Thinkers

A Levels Approach to Tactics

I like to divide tactics into five levels, with your best tactics a 2, and your worst tactics a -2. Think of your game and your opponent's game as a combination of strengths, average aspects, and weaknesses. There are nine possible combinations, divided into the five tactical levels.

- **Level 2 tactics**
    - Your strengths against opponent's weaknesses
- **Level 1 tactics**
    - Your strengths against opponent's average
    - Your average against opponent's weaknesses
- **Level 0 tactics**
    - Your strengths against opponent's strengths
    - Your average against opponent's average
    - Your weaknesses against opponent's weaknesses
- **Level -1 tactics**
    - Your average against opponent's strengths
    - Your weaknesses against opponent's average
- **Level -2 tactics**
    - Your weaknesses against opponent's strengths

The next time you play a match, why not analyze your game and your opponents, and see what level tactics you are using? For example, do you have a good loop, and your opponent doesn't block well? Then looping is a Level 2 tactic. If his blocking is average, then looping is a Level 1 tactic. If his blocking is a strength, then looping is a Level 0 tactic. If your loop is a weakness, and you're up against a good blocker, then looping becomes a Level -2 tactic—so looping becomes a tactical weakness, unless you are using it to get into some other type of rally that favors you, such as a fast topspin rally, where you are stronger.

Are you mostly using Level 1 and 2 tactics, or are you falling into negative territory? (There's nothing wrong with using Level 0 tactics. If you are a looper and you're up against a blocker whose level of play is about the same as yours, then you'll be doing a lot of looping and he'll be doing a lot of blocking. Then you'll have to find tactical ways to weaken his blocking, such as using placement, variation, etc.

Tactics Early in a Match

There are basically two ways to play tactically early in a match. You can either feel your opponent out to see what he can do and then adjust your tactics based on this ("The Explorer"); or you can force your game on the opponent right from the start, making tactical adjustments as you go on ("The Dominator").

The Explorer uses a variety of tactics early on as he tests his opponent. He uses all his shots—pushes, blocks, hard and soft loops, counter-drives, etc.—and puts the ball all over the table at various speeds. He uses all of his serves and receives as he judges the best tactics to use in the match. Some players in this category fall into the trap of over-adjusting to an opponent, either by trying to adapt to the opponent's strengths rather than take them away, or by forgetting to bring in their own dominating strengths. Being an Explorer doesn't mean you simply adjust to the opponent's shots; it means you are willing to risk falling behind early on as you search for the best tactics. Ideally, the explorer will find a way to use his strengths against the opponent's weaknesses.

The Dominator comes in with his best shots right from the start, forcing the opponent to adjust to his shots. Some players in this category fall into the trap of never learning or adapting to the opponent's strengths and weaknesses, and often lose due to this lack of flexibility. Being a Dominator does not mean you simply throw your best shots at the opponent and hope for the best; it means you start off with your best game, and then make tactical adjustments as necessary.

Are you an Explorer or a Dominator? Whichever you are, perhaps you should experiment with a little of the other. To be at your best, you need some of both.

Always Have Something Ready at the End

Many a close match is won not by the player with the best skills, but by the player who knows what to do near the end of a match. It might be something conventional, like a short serve that you know will set up your attack. Or it might be something tricky. It might be a new variation of a serve, or perhaps the same serve with a different motion. It might be a fake loop or push that looks spinny, but is dead (i.e. spinless). It might be the reverse, a suddenly very spinny loop or push. It might be a different return of serve than what you had been doing. Or it might be a conventional shot that you have great confidence in, and which you use tactics to get into play. Whatever it is, it's always a good idea to learn a few "tricks," and learn when to use them. Most important, always have something ready at the end that you have great confidence will win you the match. With experience and tactical thinking, you'll learn what to do to win the close ones.

Table Tennis Tactics for Thinkers

COMMON TACTICAL THINKING PROBLEMS

Tactical Rigidity and Habitual Tactics

There are players who have spent decades playing exactly the same way. The same strokes, the same serves, the same receives, and the same tactics. Some do it on the theory that if they keep doing the same thing over and Over and OVER, they'll keep getting better at these things, and their overall game will improve. And there is some truth to this. Others do this because they simply enjoy playing that way. If either of these work for you, that's fine.

You'll be a much better player if you constantly learn and expand on your tactics. First, it's likely that as time goes by, parts of your game will invariably become weaker, especially the lesser-used parts. Second, opponents will get used to what you do, and will develop their strategic and tactical game to beat you, while you won't be doing the same. Third, isn't it a little boring to do the same thing over and Over and OVER?

Your game should constantly be growing and expanding. Some may overdo this, trying out new techniques and tactics so often they never really develop the old ones they were trying out before. You should experiment to find the things you want to develop, and then develop them.

One top U.S. player, Dave Sakai, had a simple way of doing this. He plays a very conservative all-around game centered on pushing, blocking, and countering, and he's played this way for many decades. Every year for many years he would add one new technique to his game. One year he decided to learn to backhand loop. One year he worked on hitting his forehand down the line. Another year he put antispin on his racket and learned to play with that, flipping throughout the point. (He later went back to inverted.) Sometimes it's a new serve. But the result was he always had something new to work on, and something new to throw at opponents.

Dave Sakai
Photo by John Oros

I'm always experimenting with serves. I'm not really looking for new primary serves so much as I'm looking for more variations or nuances of current serves to keep opponents off guard—especially ones who have played me regularly and so know my serves pretty well. I also like to experiment with different ways of messing opponents up with my receive, such as last second changes of direction or varying the depth.

Even if you are somewhat set in your techniques and tactics, you can always learn new things to throw at opponents as variations, especially serves. These not only win "free" points, but they make the opponent think about it and have to be ready for the next time you do it. The rest of your game becomes stronger because your opponent is busy worrying about that serve. You like to serve short backspin to set up your loop? Learn a short side-top serve that they have to watch out for. Or a no-spin serve that they'll pop up. Or a sudden fast serve so they can't be leaning over the table waiting for your short serve. One of the best combos is short to the forehand or deep to the backhand—it's very hard for a receiver to be ready for both.

Simplify, and Choose the Best Few Tactics

Remember KISS? There's a myth that top players (in particular the ones known as "smart" players) use complicated tactics to defeat opponents. Perhaps as they are about to serve they are planning out their first three or four shots? After all, chess players plan things out many moves ahead, and table tennis has been called chess at light speed.

That's not what happens in table tennis. Top tactical players don't work out complicated tactical schemes; they look at all the complexities and find simple patterns to disarm an opponent. There are just too many variables to plan too much. It's better to focus on a few simple tactics that will tend to favor what you want to do. The key is choosing those few simple tactics out of countless possibilities. That's your primary goal in the first game of a match, probably equal in importance to actually winning that game. (Chess players do roughly the same thing. In complicated positions they don't analyze every possibility; they quickly narrow it down to a few "obvious" possibilities, and analyze and choose from those.)

Many or most tactics are for setting up your own strengths. For example, if you have a powerful loop against backspin, you might serve backspin so you get a lot of push returns. If the receiver pushes at wide angles, you might serve backspin low to the middle, thereby taking away some of the angle. If you have trouble with heavy backspin, you might serve no-spin, which is more difficult to push heavy, and is often popped up as well. If you have a good smash, you might serve varying sidespin, topspin, and no-spin serves, with varying speeds and depths. If you are quicker than an opponent, you might serve topspin so you can get right into a quick topspin rally.

Other tactics are to take away an opponent's strength. For example, if an opponent has a powerful forehand, a simple remedy would be to serve

Table Tennis Tactics for Thinkers

short to the forehand, and then attack out to the backhand, thereby taking the forehand out of the equation. If an opponent has a strong push that is difficult to attack, then perhaps serve topspin. If an opponent has a strong forehand and backhand, perhaps go after his middle, the changeover spot between forehand and backhand. And so on.

Similarly, you can use tactics to play into an opponent's weakness or to avoid exposing your own weaknesses. See if you can come up with your own list of tactics of this type. Ideally you'll learn to play your strengths against an opponent's weaknesses. But do not become predictable. Sometimes you'll play your medium shots to the opponent's weaknesses, or your strengths to the opponent's medium shots.

Ultimately, pretty much all successful tactics are used to set up your strengths, to hide your weaknesses, to take away an opponent's strengths, or to play into an opponent's weaknesses. Find the simplest (and usually most direct) way of achieving these four goals and you are well on your way to tactical brilliance.

Most top players do all this with just a few tactics—perhaps two or three serve tactics, one or two receive tactics, and one or two rally tactics. This doesn't mean they don't use other tactics as the situation comes up, but they are standard tactics that are ingrained from years of playing and thinking about the sport. The specific tactics against a specific player are far more limited, and yet, if chosen properly, will pay off dividends.

Tactical Over-Anticipation

Tactical over-anticipation is when a player gets so caught up in tactics that he over-anticipates what the opponent will do. This is fine if the opponent is predictable, as many are. But often this is not the case.

This is an example of where the myth of thinking too much comes from. If you think tactically between points, but blank your mind out during a point, you'll simply respond, as you should do. Tactics (other than serves) comes mostly on *how* you respond, not trying to react too soon and thereby often incorrectly. For example, if you decide you need to return an opponent's short backspin serve with a short push, then you might over-react by deciding to push short as if the ball had backspin no matter what, and so pop up a short topspin, sidespin, or no-spin serve. Instead, learn to rely on your subconscious to do the right thing. If you think enough about returning a short backspin serve with a short push, and practice doing this, your subconscious will get the message. At the same time, if you let it just respond, your subconscious will probably only do this when it sees a short backspin serve. It won't try to push the same way against topspin, sidespin, or no-spin. (You can push these serves back, even short, but you have to chop down on the ball—and it takes practice. Try it, and add another tactic to your arsenal!)

Sometimes you do want to anticipate what an opponent is doing. When I give lectures on return of serve, I often jokingly point out that against most beginning and intermediate players (and surprisingly many advanced ones), you can serve backspin to their backhand, then turn away and go for a walk. When you come back, just go to your backhand corner because the return, over and over, will be a deep push to the backhand. From a tactical point of view, you don't want to be the type of player who keeps pushing to the same spot, or has some other predictable pattern. (There are exceptions—if the opponent really can't handle this shot, or doesn't notice you are doing it over and over, or if you are just overwhelmingly good at responding to whatever an opponent might do against it, then by all means keep doing it.)

Once you realize your opponent is predictable on some shots, take advantage of it. For example, if you have a strong forehand and you know your opponent is almost for sure going to return a serve or some other shot to your backhand, then by all means step around as early as you can (but not so soon that he will see it and eventually cross you up with a shot to your forehand) rather than wait to see if the opponent really does what you are sure he will do. If you put a ball to your opponent's forehand and you are almost certain he's going to loop it to your forehand, then by all means move to the forehand side early (though again, not so early that the opponent sees this and changes direction). And so on. Just remember that these are tactical choices, and that the opponent might figure these out and adjust—so be quick to change your own tactics on this.

Tactics and the Subconscious

The hardest part about tactics during a point is that you really don't have time to think; you only have time to respond and do the shot. When serving, you get to think things over, but the rest of the time you don't have that luxury. How can you play tactics when you don't have time to think?

Imagine an opponent who goes way out of position to loop with his forehand from his backhand side, and he loops to your backhand, leaving his forehand side wide open. You don't have time to stop and say to yourself, "He's wide open on the forehand, so I should block the ball there." In fact, you shouldn't take time to think at all—from years of experience, you should just block there automatically, reflexively. This is no different than getting the right racket angle to block his loop. You don't stop and calculate the racket angle needed, or tell yourself what angle the racket should be. From years of experience, you automatically get the angle right (usually!), without any conscious thought. This is exactly how you play tactically in a rally.

What is it that responds almost instantly as it guides your racket angle against a loop, and blocks to that wide open forehand? Your subconscious.

Table Tennis Tactics for Thinkers

It may appear to you that you consciously saw that open forehand side and consciously told yourself to block that way, though of course not with actual words in your mind. And you quite possibly did. But you were likely *reacting* to what you saw while your subconscious, which responds much faster than the conscious mind, was already doing, or at least getting ready to do the shot. You were aware of the tactical shot you reflexively did, like blocking to the open court or the weaker side, but it is the subconscious that reflexively does these shots.

This assumes you are an experienced player. A beginner hasn't yet built up the reflexive tactical responses, and so his subconscious doesn't know what to do, and so the beginner may have to consciously, and very awkwardly, tell himself what to do tactically in the middle of a rally, or else he'll just blindly return the ball without any attempt at tactics. An intermediate player may also not have yet built up these responses, which is why he needs to think tactics enough so that he learns to do so instinctively.

There are exceptions, especially in slower rallies, where you might make conscious decisions. For example, if an opponent lobs and leaves his forehand side open, you might consciously decide to smash to his forehand. Yet it's likely that your subconscious, trained in tactics the same way you were, would have done the same. Or in a pushing duel, you might consciously decide to loop the next ball or perhaps quick-push to the forehand. But these are the exceptions, the times when you have time to actually think. (And one key here is that while you may consciously decide to smash the lob to the backhand or to loop the next push, it is your subconscious that should actually execute the shot.)

In general, you should take conscious control of your tactics during a rally only if your goal is to play poorly. Or you can let your subconscious do what it's been trained to do, or that you are training it to do, and then have a chance of playing well.

Your subconscious is your friend and partner. It's always there, doing the boring stuff you don't have time or interest in doing, such as executing the strokes you have spent so much time practicing, calculating racket angles and, yes, implementing the tactical plans you have formulated. You're the boss, and it's your dedicated servant—but only if you tell it what to do.

Remember what Werner Schlager said—and this is the third time I've quoted this so you know it's important: "The faster you play the more important subconscious tactical decisions become."

How do you tell your subconscious your tactical plans? By constantly thinking about tactics. Just as your subconscious gets the message that you want to block loops on the table, and so learns what angles will do this, it will get your tactical messages if you think about them enough.

CHAPTER FOUR
All About Spin

Spin is such an integral part of tactics that we're going to devote an entire chapter to it, even though it may seem somewhat out of place in a tactics and strategic development book. I don't want new players to get lost later on! Much of this chapter is basic; some is a bit more advanced. It's important that players understand these fundamentals or much of the book will not make sense. For advanced players, this chapter is a good review, and there are some ideas you might learn from it. Or you can skip this chapter (and perhaps the next, "Beginning Tactics") unless you plan on coaching beginners.

The biggest difference between a serious table tennis player and a basement player is spin. Serious players use spin on both their serves and rallying shots, both to control the ball and to force errors from their opponents. What we are going to do is go over the types, effects and purposes of the various spins, how to create spin, how to read spin, how to handle spin, and how spin actually makes a ball curve in flight.

The Types of Spin

How many basic types of spin are there in table tennis? The most common answer is four: topspin, backspin, and sidespin in both directions. For many players, this is an adequate answer. However, the more correct answer is seven, plus an infinite number of combinations.

The ball can rotate in three different axis that are perpendicular to each other, and the ball can rotate in two directions on each of these axis. Assume you've just hit a ball away from you, and are watching to see how it rotates.

- If the top of the ball is rotating away from you, it is topspin.
- If the bottom of the ball is rotating away from you, it is backspin.
- If the right side of the ball is rotating away from you, to the right, it is "right" sidespin.
- If the left side of the ball is rotating away from you, to the left, it is "left" sidespin.
- If the ball is spinning clockwise (relative to you), it is "right" corkscrewspin.
- If the ball is spinning counter-clockwise (relative to you), it is "left" corkscrewspin.
- If the ball is not rotating at all, it's no-spin!

Table Tennis Tactics for Thinkers

No-spin is considered a spin on its own. In fact, if you listen to top players, you'll hear them refer to "heavy no-spin," which sounds rather contradictory. It's actually a no-spin shot (usually a serve) that is faked to look like heavy spin (usually backspin).

Corkscrewspin is rarely seen except in serves by advanced players. It generally can only be produced with a high-toss serve. If you ever face this corkscrewspin, read over the difference between sidespin and corkscrewspin carefully. If you imagine the axis of rotation, it's easier to understand. For sidespin, the axis is up and down. For corkscrewspin, the axis points straight at and away from you. (For topspin/backspin, it is left to right.)

Four types of spin: topspin, backspin, and sidespin both ways.

If the ball rotates around the arrow on the left it would be corkscrewspin.

For the truly nerdy, there are really 27 specific combinations of spin, by taking every possible combination of backspin/topspin, sidespin and corkscrewspin, rotating in either direction. (Yes, there are even eight spins that combine all three—you can do that! For example, a left sidespin/right corkscrewspin/topspin serve.) We'll leave it as an exercise to list all 27. (Don't forget no-spin.)

Effects of Spin

All spins have three major effects: how they travel through the air, how they bounce on the table, and how they bounce off the opponent's racket. Here is a listing of each spin's major effects.

<u>Topspin</u>
- In the air: Curves downward
- Bounce on the table: A low, fast bounce
- Rebound off opponent's racket: Jumps upward and fast

<u>Backspin</u>
- In the air: Tends to float
- Bounce on the table: Ball slows down
- Rebound off opponent's racket: Shoots downward

<u>Sidespin</u>
- In the air: Curves sideways
- Bounce on the table: A slight sideways bounce, but not too much. After bouncing on the table the axis of rotation of a pure sidespin changes and converts partly to corkscrewspin, and so the second bounce jumps more sideways
- Rebound off opponent's racket: bounces sideways

<u>Corkscrewspin</u>
- In the air: The spin barely affects the flight
- Bounce on the table: Very sharp sideways bounce
- Rebound off opponent's racket: Not too much effect off opponent's racket, unless the opponent's racket is very open or very closed, in which case it bounces sideways

Purpose of Spin

Spin is used when serving or rallying either to control the ball or force an opponent into error. Let's examine the purposes of each type of spin.

Topspin

When serving, topspin is used primarily to force a high return or a return off the end. If an opponent doesn't make an adjustment (i.e. aim low), the topspin will force either a high return or a return that goes off the end. Often players use a very fast motion to fake a backspin serve, but actually serve topspin, fooling their opponent into an error.

In a rally, topspin makes the ball drop very fast, and so allows a player to hit the ball very hard and still have it drop down and hit the table. Not only does it allow a player to attack a very low ball, but it gives a larger margin for error on all rally shots, with the topspin pulling down balls that would otherwise go off the end. One way of thinking of it is as follows. If you hit a relatively low ball hard but without topspin, the ball might only have enough time to drop so as to hit the last foot of the table. With topspin, it might be able to drop and hit anywhere on the last three feet. This means your target is three times as large!

Just as when you serve, the topspin you put on the ball will make your opponent tend to return the ball either high or off the end. The loop drive, which has extreme topspin, is the most important rallying shot in table tennis. It forces an opponent into either a defensive return or a difficult counter-attack.

Backspin

*South Korea's Joo Se Hyuk chops another one with backspin.
Photo by Diego Schaaf*

When serving, backspin is used to try to force an opponent into returning the ball into the net. It is also effective in forcing a defensive return that you can attack. Often players fake either topspin, sidespin, or no-spin when serving backspin, trying to trick the opponent into an error.

In a rally, backspin is a relatively defensive shot. Against an incoming backspin, a backspin return (a "push") is a way to jockey for position, and against many players, it is quite effective. However, it gives the opponent the opportunity to attack (especially with a loop drive), and so should not be overused.

There are also many defensive players who back off the table and return topspin attacks with backspin ("chop") returns. Again, this gives the opponent the opportunity to attack, but some players do quite well this way, returning ball after ball with backspin until the opponent either misses or gives an easy ball to put away.

Sidespin

Sidespin is used primarily when serving. The purpose is to try to force an opponent into returning the ball off the side, or into returning the ball where you want him to. Also, since sidespin jumps off the paddle relatively quickly, it forces opponents into hitting many off the end as well as off the side. Often sidespin serves are disguised as backspin serves, and opponents push them back, and so the ball goes off the side. (They also pop up since the receiver is aiming up to compensate for backspin that is not there.) Sidespin is also mixed with topspin when serving to force mistakes—opponents have to worry about going off the side and going off the end.

Sidespin is not used much during a rally except at the higher levels. Top players sidespin loop, sidespin lob, and sidespin push. Beginning and intermediate players should learn to do these shots early on as well. That way, when they reach the higher levels, they'll be able to control these shots.

Corkscrewspin

Corkscrewspin is not too common in table tennis, and is usually only used by advanced players when serving. It is difficult to produce except with a high-toss serve (i.e. a serve where the ball is tossed relatively high into the air). Sometimes, a player out of position will scoop a ball off the floor, and when the ball hits the table, it jumps sideways because of corkscrewspin. Lobs and counterloops also may have this type of spin.

When done on the serve, it can be very effective. When the ball hits the table, it jumps sideways, throwing an opponent off. This is because the ball contacts the table with the fastest moving part of the spinning ball (shooting it sideways), and not on the axis of the ball (as with a straight sidespin). Note that a pure sidespin ball doesn't bounce sideways much on the first bounce (on the server's side of the table) when serving, but the axis of rotation changes when it hits the table, and it becomes more of a sidespin-corkscrewspin serve—which is why sidespin serves noticeable jump more when it bounces on the opponent's side of the table. In fact, a good corkscrewspin serve is actually served with about half sidespin, half corkscrewspin, so that after it bounces on the server's side of the table it becomes more or less pure corkscrewspin, which maximizes the sideways jump on the receiver's side of the table.

Additionally, an opponent's instincts for returning corkscrewspin are often off. Suppose you serve with a corkscrewspin so that the ball is rotating clockwise as it travels away from you. If your opponent hits under the ball (a push), the ball will jump to your right. If your opponent hits toward the top of the ball (a drive), the ball will jump to your left. Imagine the rotation of the ball and which way it jumps on contact with an opponent's paddle, and you'll see.

No-spin

No-spin serves are extremely effective because it is relatively easy to fake spin, but put no spin on the ball. If you can convince your opponent to react to a spin that isn't there, you don't need to put spin on the ball. However, for this to be effective, you need to have spinny serves as well. It's not hard for an opponent to adjust to no-spin and lightly-spun serves, but if they are guarding against spinny serves, then the no-spin serve becomes a serious weapon.

Most often, players fake a backspin serve, but contact the ball near the handle (where the racket moves slowest) and just pat the ball over the net with a vigorous but non-spin producing serve. If you pull the wrist back slightly as you contact the ball (on any spin serve), you can make the racket rotate at this contact point near the handle (instead of your wrist), and so the racket is barely moving where it contacts the ball. (It'll actually be rotating in a circle, but that won't put much spin on the ball.) If you use a big wrist snap after contact, and a big follow-through, your opponent will probably think there is spin on the ball—when it's actually "heavy no-spin"!

In a rally, no-spin is also used to fool opponents into thinking there is spin on the ball. Most players open their rackets when pushing against a backspin push, so if you give them a no-spin push, they will pop the ball up. If they attack, they'll tend to lift the ball off the end. Similarly, you can fool players by using a no-spin loop. (You do this with a regular looping motion, but hold the wrist rigid, and accelerate into the ball just *after* contact. You can also contact the ball near the handle to minimize spin, though this takes good timing.)

Another good use of no-spin is with a fast serve. If your opponent thinks your fast serve has topspin, he closes his racket slightly. If the serve actually is no-spin, the ball goes into the net. What makes this effective is that the serve must be fast enough so that the opponent doesn't have time to react to the ball's spin (or non-spin).

A ball with spin will jump off the paddle with energy both from the ball's velocity and its spin. A no-spin ball has no spin, and so bounces out slower. This means that players often put no-spin balls in the net because the ball doesn't bounce out as fast as they expect. Similarly, players often put spin balls off the end by not taking the extra bounce from the spin into account.

Creating Spin

Spin can be created at two times: when serving or when rallying. The main difference is that when serving, you are in complete control of the ball—you can toss it up just the way you want to. In a rally, the ball comes at you in different ways that you have to react to.

To create a good spin, you need three things: racket speed, a grazing contact, and a grippy racket surface. (With a non-grippy surface, you can't put as much spin on the ball. However, you can return an opponent's spin—but that's not quite the same as creating spin.)

It's important to be loose and relaxed if you want to create a good spin. If your muscles are tight, your muscles won't work together properly, and you'll get little spin. Imagine hitting something with a whip, and then with a rigid stick. Notice how the tip of the whip travels much faster than the tip of the stick? That's the difference between loose, relaxed muscles and stiff (stick-like) muscles.

Service Spin

There are an infinite number of service motions where you can put spin on the ball—but that's outside the context of this book. What we want to go over are the principles behind getting that spin when serving.

To get maximum spin, you should use a grippy inverted surface. A less grippy surface, such as pips-out, can create spin, but substantially less. To really spin that ball, you need a surface that really grips the ball.

You need the racket to really be moving at contact—you want to accelerate the racket through the ball. With whatever service motion you use, you need to start with the arm moving, and then snap the wrist as you contact the ball. Most of the racket speed comes from the wrist—perhaps 70%—so work on using as much wrist as you can.

Lastly, you need to just graze the ball at contact. The finer the contact, the more spin you will get. Top players with really spinny serves can be almost violent as they move their racket to the ball during the serve—yet, since they only graze the ball, the ball moves very slowly, often barely making it to and over the net. Nearly all of their energy is being used to create spin, not speed. It will take time to develop spinny serves, but they are a necessary tool in your tactical toolbox—so get a bucket of balls, and start practicing!

A good way to practice getting spin on the serve is to serve onto the floor, away from the table. Try to put spin on the ball so the ball bounces sideways or backward on the floor. If you put a good backspin on the ball, it should bounce a few times away from you, come to a stop, then bounce or roll back at you! If you put a good sidespin on the ball, it should bounce sideways after a few bounces. Put some targets on the floor and try to spin the ball so it bounces around the targets.

Rallying Spin

During a rally, you normally will use mostly topspins and backspins, with an occasional no-spin or sidespin thrown in.

Most drives have some topspin, but when you want to really produce a heavy topspin, you have to loop the ball. To loop the ball well with lots of topspin you need to use your entire body, like a tennis player.

Table Tennis Tactics for Thinkers

The technique for looping is outside the scope of this book, but the principles are the same as when serving—racket speed, grazing (though you normally sink the ball more into the sponge when looping since you often want speed as well), and a grippy surface. Also, see above about relaxed, loose muscles—be a whip, not a stick!

The nice thing about looping, and topspin in general, is that not only does the topspin give you a wider margin for error, but the topspin often sets you up to attack the next ball as well. Especially on the forehand side, players learn to loop the ball over and over until they see an easy ball to put away, or the opponent misses. (At the higher levels, many loop just about everything on the backhand side as well.)

Topspin is also used when lobbing. A high ball with a lot of topspin (and often sidespin) can be tricky to smash. The topspin makes the ball take a fast bounce off the table, and the topspin will make it jump out when it hits your racket. At the higher levels, lobbing is one of the most spectacular shots, and it can be quite effective against many players.

Backspin is used during a rally when pushing or chopping. A push is a defensive or neutral backspin shot against an incoming backspin shot. Many players are very good at attacking pushes, so choose when to use this shot carefully. Many players overuse it, especially when returning serves—often trying to push even against a sidespin or topspin serve. (Which leads to disastrous returns high in the air, off the end, or off the side.) However, a good push can be valuable. The key is to make sure it is an *effective* push. Learn to put a good backspin on the ball, keep the ball low, and push to a wide angle. You should also learn to push quick off the bounce (so the opponent has less time to react), and perhaps to push short by just touching the ball lightly (so that it bounces very short on the other side of the table, making it hard to attack). At the highest levels, players often push short. But this is a tricky shot, so I'd recommend learning a good deep push first. If you are pushing deep, try to push very deep, so the ball goes within at least a foot of the end line. (How important is pushing? There's an entire chapter in this book devoted to pushing tactics.)

Sidespin is rarely used in rallies except by relatively advanced players. It can be used when pushing, blocking, looping or counterlooping. It is used basically to throw the opponent off and force a mistake. (Jan-Ove Waldner, arguably the greatest player of all time, was a master at this—he is famous for sidespin blocks and sidespin pushes.) When looping, especially against a block or a topspin (especially when counterlooping), you should usually put some sidespin on the ball, normally so that the ball hooks to the left (for righties). A stroke with about 15% sidespin is more natural than trying to loop with pure topspin. Advanced players can sidespin both ways—for righties, hooking to the left (more natural) and fading to the right (takes more practice).

Reading Spin

The single hardest thing to learn to do in table tennis is to learn to read spin, especially against a good serve. Because there are no simple, easy-to-follow methods, it takes a lot of practice and experience. However, many players play for years and never gain this experience because they don't understand the principles of reading spin. Although it is best to read spin from the racket's contact with the ball, you can't always do that perfectly. You should use a number of pieces of "evidence" to really read the spin. What follows are eight factors to take into account when trying to read spin, especially when returning serve.

1. **The grippiness of the racket surface the opponent is using.** Inverted racket surfaces usually give the most spin, but inverted surfaces run the range from extremely grippy surfaces that will create huge amounts of spin to very slick surfaces that will not (antispin). Pips-out surfaces will not create as much spin as a grippy inverted surface, but most shorter pips can create a surprising amount in the hands of an expert. Longer pips don't create too much spin. (Note the difference between creating spin and returning an opponent's spin—item 8) below.)

2. **The amount of spin from the racket's contact with the ball.** The amount of spin is related directly to the racket's speed and grazing motion at contact, in addition to the grippiness of the racket surface. The faster the racket is moving at contact, and the more the racket grazes the ball, the more spin. You should be able to see the racket speed, but make sure you are watching the part of the racket that is actually contacting the ball. Many players use a fast racket motion, making it seem like there is a lot of spin, but contact the ball near the racket's handle, where the racket isn't moving as fast. The result is less than the expected spin, which is effective if the opponent thinks there is more spin on the ball.

    You can tell how much the opponent has grazed the ball in several ways. First, see how fast the ball comes off the racket. If the racket was moving very fast at contact, but the ball came out slowly, the energy had to go somewhere—it went into spin, via a grazing motion. Second, see how the racket approached the ball at contact—you can see if it was a grazing contact, if you watch

Table Tennis Tactics for Thinkers

closely. Third, the sound gives it away, unless you are in a loud playing hall. A grazing motion is very quiet, with at most a high-pitched "hissing" sound. If there's a "thumping" sound, there is less spin. (Many players, including me, play poorly if there's a lot of background noise since they can't hear the contact and so have difficulty reading the spin.)

3. **The type of spin from the direction of contact with the ball.**
   The type of spin comes directly from the direction the racket is moving at contact with the ball. Often, this is easy to tell—just watch which direction the racket is moving at contact. It gets tricky, however, when the opponent uses a "semicircular" motion. This means the racket changes direction during the serving motion. Your mission is to try to see what direction the racket was moving at contact.

   There are two ways of doing this. First, you can try to get a very short "video" of the contact in your mind, and from that, see what direction the racket was moving at contact. If you can learn to create this video in your mind, soon you'll be able to pick up the contact more consistently. Second, try to see which direction the ball comes off the racket. If it comes up slightly, it is topspin; if it comes off sideways, it is sidespin; if it comes off going down, it's is backspin. However, since the racket may be moving very fast, it is not always that easy to judge this.

   In both cases, when you are learning how to read the type of spin, call out to yourself (in your mind!) the type of spin on each serve, until it becomes second nature.

4. **How the ball bounces on the table.**
   If you aren't sure of the spin from racket contact, you can pick it up from the way the ball bounces on both sides of the table. If the ball has topspin, it will take a low, fast bounce. If it has backspin, it will tend to die and bounce short. If it has sidespin or (especially) corkscrewspin, it will bounce sideways.

5. **How the ball travels through the air.**
   You can read the ball's spin from its flight in the air. A topspin arcs through the air and drops rapidly. A backspin tends to float, with a flatter arc. A sidespin curves sideways. A corkscrewspin doesn't curve much in the air, but its sideways bounce off the table makes it appear to do so.

6. **Seeing the ball spin (or not spin) itself.**
   You can read the spin (or non-spin) from the ball itself. Some players can read a no-spin ball by seeing the label. Many advanced players claim to be able to read spin directly off the ball, most likely from how blurred the ball's label is. This is not easy to do, and while some players claim they can do this, others claim it is impossible. My verdict? I'm pretty sure I can pick up the spin a bit from the blur of the spinning ball, but only barely.

7. **Amount and type of spin on previous similar serves/shots.**
   Even if you can't read the spin from any of the above indicators, you can read it from experience. If you misread a spin one time, the next time you see that motion—even if you can't really read it—you can tactically guess it is the same spin. For example, if you think you see a backspin serve, but every time you return it, it pops up or goes off the end, you are probably misreading a topspin. When you see this "backspin" motion again, put aside your natural reflex, and treat it like a topspin. The major problem with this, of course, is that your opponent might vary the spin with a similar motion—and if you aren't really reading the spin, you'll have great trouble reading any changes. (Fortunately for some, most players aren't able to do this except at the higher levels.) So use past indicators to make corrections to your reading of spin, but only in combination with the above indicators, or as a last resort.

8. **In a rally, how much spin was already on the ball, and how much of it is being returned.**
   If you put spin on the ball, your opponent might simply return your spin back to you. This happens most often if your opponent has a less grippy surface, especially long pips. Surfaces such as long pips (but also short pips and antispin) can return your own spin back to you. For example, if you put a heavy topspin on the ball, a player with long pips can give you all of your spin right back at you without doing much. A player with a more grippy surface can also return your own spin, but to a much lesser degree.

Handling Spin

Handling spin is mostly an exercise in racket angles and stroke direction. For every spin, there is a racket angle that will compensate for it. There is also a stroke direction that will compensate for it. Choosing which to use is the question. In general, use an upward stroke and open racket to compensate for backspin, while using mostly racket angle to compensate for other spins. (Open racket means aim racket upward; closed racket means aim racket downward.) You especially open the racket against backspin when pushing, and stroke more upward when attacking.

Against a sidespin, the more aggressive you are, the less the spin will "take" on your racket, and so the less it will affect you. The softer your contact, the more the ball will jump—so tentative players often have more trouble with sidespin than aggressive players.

When learning to read spin on a serve, it's a good idea to wait on the ball, and take it as late as possible to give yourself more time to respond. As you improve, you should start taking the ball quicker. However, even advanced players often take the ball later against a player with tricky serves.

Here is a rundown on how to return the various spins.

Topspin. Close your racket (i.e. aim the hitting surface downward). This will compensate for the tendency to hit the ball off the end or pop it up. Against a heavy topspin, you'll most likely use a simple block to return the shot. Take the ball quick off the bounce—otherwise, you'll have to contend with the ball's low, fast bounce.

Backspin. Open your racket (i.e. aim the hitting surface upward). This will compensate for the tendency to hit the ball into the net. If you are topspinning, stroke upward and lift the ball upward with your racket only a little more open than normal. This is the perfect time to loop with heavy topspin!

Sidespin. Aim the opposite way. A good rule to remember when returning sidespin serves is to aim in the direction the server's racket came from. If you return the sidespin somewhat aggressively with a topspin, you can treat the incoming sidespin almost like it were a topspin, and the sidespin will only change the direction of your shot a little bit.

Corkscrewspin. Anticipate the sideways bounce on the table, and be in position for it. Don't get too caught up trying to learn how to handle this spin too much as it is usually only seen at the higher levels. However, it is interesting to note that if you push against a corkscrewspin (with an open racket, hitting toward the bottom of the ball), the ball will bounce sideways off the racket. If you topspin it back (with a closed racket, hitting toward the top of the ball), the ball will bounce off your racket sideways in the opposite direction. Imagine the incoming spin and how it will "grab" your racket based on whether you hit toward the top or bottom of the ball, and you'll see this.

What Makes A Spinning Ball Curve In The Air?

Now we get into serious science, so those less science-minded, here's your cue to leave and go practice! This has nothing to do with tactics, but will give you a better understanding of this game of spin.

Imagine a ball with topspin. As it travels through the air, the forward movement of the top of the ball forces air forward (or more precisely, slows down the movement of air over the top of the ball). This causes air to be "clumped" together toward the front top of the ball, creating an area of high air density. Similarly, the backward movement of the bottom of the ball pulls air backward quickly, creating an area of low air density toward the front bottom of the ball. The high density air mass at the top of the ball forces the ball downward; the low density air mass at the bottom of the ball "vacuums" it downward. The result: the ball drops. That's what makes a ball with topspin drop. (It's called the Magnus effect.) The same applies to all spins, but as the spin orientation changes, the movement of the ball changes. For example, a sidespin creates a high-air density area on one side of the ball, a low-air density on the other, which forces the ball to curve sideways.

Backspin doesn't really curve up, but that's because of gravity. The backspin is pulling the ball up; gravity is pulling it down. The result is a ball that tends to travel in a line at first (to float) before the backspin is finally overcome by gravity. If there were no gravity, then a backspin ball would curve up just as much as a topspin ball curves down.

Conclusion

Spin is the biggest difference between "basement" stars and advanced players. Players may learn to rally better than others, but if they can't handle spin—or create their own—they're at a huge tactical disadvantage. Learn to use and handle spin, and you'll quickly leave the basement players (and most tournament players) behind.

Table Tennis Tactics for Thinkers

CHAPTER FIVE
Beginning Tactics

*John Hsu (left) and I work with beginning juniors.
Photo by Chaoying Gong*

    This chapter is for beginning players and players who haven't really given tactics much thought. New players may be overwhelmed by all the talk of spins and loops and smashes and other advanced-sounding shots, or tactics of keeping the ball long or short when a beginner is just trying to keep the ball on the table. So let's discuss beginning tactics. Advanced players may want to read this section as well as they might someday coach beginning players. Plus, of course, some "advanced" players (and many intermediate players) may never really have spent a lot of time thinking tactically, and so they may want to begin here with the basics.
    The most important "tactic" for a beginner is to develop the fundamentals, which is actually strategic thinking. If you can't execute a tactic, the tactic is useless. Telling a beginner to, say, go to a strong forehand player's forehand so he can come back to their backhand doesn't work if he can't handle the first forehand shot. You need to develop your own toolbox of shots for your tactical use. Besides developing the basic shots, you also want to develop strengths that threaten your opponent. If you don't have anything that threatens your opponent, how can you beat him?
    Much of beginning tactics are conventional tactics at a simplified level, so make sure to study that chapter.

Beginning Service Strategy

    You want to develop both backspin and topspin serves; some sort of sidespin serve; and a fast serve that you can place anywhere on the table.

With these tools, you have tactical weapons you can use.

What are your strengths and weaknesses, and what are your opponent's strengths and weaknesses? At the most basic level, you want to serve to the opponent's weaker side so he has to do his weaker shot. Or you might want to serve wide to his stronger side, and return his first shot to his weaker side, thereby forcing him to both move and hit with his weak side. This latter is one of the most under-used tactics at the beginning level. A beginner might have trouble with that first shot from the stronger side, but the only way to learn to deal with it is to play into it.

Since most players tend to hit crosscourt, you might consider serving to the side diagonally away from your strong side. If you have a stronger backhand than forehand, then a serve to the backhand will often come back to your backhand.

Are you better in topspin or backspin rallies? Topspin serves tend to be returned with at least some topspin, while backspin serves tend to be pushed back with backspin. Take your choice! But don't be afraid to vary the serve to force mistakes. If your opponent pushes your backspin serve back several times in a row, a slow topspin or sidespin serve might also get pushed back, and so pop up or go off the end or side of the table.

Sidespin serves will force mistakes both from the ball jumping on the table and off the opponent's racket. They also tend to force the opponent to return the ball to one side. For example, a backhand sidespin serve (with racket moving from left to right) will create a sidespin that will return the ball to your forehand or off that side, if the opponent doesn't adjust. The opposite will happen to a forehand pendulum serve (with racket moving from right to left). So choose your sidespin and placement to maximize the chances of getting a return where you want it.

If you have a good forehand from the backhand corner, you might consider doing what many "pros" do—a forehand pendulum serve from the backhand corner. This will tend to be returned to the backhand, allowing you to play your strong forehand from the backhand corner. The main advantage of this is that it puts you in position for two forehands—the one after the serve, and the next one as well. In fact, you might be able to keep playing forehands the rest of the rally until the opponent goes to your wide forehand (giving you one more forehand) before finally coming back to your backhand. With all those forehands, you should win most of the points.

A serve with forehand pendulum type spin will break to the right, and so if you serve to your opponent's backhand, it'll break away from him. To return it, he not only has to move or reach after the ball breaking away from him, he has to angle his paddle to his left (toward your forehand), which is more awkward than aiming crosscourt. Similarly, a serve with

Table Tennis Tactics for Thinkers

backhand serve type spin (racket going from left to right) will break into an opponent's forehand, making him move or reach for the ball, and to compensate for the spin, he has to aim down the line, which is even more awkward on the forehand side for most players. In general, it's easier to return a sidespin that breaks into you than away from you. So in general, you want to favor serving forehand pendulum sidespins and similar spins to an opponent's backhand, and the reverse spin to the opponent's forehand. (But always mix it up.)

If your opponent doesn't have a good attack against backspin, a deep backspin serve might be effective. Most players push better on the backhand than the forehand, so perhaps deep backspin to the forehand will work. But beware—by the intermediate level, most deep backspin serves to the forehand, and many to the backhand, are going to be looped.

Use your fast serves creatively. You have three targets—wide forehand, wide backhand, and middle (opponent's elbow, the crossover point between forehand and backhand). Watch your opponent, remember how he returned it previously, and choose your placement accordingly. Remember that most serves are returned crosscourt, so if you serve fast to the opponent's backhand, you'll probably get a return to your backhand.

So far all these beginning tactics are just that—tactics. You also want to start thinking strategically, and develop the type of serves that will help you improve. For example, a deep serve to the forehand might work now, but other than as an occasional variation to catch an opponent off guard, it usually won't work at the higher levels. To reach those levels, you need to learn to serve and attack.

That moment of realization.

Serve and Attack

It's not enough to just serve for winners; you want to serve and attack. That's a primary difference between a beginning player and an intermediate one. At the advanced level, it's pretty much a given that the players will serve and attack, and most tactics at that level are finding ways to do this while stopping your opponent from doing so. Even modern defensive players usually serve and attack if given the chance.

What's your best attacking shot? If you are good at looping backspin, serve backspin and be ready to loop the likely pushed return. If you don't have a good loop against backspin, then you might not want to serve backspin.

But this is tactical thinking. Strategically thinking, if you don't have a good attack against backspin, you need one. So while tactically you wouldn't want to serve too much backspin—thereby getting backspin returns you aren't good at attacking—strategically you *would* want to do this so you can develop your attack against backspin. At the intermediate and advanced levels, the most basic strategy is to serve backspin (and no-spin) and loop the pushed return.

Watch strong players and see how they link up their serve with their follow-up attack. If your goal as a beginning player is to stay a beginning player but win now, then play only tactically. And there is a time for that, such as in important tournaments and league matches. Plus you can't develop your tactical skills unless you use them. But if you want to advance beyond the beginning stage, think more strategically and develop that serve and attack, especially (for most players) your serve and loop against backspin.

You also want to develop tricky sidespin and side-top serves that opponents will pop up or miss outright. One of the best ways to develop your forehand smash and footwork is to develop such serves, which will give you lots of practice moving and smashing. This will also raise your level of play, allowing you more opportunities to play stronger and stronger players, thereby giving you the experience you need to improve even more. (This is exactly what happened to me. When I started out, I developed a tricky forehand tomahawk serve that players kept popping up, and so I constantly served and smashed—and the result was I developed my footwork, my smash, and my overall level from playing stronger players. It also delayed my developing a good forehand loop for a time.)

Return of Serve

Returning serves is all about control. You'll see top players attacking the serve, but that's because 1) they are top players, and 2) what looks like an aggressive return to a beginner is not so aggressive to a top player. It's all relative. Plus, you'll see top players push serves back all the time, both long and short. They understand that ball control is top priority when receiving; a consistent, well-placed return is more effective than an erratic attack.

If you have trouble returning serves, don't worry; you're not alone. Receive is probably hardest thing to learn in table tennis. There are just too many variables to respond to. And yet, if you learn a few basic concepts, you can develop a solid receive game.

At the most basic level, there are three things a beginner should focus on. What type of serve is it? How should I return it? Where should I

return it?
What Type of Serve Is It?

Reading the serve means quickly reading if the serve is a fast serve or a spin serve, or perhaps both. (If neither, then it probably isn't a good serve. And note that no-spin is a spin serve, but only effective if it looks like spin.)

If it is a spin serve, then you have to read the type of spin. What direction was the racket moving *at contact*? (Ignore any motion before and after contact.) If downward, then it's a backspin serve; if upward, it's a topspin serve; if sideways, it's a sidespin serve. If the racket was moving sideways and up, then it's sidespin-topspin. If it's moving sideways and down, then it's sidespin-backspin. Since there are two types of sidespin (spinning left or right), this doubles the number of sidespin serve possibilities. (We won't worry about corkscrewspin since you rarely see that at lower levels.)

With all the possibilities, and with you only having a split second to react, how can you possibly make a good return? This is where your choice of receive becomes important.

How Should I Return It?

If it's a fast serve, your options are simple. Move to the ball and return it with a forehand or backhand. (This could be a block, a drive, or a loop, depending on your game.)

You can simplify things by dividing spin serves into two types: those with backspin, and those without backspin. Then all you have to do is push back those with backspin, and use a regular forehand or backhand against anything else. There, wasn't that simple?

If you push a sidespin-backspin serve, it will only break a little bit. And so you can just push toward the middle, and it'll usually stay on the table. (If it really jumps sideways off your paddle, it was probably a pure sidespin or side-top serve, and you shouldn't be pushing.)

Similarly, if you hit a topspin serve, a sidespin-topspin serve, or a sidespin serve with a regular forehand or backhand, the ball will go back almost the same. There'll be some break, but not enough to throw you off too much. The sidespin on a serve might make a drive go a little bit to the side, but not much. (Contrast this with pushing a sidespin serve, where the ball shoots off to the side.) It may be counter-intuitive, but the more aggressively you return a sidespin or topspin serve, the less the opponent's spin takes on your paddle, and so the more control you have over the spin. However, if you get too aggressive, you also lose control. You have to find a balance.

Against no-spin serves, you can push or drive. Take your pick. Just remember that a spinless ball is rather dead, and if you drive it, you'll have to put a bit more energy into the shot. You'll also find that you have to push more into a spinless ball to create backspin, since you won't have the incoming backspin to rebound back as backspin.

Where Should I Return It?

You could simply return the ball to your opponent's weaker side. However, it's often best to go to the stronger side, and then come back to the weaker side. This allows you to choose which ball the opponent gets to use his strong side against, and then making him move to hit from his weaker side. If you just play to the weaker side, such as the backhand, the opponent doesn't have to move to hit the shot, and he can choose when he wants to step over and use his strong forehand out of the backhand side. If you go to the forehand first, he has to move to that side, which opens up the weaker backhand, and makes him move to hit it. However, at lower levels and against slower opponents, you might want to just go mostly to the weaker side. You'll have to judge how often to do each.

But first you have to be able to put the ball where you want it. I've already mentioned that if you attack the sidespin and topspin serves, and push the backspin and backspin-sidespin serves, the sidespin won't affect you too much. But they will affect your return some, and you should learn to compensate for the sidespin or you will lose accuracy. To do this, you'll want to aim away from where the sidespin is pulling your return. How do you do this?

There's a simple rule to follow: aim where the racket started. For example, against a backhand sidespin serve, your return will tend to go off to your left, which is your opponent's forehand. His serve motion started on his backhand side and moved to his forehand side. So aim where the racket started—his backhand side. Similarly, since a forehand pendulum serve starts from a server's forehand side and moves to his backhand side, you'll want to aim to his forehand side. Experiment with this and soon you'll gain greater control over your receive.

Rallying Tactics

Once into the rally, it's all about consistency, placement, and picking your shots. Consistency is key; you'll remember that I said near the start of this chapter that "The most important 'tactic' for a beginner is to develop the fundamentals, which is actually strategic thinking." Now it's time to put this into practice. Hopefully you are taking the initiative on your serve while neutralizing your opponent's serve. Once into the rally, what do you do?

Again, consistency is key at all levels. What you should learn from

Table Tennis Tactics for Thinkers

watching the top players is not that they can attack almost any ball, but that all of their shots are *consistent*. Take that to heart, and keep upping the level of the shots you can do consistently.

You want to find ways to get your best shots into play against your opponent's weaker shots. You do this with serve and receive, and with your own rally shots. For example, if you have a good forehand from the backhand corner, if you are in a backhand-to-backhand rally, look for a chance to hit one a little quicker and more aggressively to the opponent's wide backhand or elbow. This will likely get you a return that's a bit weaker and allow you to step around and attack with your forehand.

Or if you push and block well, place your pushes where the opponent doesn't have an easy attack. Or if you have a good backhand, then keep your shots deep and aggressive to the opponent's backhand, so he doesn't have an angle into your forehand, and so you'll be able to keep hitting backhands or easy forehands.

But don't forget the strategic thinking. If you have a strong backhand and a weaker forehand, perhaps, just maybe, you'll want to consider playing rallies where you use your forehand more, and thereby develop it.

In general, focus on keeping the ball to the wide corners or the opponent's elbow; keep the ball deep in most rallies; and focus on serves, receives, and rallying shots that set up your strengths or set you up to go after the opponent's weaknesses. Choose whether to play mostly to the opponent's weaker side, or whether to draw him to the other side by playing to the strong side, and then coming back to the weak side.

Read over the many tactical tools covered in the following chapter on Conventional Tactics. Find what tools you have, or can develop, and use them. Write down the tactical tools that help you win, or ones you need to develop strategically. Then play practice games where you focus on using and developing those tactics. Don't get stuck using just a few tactics; experiment and find out what works.

Rushing

Perhaps the biggest stumbling block to good tactics for beginners is a tendency to rush, where players practically grab the ball and serve without thinking. Take your time between points, think things over (especially when serving), then clear your mind, focus, and play.

On the other hand, if your opponent is falling apart, whether mentally or physically, that's the time to play fast. Why give an opponent time to recover?

CHAPTER SIX
Conventional Tactics

Conventional tactics are the backbone of your tactical game, and you should develop them strategically. Unconventional tactics, covered in the next chapter, often win matches, but in most cases something more conventional works. So focus on conventional tactics; there is a reason they are "conventional," and that is because they work.

Far too often a player is struggling to figure out how to stop an opponent from dominating play, and a coach will say something simple that changes everything, such as "Serve short," or "Keep the ball deep," or "Stop pushing every serve back," or "Attack after your serve." There are lots and lots of conventional tactics. They are the standard tactics that coaches tell players over and Over and OVER. I think they should be put on a large poster and plastered on walls at every club.

2004 Olympics Men's Singles Gold Medalist Ryu Seung Min of South Korea plays a conventional penhold looping game - run around and loop everything with the forehand!
Photo by Diego Schaaf

Depth

One of the most important weapons you have is depth. If you keep the ball deep on the table during a rally, your opponent will have great difficulty in attacking effectively. He'll be pushed off the table, he won't be able to get good angles against you, and you'll have more time to respond to his shots. Since your opponent will be farther off the table, he'll be farther from your side of the table, making his target farther away, and so making it harder for him to keep the ball deep. And so you end up controlling the table, hitting balls over the table aggressively and at wide angles (or to the opponent's elbow), while he has to run the shots down.

This is especially true when playing "weird" styles. If the opponent uses a surface you are not used to, or hits the ball in a strange fashion, then you need more time to respond, and depth gives you that time. If you put the ball short, you'll have far less time to respond to these weird incoming shots.

Table Tennis Tactics for Thinkers

Two classic examples of the importance of depth are in regular topspin rallies and pushing. Often a player will complain that his opponent's smash is too good. A coach would probably tell him it's because his shots aren't going deep enough, giving the opponent an easy smash. Or a player will complain that his opponent's loop is too strong. A coach would probably tell him it's because his pushes aren't going deep enough, thereby giving the opponent an easy loop.

Short Balls

As important as keeping the ball deep is, it is equally important at the start of the rally to be able to keep the ball short. (Short means that, given the chance, the ball's second bounce on the opponent's side would hit the table.) This is especially important when serving. A long serve is much easier to attack then a short, low one. This doesn't mean that you should *always* serve short, but at the higher levels, the large majority of serves are either short, or half-long (also called "tweeny" serves), where the second bounce, given the chance, would be right around the end line. (At the higher levels, many players favor serves where the second bounce goes just off the end, inviting the receiver to loop—but because the serve just barely goes off the end, with the table in the way, the receiver often loops weakly, giving the server an easy counterloop or smash. This takes great serve control, fast footwork, and a strong attack against a soft but possibly spinny loop.)

In a rally, it is very difficult to keep the ball short and low, which is why it is more important when serving. However, against a low, short serve with backspin, often the best return is a short push. This makes it difficult for the server to attack with a loop. At the higher levels, many rallies start with a short serve, a short receive, and sometimes another one or two short pushes before a player finds a ball to attack.

Varying Depth

If your shots are unpredictable, then you put pressure on your opponent. So it is important to vary your depth. Sometimes serve or return the serve long, sometimes short. In rallies, while you should mostly go deep, you should mix in change-ups where your ball goes slower and shorter on the table, especially against a player who has already backed up. Some players like to get into a pocket a few feet off the table where they steadily attack deep balls; a short ball throws their timing off while drawing them out of that comfortable pocket, leaving them vulnerable to an attack.

Placement

You almost always want your shots to go to one of three spots: wide to the backhand, wide to the forehand, or to the elbow (the middle).

Why go to the middle backhand or forehand, where the opponent is waiting, when you can make your opponent move to hit the ball? Not only do they have to move to the ball (forcing errors), but they have to go out of position, often leaving them open on the next shot. Even when warming up, make a practice of hitting your shots to the wide corners so that you'll do the same in a match.

When going wide crosscourt there are really two placements: to the corner itself (which maximizes how much table you have to aim for), and outside the corner (which often puts the shot out of range of your opponent). You should look to go outside the corner against short balls, when hitting from your own wide angle (which gives you a wide angle back), and often when looping wide (since the extra topspin pulls the ball down, so you don't need as much table to aim for), especially if you can sidespin loop so the ball breaks left (i.e. a hook loop).

Often the best place to go is the opponent's elbow, the transition point between forehand and backhand. (If a player favors one side—forehand or backhand—then the transition point might be a bit to the side of the elbow, so make sure to figure this out early.) For most players, it's easier to move wide to a corner and stroke than to move to the middle and do so. First, you have to make a decision on whether to play forehand or backhand. Second, when moving wide, you can actually use the movement to rotate into the shot. When moving to the middle, you are going the wrong way, and so timing it and making a strong shot can be tricky.

Going to the middle also opens up the court. If your opponent plays a forehand from the middle of the table and he doesn't have fast footwork, his forehand side is open. If he moves to cover it, he's moving away from his backhand side, and may leave that open. So it's a common strategy to attack the middle, and then go after a corner. However, beware-- an opponent with good footwork who makes a good loop from the middle will often dominate on the next shot as well.

Disguised Placement

If you always aim your shot to one of the three main placements (wide corners, middle), and then go there, the opponent can get into a rhythm and respond to these shots by simply watching where you are aiming. It's important to be able to disguise your placement as long as possible. This is somewhat advanced, and you should make sure your strokes are developed before overdoing this, but you need to start developing this habit early so that it becomes ingrained.

Learn to aim for one spot, and at the last second, just before you start your forward swing, go somewhere else. For example, set up to play your forehand to the left. Then, at the last second before you start your

Table Tennis Tactics for Thinkers

forward swing, rotate your shoulders back and go to the right. Or aim to the right, and at the last second, whip your shoulders around and go left. It's even easier on the backhand to change placement at the last second. For regular backhands, you'd want to face the direction you are going to hit. To be deceptive, at the last second rotate the shoulders so you aim the other way. If you are backhand blocking, it's even easier, especially if aiming to the right before going to the left—just pull your wrist back at the last second so the racket aims left.

Consistency

At every level, consistency is king. At the lower levels, whoever is more consistent usually wins. At higher levels, even where players are going for shots, a player who isn't consistent with his shots isn't going to do very well. If you watch top players, you probably see how well they attack, but notice how consistent they are with *all* their shots? They rarely make unforced errors. One of your best weapons is to simply be more consistent than your opponent. If you make only two unforced errors per game, and he makes six, he's spotting you a 6-2 lead. At its most fundamental level, tactics is all about consistency—if you aren't consistent (relative to your opponent), then your other tactics won't help much. You should use tactics to get into rallies where you are comfortable and therefore consistent, while avoiding ones where you are inconsistent. (Meanwhile, you should strategically work on developing the shots you need that are inconsistent.)

Height

Generally you want to keep the ball low, or you'll be picking up your opponent's shot at the barriers. However, sometimes you can arc the ball high and deep with topspin, and this will throw opponents off. For example, many blockers have more trouble blocking against a high-arcing loop then against one that comes at them straighter. And when off the table, a higher topspin return (especially combined with sidespin) increases your consistency while creating a fast, arcing bounce on the far side that can give an opponent trouble.

Spin

Table tennis is a game of spin. At the most basic level, you learn to serve and rally with some topspin and backspin, and use both of these and sidespin on your serves. As you get more advanced, you learn to use all types of spin on your serve, and to rally with lots of topspin or backspin, and sometimes sidespin.

When serving, you want lots of spin, variation, and deception. In general, you want to be able to produce great spin, with all or most of the many variations possible—topspin, backspin, sidespin in both directions, perhaps corkscrewspin in both directions, and combinations of these. You also want deception—a spinny serve that's easy to read isn't as effective as a less spinny serve that is misread. (In fact, one of the most effective serves is a no-spin serve that looks spinny—a "heavy no-spin serve.") All of this will be covered in more detail in the chapter on serving tactics.

When rallying, you want to be able to attack with topspin, whether with the extreme topspin of a loop, or the more moderate topspin in a drive. You also want to be able to produce heavy backspin when pushing, and for some players, when chopping against an opponent's attack. Sidespin is used less often in rallies, but many players use it effectively when pushing, blocking, counterlooping, and lobbing.

Quickness

The quicker you hit your shot, the more rushed the opponent will be. This is the basic strategy of a blocker, especially a jab-blocker, who takes everything off the bounce with aggressive, well-placed blocks. Whoever is quicker often controls the table, forcing the opponent off the table. If your opponent is quicker than you, then you have to take this into account when working out your tactics—but note that even if the opponent is quicker, you can use tactics so that you get the first quick, aggressive shot, thereby putting pressure on the opponent before he can do this to you.

Speed

Ultimately, the most effective weapon in a player's arsenal is pure speed. A good smash isn't returned very often except by top players, and even then it is usually returned so that you can smash again. And so most top players base their game on looking for a shot to put away, either by smashing, or (more often at the higher levels) with a loop kill. The problem, of course, is that it is difficult to smash or loop kill most shots (at least for most of us), and so you have to work for that shot—i.e. use tactics to set up your putaway.

Varying Speed

It's not all about hitting at high speeds. Varying the speed of your shots will throw off your opponent's timing. Rather than hit three aggressive balls at the same speed, which an opponent can get into a rhythm against, hit one or two hard ones, then when the opponent is expecting another, hit the next one a little softer, and watch him struggle with it.

Table Tennis Tactics for Thinkers

The Serve

The serve is a unique weapon—you have complete control over it. You don't have to worry about your opponent interfering with your serve; your serve is as good as you make it. So turn it into a weapon, one that both wins points for you and sets you up to attack. (See the chapter on Service Tactics.)

Serve and Attack

This is different from service alone. If you develop your serves, and develop your attack, you should be able to turn them into a dynamic duo. There are few things more important, and less used at the beginning and intermediate level, as serve and attack. It's a basic tactic that should be central to your game.

Other Shots

Everything else you do can be a weapon. I'm not going to list every shot and its value here, though I hope to go over most of them later on. Suffice to say that any shot you do well can become a weapon, if used properly.

Pattern Play

All experienced players develop various types of pattern play. These are shot sequences that consistently win them points. For example, a looper might serve backspin, loop the push return at the opponent's middle to draw the opponent out of position, and then loop a winner to a corner. Or he might serve no-spin short and low to the middle, and reasonably expect a deep return he loops, say, down the line for a winner, perhaps faking the loop the other way first to mess up the opponent. Or a player might serve backhand-type sidespin (from several possible serve motions) to an opponent's forehand, and expect a return toward his forehand side, which he then loops or hits to the opponent's wide forehand, catching him as he moves back into position away from the forehand side after receiving there. Or a player might serve slightly long (a half-long serve), and smash or counterloop the expected weak loop receive. Or against a two-winged looper, he might block one hard to the forehand to get the looper off the table, then dead block to the backhand to get the looper to backhand loop soft, then counter-attack the softer loop to the looper's middle.

The patterns are infinite—develop your own, and perhaps write them down to help remember them. They become your bread and butter point-winners. Weaker players and many peers won't be able to stop you from doing your favorite patterns, and they may threaten stronger players as well.

At the same time, don't get so addicted to pattern play that you are unable to deal with an opponent who breaks up your patterns. Learn to play the ball as it is played, whether it is part of a favored pattern or not. The best players in the world have their own patterns, but they are the best in the world because they can respond strongly to whatever the opponent throws at them.

Locking Up Your Opponents

The easiest and simplest way of beating a player is to "lock him up." This basically means forcing him to do what he doesn't want to do. The classic case is to force a player with a weak backhand to go backhand to backhand. Another example would be take away an opponent's strong loop and force him to instead block by looping first each rally.

How do you "lock someone up"? Often, the best bet is to base much of your tactics toward this goal. It often takes some thinking to figure out how. You've got to figure out what your opponent doesn't want to do. Then you have to figure out how, using your own weapons, you can force him to do this. Too often players think only about what they want to do, and forget about forcing their opponents to do what they don't want to do.

I'll give an example here of how some smart opponents with strong forehands through the years have "locked me up." Anyone who plays me knows I have a steady backhand in fast rallies, but that I don't counter-hit that strongly with it. I make up for this by usually keeping the ball very wide to the opponent's backhand to avoid the opponent's forehand. I don't go down the line as much as I'd like because the shot simply isn't consistently strong enough to give a good forehand player difficulty. Some opponents have realized that when they attack my backhand, they didn't have to wait and see where my return would be or how strong; they would anticipate that steady but not-too-strong return to their wide backhand, and step around to attack it with their forehand before they could see for certain that that was where I was going. They knew that even if I changed directions and went to their forehand, it usually wouldn't be that strong a shot, and so they'd have time to react to it. Meanwhile, players who didn't anticipate the softer returns and waited until I committed wouldn't have time to step around against it because of the placement to their wide backhand, and so I'd take them down, backhand-to-backhand. The result? The smart ones would sometimes "lock me up," while I'd lock up the not-smart ones, the ones who'd wait to see what should be a somewhat predictable shot. (If you are from my club and we play practice matches, please refrain from reading the above.)

Table Tennis Tactics for Thinkers

Forcing an Opponent Out of Position

There are a number of ways to effectively force an opponent out of position. You can do this by either moving him side to side or in and out or some combination of this. In practical terms, here are some ways to do so.

Corners—You play one ball wide to either the forehand or backhand. As the opponent moves wide to return the shot, he either leaves the other wide corner open, or he moves to cover that side so quickly that he leaves the other corner open. (This is really two tactics, since you can start by going wide to either the forehand or backhand.)

Middle—You go to the opponent's middle (playing elbow), usually aggressively so as not to set him up for an easy shot from his stronger side. If he moves to cover it with his forehand, he leaves his forehand side open, and if he moves to cover it with his backhand, he leaves his backhand side open. You either play to the open side, or if the opponent moves to cover that side too quickly, you go the other way.

Short to forehand, deep to backhand—You serve or push a ball short to the forehand, bringing the opponent in over the table. Then he's jammed over the table and vulnerable to a deep ball to the backhand. Sometimes the opponent moves so quickly to cover the wide backhand that he's vulnerable to another short ball to the forehand, or to deep to the wide forehand.

Short to backhand, deep to forehand—You serve or drop a ball short to the backhand, bringing the opponent in over the table. Then he's jammed over the table and vulnerable to a deep ball to the forehand. Sometimes the opponent moves so quickly to cover the wide forehand that he's vulnerable to another short ball to the backhand, or to deep to the wide backhand.

Deep to backhand against a forehand player—Against a forehand-oriented player, you play the ball deep to the backhand over and over, often by pushing, until the opponent steps around to attack with his forehand. You quick-block the ball to his wide forehand, or if he moves too quickly to cover that, come right back at his backhand again.

In the scenarios given above, I've given two places to place the ball after forcing the opponent out of position. In each case there is a third option—if the opponent is hustling to cover the corners, you can go after his middle. It's hard to cover the middle when you are moving to get back into position. (This is why it is rarely a good idea to be moving back into position when the opponent is hitting the ball. It's better to be slightly out of position than in motion as the opponent is making his shot.)

How to apply the above? Study your opponent, and focus on using your serve, receive, and rally shots to set up the above, and turn your opponent into a puppet—and you hold the strings!

Moving opponents in and out

We've already talked about depth and moving players both side to side and in and out, and now it's time to elaborate. Most players learn early in their table tennis lives the importance of moving opponents side to side, playing the three spots—wide backhand, wide forehand, and the opponent's middle. However, a quote from Dan Seemiller at a camp many years ago has always stood out for me. He said moving an opponent in and out was even more important than moving them side to side. The two main examples of this are:

- Serving short or pushing short, and then attacking deep, especially if you use the diagonals, i.e. go short to the forehand and attack the deep backhand, or short to the backhand and attack the deep forehand. Or in both cases, after dropping the ball short, attack the middle. This involves moving an opponent both in and out and side to side.
- Forcing an opponent off the table in a rally, and then dropping the ball short with a drop shot or dead block. Again, use the diagonals when possible, dropping to the short forehand and attacking the deep backhand, or short to the backhand and attacking the deep forehand. Or in both cases, after dropping the ball short, attack the middle.

In both of these cases you shouldn't always go short and then long; sometimes it's better to go short a second time, catching the opponent as he moves back to react to the expected deep ball.

These types of tactics are rare at the beginning level, are used by some at the intermediate level, and are central to most advanced games. At the higher levels you'll see receivers constantly mixing up short serve returns and attacks, with the server sometimes tied up trying to cover for both. Most serves at that level are short (or half-long), and if it was returned short, the server would either attack or sometimes drop it short again, forcing the receiver to cover for both.

Once an opponent is forced off the table, most players keep blasting the ball until they win the point. In most cases, while a short ball may set up the attack that forces the weak ball to put away, once you get that weak ball it's often better to keep attacking until you win the point. However, against a player who is returning your attacks consistently from off the table, sometimes it's better to take something off the attack to throw off the opponent's timing, and then blast the next ball. Perhaps take something off one of your smashes, forcing the opponent to adjust his timing, and then smash the next one at normal speed, forcing the opponent to adjust again. Or throw in a dead block to bring him in, and then attack

Table Tennis Tactics for Thinkers

again with the opponent now too close to the table to defend. Dan Seemiller, both now and when he was winning his five U.S. Men's Singles titles, would constantly mix up strong attacks and dead blocks.

So learn to turn your opponent into a marionette, and learn to yank his strings as you move him in and out.

2-2-1 Placement Rule

Where do most players block best? On the backhand. Where do most players attack the most? To the opponent's backhand. This never made sense to me.

When attacking there are three places you should normally go for: the wide forehand, the middle (the opponent's crossover point between forehand and backhand, usually around the elbow), and the wide backhand. Most beginning and intermediate players probably attack to the backhand twice as often as to the forehand, and almost never to the middle. We'll call it the 1-0-2 rule, i.e. they proportionately go once to the forehand, zero times to the middle, and twice to the backhand.

Instead, try the 2-2-1 rule, where you proportionately attack twice to the forehand, twice to the middle, and once to the backhand. (This assumes your opponent isn't able to counter-attack with his forehand consistently, as they often do at the higher levels, usually by counterlooping. If they do, change your attack placement accordingly, though it also might mean your attack is too soft, too short, or too predictable.) Few players block on the forehand as well as on the backhand, and nearly everyone's vulnerable at the middle. So why not go where the opponent is vulnerable?

There are exceptions to this rule. If you are going for a difficult attacking shot from a wide corner, go crosscourt, where you have more table. (The table is 9 feet long, but about 10.3 feet crosscourt, about 13.5 inches longer, almost seven more inches on the far side.) You also use the attack to set up your own follow-up shot, which means you might want to attack the spot opposite your own stronger side (since most attacks are returned crosscourt), so if your backhand is your strength, you might want to attack more often to the opponent's backhand so you get returns to your backhand. (But strategically, you might want to move the ball around more and develop your forehand.)

Also, you have to take into consideration your own positioning. For example, if you are attacking with your forehand from the wide backhand corner, if you attack down the line you are vulnerable to a crosscourt block to your forehand (unless you are fast on your feet), so you might go to the middle or backhand. And, as noted above, if the opponent is able to consistently counter-attack with his forehand you might want to attack there less often.

If You Have a Big Lead, Should You Experiment?

With games to 11, few leads are really safe. It only takes a short series of careless shots, and what seemed like a big lead becomes a big loss. However, if you do have a big lead, and the match won't be over if you win that game, consider experimenting with tactics for the next game. Don't do anything that's probably low percentage—but perhaps try out a new serve or new serve & follow, or a different receive, and see what happens. Often you'll find something that'll be useful later on. But caution—the first priority is to win the current game, so use some judgment here. If you do find a new tactic, you might then consider holding back on it in the next game, and do whatever you did to get your big lead in the previous game. After facing your "new" tactic, your opponent might not be ready for the tactics you had been using, and you now have an "ace in the hole."

Should You Stick with Your Best Shot if It Is Missing?

The situation: Your best shot is missing, and you are essentially spotting your opponent points and losing because of this. Should you keep using it, or abandon it? It takes lots of match experience and hard thinking before a player can consistently make a sound judgment in a situation like this as to whether to change his tactics, or keep using the shot that is missing in order to get it going again.

There are three possible reasons why you are missing your best shot: You are nervous, your opponent is doing something to throw you off, or your timing is simply off.

Psychologically, you have to learn to be calm during a match. That's mostly separate from the tactical side. If you do get nervous, that's a good time to take a one-minute time-out, or at least take your time to get yourself together. Nervousness is the most common reason for a player's best shot to start missing.

The majority of players, even at the advanced levels, do not recognize when an opponent is doing something that is throwing them off. Those that don't recognize these strategies often talk and think strategy quite a bit—but only from their point of view, forgetting to take the opponent's tactics into account. Ideally, you neutralize your opponent's strategy by dominating with your own—but to do so, you need to know what the opponent is doing, or is capable of doing. So the first thing to do is figure out whether you are missing because you are really off, or because your opponent is doing something to throw you off. If the latter, then you have to find a way to counter it.

Finally, there are those times when, for inexplicable reasons, you are simply "off," and your best shot keeps missing. That's when the judgment from lots and lots of match play can pay off as you judge whether to keep

Table Tennis Tactics for Thinkers

using the shot, in the hopes that it will come back, or switch to other shots and tactics.

A good general rule is that you have to get your best shot going in any competitive match, or you'll probably lose. Against stronger players, you almost certainly are going to need your best shot, so keep using it. Against a weaker player you might retire the shot and find other ways to win. Against players around your own level, you will probably need your best shot. However, if you see a way to win without your suddenly-erratic best shot—perhaps by tactically taking away your opponent's own best shot so both of you are going with your "B" games—then perhaps you should take it.

Should You Choose to Serve at the Start of a Match?

The time when a player is most likely to miss easy shots is at the very start of the match. That's when a player may not yet be fully warmed up or used to his opponent's shots yet. So it's often best to let the other guy serve first, let him mess up on his serve & attack at the start, and then get your chance to serve, when you are more into the match.

There's another, more mathematical way of looking at this. Suppose in a given match, the server will score 60% of the points. (In reality, it is not that high in competition matches—more like 55% or so.) So you figure every time you serve a point, you should score an average of 0.6 points. That means if you mess up on your serve and lose two in a row because you aren't yet warmed up, you've mathematically lost 2 x 0.6 points, or 1.2 points. If you do so when receiving, you've only lost 2 x 0.4 points, or 0.8 points. In other words, you can more easily afford to lose a point on the other guy's serve than on your own—so let him serve when he's not warmed up, and put off your own serving until you are slightly more warmed up.

The exception, of course, is the player who needs to get a quick lead to build up confidence. If you lose confidence when you fall behind and don't play as well, then by all means serve first. But in this case, you need to work on your mental game.

Time-Out Tactics

Each player is allowed a one-minute time-out during a tournament or league match. (Often a coach calls the time-out, but the player can waive that off if he doesn't want one at that time, except in a team match.) When should you call a time-out? Here are some scenarios where you should call a time-out—but remember, you are only allowed one, so choose carefully. I've put them in order of priority. There are also times you shouldn't call a time-out, such as when you are in the zone (i.e. focused and playing well), and a time-out might only disturb your concentration. If a coach calls a time-out and you really, really don't think you need one (and want to save it for later), then waive him off. (You might want to let him know in advance you might do this.)

When to Call a Time-out
1. **When losing focus before a key point.** This is the most important time to call a time-out. A time-out is a good way to get your concentration back.
2. **To think about or discuss tactics at a key point.** Generally do this when you are about to serve, since you have complete control over choosing your two serves. If you have a coach, he might be able to help choose two serves to use. Call it when you are receiving mostly if you have a good idea what the opponent will serve, and are debating how you should return that serve. Or call it to think or discuss any other tactical plans. It's also valuable to call a time-out when you are winning a relatively close game (especially late in a match), such as at 10-8 or 9-7, so as to clear your mind, think tactically, and close out that game. This is often when the Chinese team calls time-outs.
3. **When falling behind in a key game.** It's useful to call a time-out if you lose the first game and are falling behind in the second (since you absolutely do not want to fall behind 0-2), or if you have already lost two games and will lose the match if you lose another. The key is not to wait until you are way behind; instead, call the time-out when you are still relatively close and can still find a way to come back. The time-out allows you to make sure you are focused and to rethink your tactics. It's also a good way to give your opponent a chance to cool off if he's playing well—there's nothing wrong with calling a time-out in hopes of disturbing his concentration or throwing off his rhythm.
4. **Desperation tactic.** Far too many players call time-outs as a desperation tactic near the end of a match when they are way behind and are pretty much out of it, but this rarely leads to a win. If you are losing badly, why wait until you are way down in the last game? It's far better to call the time-out earlier in the hope of not being in this situation, where the time-out will rarely help.

CHAPTER SEVEN
Tactical Examples

U.S. Women's Coach Doru Gheorghe (right) coaching U.S. #1 Gao Jun at the 2003 World Championships. Pips-out penholder Gao often won with "unconventional" tactics, such as constant drop shots and change-of-pace blocking with backspin and sidespin.
Photo by Diego Schaaf

Conventional and Unconventional Tactics

In most cases, conventional tactics are your first choice; that's why they are conventional. However, you should be flexible in your thinking, especially when facing an unconventional player, or a conventional player with some unconventional aspect to his game. The higher the level, the less unconventional tactics work—but used intelligently in the right circumstances, they work at all levels. (And many "unconventional tactics" are just conventional tactics that aren't used that often.)

For example, at the higher levels, most players serve short so the opponent can't loop the serve. However, what if they play a pips-out penholder who doesn't have a very good loop, but is a great blocker and hitter? The pips would handicap him when looping deep serves, but are a tremendous advantage against short serves. Spin doesn't take on the pips as much, and they give maximum control in hitting and in pushing long or short against short serves. And yet, many top players, when faced with this type of game, will use their usual short serves as if they were playing a looper, and handicap themselves. Better tactical players would serve long as often as possible, thereby handicapping the opponent. A player may not be comfortable using these other service tactics against less conventional styles, but the only way he'll get comfortable doing so is by using these service tactics until he becomes comfortable doing so—it's strategic thinking.

What I'm going to do now is give examples of both conventional and unconventional tactics that I've coached, used, or seen used successfully. While you may be able to use some of these tactics, it's just as important to understand the type of sideways thinking that led to some of the unconventional tactics. Often if you really understand how the opponent plays, and what he does well and has trouble with, you'll find an unconventional tactic that will win the match for you. You'll also note that in many or most cases, what I call "unconventional" tactics might in other circumstances be completely conventional.

Inventing a Serve

At the Junior Olympics one year I was coaching Andy Li in the final of Under 16 Boys. (The opponent, from California, was the top seed and a pretty big favorite. (He was rated about 2350, while my player was about 2150.) The Californian was a conventional looper, but had one unique aspect to his game—he held his index finger down the middle of the paddle, like 1967 World Champion Nobuhiko Hasegawa. Andy had a big forehand loop, a pips-out backhand, relatively slow footwork, and a very good forehand pendulum serve that unfortunately always went long.

*Junior Olympic Champion Andy Li.
Photo by Houshang Bozorgzadeh*

In the first game, the Californian looped the serve over and over, and easily won. (This was when games were to 21, and was a best of three.) Between games I asked Andy if he could serve backhand. He said he hadn't served backhand in a game in his life. I said, "Can you just tap the ball over the net to the guy's forehand with a backhand serve?" He said yes, but why would he do that? We didn't have time to elaborate, but I convinced him to give up his strong forehand pendulum serve, which had dominated all his previous opponents but was ineffective here, and went for this simple little dink serve over the net.

It worked. Because of the opponent's grip, he couldn't flip the ball down the line effectively to Andy's backhand. And so every return either was soft to Andy's backhand (he'd crunch it), or came out aggressively toward Andy's strong forehand. Andy serve and looped over and over, won the next two games, and the national championship.

Note that what was unconventional about this was that the player had to learn and use a new serve in the middle of a match. If he already had a good serve that would go low and short to the forehand, then using that serve would have been completely conventional.

Simple Angle Shot Wins Title

In the final of Under 12 Boys at the Junior Nationals, the opponent won the first game easily by serving short backspin and no-spin to my player's backhand or middle. My player, Amaresh Sahu, would push the ball back to the corners, but the opponent was able to forehand loop all these pushes with great power. Since Amaresh didn't have an effective short push at that time, there didn't seem to be a way of stopping this.

Table Tennis Tactics for Thinkers

Amaresh Sahu
Photo by Terry Berman

But I noticed that the opponent seemed to move robotically when stepping around his backhand corner, always to the same spot, where he could cover his backhand corner. So I told Amaresh to take every serve right off the bounce, and don't worry about popping it up, just return it softly at an *extreme* angle to the opponent's backhand. All that mattered was to get the ball well outside the corner—and lo and behold, the opponent, so grooved from years of drilling to go to that one spot around his backhand corner, couldn't take the extra quarter step to attack this ball, even if it was weak. Since he didn't have a strong backhand attack, a simple well-angled push—even a weak one—stopped the opponent's attack, and won the national championship for Amaresh.

Using a similar tactic, I won a match against an older but probably stronger opponent. He was a pips-out penholder with a good block and a great smash. But like the player above, he was drilled into stepping only so far around his backhand side. So the entire match all I did was return serves and backhands to his wide, wide backhand, thereby taking out his scary forehand despite many of my shots being soft and very smashable.

Forehand Blocking and Service Cycling

I was coaching then nine-year-old Derek Nie (top two of his age in the U.S.) against a much stronger player. Derek had a very nice forehand smash, but he simply couldn't hit hard enough against the opponent, who returned shot after shot. Derek mixed in blocks, but they also weren't effective. Then I noticed something—when Derek smashed, the opponent positioned himself to guard against the crosscourt shot, but was fast enough to cover the

Derek Nie
Photo by Paul Derby

down-the-line smash. However, his positioning meant that he had a long way to go to cover a dead, down-the-line block. So I told Derek to fake crosscourt smashes to the opponent's forehand, but then do a forehand block soft to the opponent's backhand. The opponent was unable to make a good return against this shot, and too close to react to the next smash, so Derek began to dominate these rallies.

The opponent handled Derek's serves pretty well, except for one. If that one was overused, the opponent would get used to it. So I told Derek to just throw every serve he had at the player, and just keep cycling through them all. Because of the huge number of different serves, the opponent was unable to get into a rhythm, and he ended up struggling against serves that early on he'd handled better, while never getting used to the one he had trouble with.

Between the dead forehand block and the serve cycling tactics—and excellent overall play!—Derek won.

Multiple Tactics for Multiple Styles

There's a top player who is equally good playing an all-out forehand looping game or playing a two-winged attack. (Actually, there are many who can do this, but with this particular player it's very distinct when he goes from one to the other.) There are simple tactics you can use against either of these games, though you still have to do these tactics at a high level to make them work. The problem is that this player is good at switching from one style to the other, and the tactics that work for one do not work against the other. For example, when he's playing all-out forehand, he's vulnerable to aggressive shots to the wide forehand, but if you do this when he's playing two-winged attack, he rips the ball. When he's playing two-winged attack, he's vulnerable in the middle, but if you do this when he's playing all-out forehand attack, he also rips the ball. What to do?

Fortunately, you don't play these two styles from the same stance. When the player plays all-out forehand attack, he's in a forehand stance, with his right foot back, plus he's edging toward his backhand side. When he's playing two-winged attack, he stands neutral, with his feet pretty much parallel to the table. The problem is most players aren't aware of what the opponent is doing during the point—or even at the start of the point—except as he hits the ball, and so few players notice when this player changes styles, sometimes in mid-point. If you are aware of his stance during the point, you can play the proper tactics. If you aren't aware, you better be very, very good or he will rip winner after winner past you. I've coached a few players against this player, and once they became aware of his changing stances, they learned to place the ball appropriately and learned how to (sometimes) beat him.

Table Tennis Tactics for Thinkers

Carrying an Opponent

There's a top player I was about to play who can play equally well as a penhold attacker and as a shakehand chopper with long pips on the backhand. (This was back in the days when you could change rackets at any time during a match.) Now it so happens that I eat choppers for breakfast (at least back in my prime), and I knew that he couldn't challenge me chopping. However, as a penholder attacker, things could get tricky.

He started the match as a penholder, and we battled. Then, halfway through the first game, with me leading by a point or two, he switched to his chopper blade. (This was when games were to 21.) I desperately wanted him to stick to chopping, and so I carried him. I faked all sorts of difficulties, struggling to lift his chops, mis-hitting shots all over the place, and let him actually take the lead until near the end. Then I won several points in a row, did an intentional awkward miss, and finally "pulled it out" 21-19. He had no idea that I had carried him the whole way, that I could have beaten him with ease as long as he chopped. Instead, he stuck to chopping, and I "struggled" all through the next game and just pulled it out as well. While this specific tactic no longer works (since you can't change rackets in a game anymore), the general tactic of "carrying" an opponent who plays more than one style may apply in some cases. (But only in rare cases; normally you shouldn't struggle on purpose!)

A similar version of this is to go after a serve you don't like. For example, if you have trouble with a certain short serve, flip or loop it aggressively and see what happens. If it hits, great. If it misses, seeing how confidently you went after the serve, the opponent might still be scared to use that serve again. I've used this strategy many times, especially against certain long serves that give me trouble and that I want to scare the server away from using.

Changing Service Position

At the North American Teams one year I was playing with slightly lower-ranked players as a player/coach. I was one of the three undefeated players in the division. The other two were two junior players from Canada. Our teams played in the final. Both of the Canadian juniors played the same style, which had created havoc throughout the division: big forehand looping attacks, but medium long pips on the backhand which they used to flat hit shot after shot. They quick-hit every short serve with their backhands (spin didn't take on their pips), even short ones to their forehand, and followed with their big forehands.

As I watched them play, I realized that they would have little trouble with my best serve, a forehand pendulum serve I do from my backhand corner, which sets up my forehand. No matter where I'd serve it, if it was long, they'd loop it; if it was short, they'd backhand hit it. I could use a tomahawk serve to their forehand, but that would take away my big serving strength. What to do?

When I went out to play the first of the two, I set up like I normally do to serve, in the backhand corner. Then I took two steps to my right, and spent the whole match serving forehand pendulum serves from my forehand corner. This gave me an angle into his forehand so that he'd have to receive with his forehand (or risk me going down the line to his open backhand side if he tried to cover the short forehand with his backhand), and so I was able to use my pendulum serve to his inverted forehand, something he had probably rarely had to deal with. Since he couldn't return it aggressively, I was able to move back into position after each serve to attack with my forehand. The same strategy worked against the other Canadian junior, and I won both matches. (Ironically, before the last match, the perceptive Canadian coach took the other junior off to a table and mimicked my serve over and over from the forehand side so the kid could practice against it, but it wasn't enough.) I won all three of my matches, but alas, we lost the final 5-3.

Dead Blocking Galore

Around 1990, I watched former U.S. Champion Scott Boggan play Mikael Appelgren of Sweden, who was either ranked #1 in the world or close to it. Scott's basically an all-out hitter, while Appelgren is a steady two-winged looper. Because of Scott's great smash, Appelgren stayed a bit off the table, ready to spin these shots back. Scott could have smashed shot after shot, but that's exactly what Appelgren is used to, and he would have spun them back until Scott either missed or was forced to block, and then

Scott Boggan
Photo by Mal Anderson

Appelgren would have attacked. Instead, Scott dead-blocked over and Over and OVER. Appelgren, guarding against the sudden smash and not used to all these dead balls, spun the balls back softly but was unable to attack effectively. When he saw a chance, Scott would fake a block and suddenly smash. And so what could have been an easy win for Appelgren against a supposedly much weaker player became a serious match. I forget the scores, but I believe it went the entire distance, with Appelgren finally winning something like 21-19 in the deciding game.

Table Tennis Tactics for Thinkers

The Tell-Tale Tongue and Service Telegraphing

There's a former member of the USA National Team who liked to mix in fast, deep serves every chance he could. I was coaching against him when I noticed something—whenever he served fast and deep, he'd stick his tongue out as he started to serve. I told my player, who spent the rest of the match attacking the deep serves to the point that the opponent had to give up on serving deep, and my player pulled off a minor upset. The same tactic against this player was used a number of times in future matches by other players I coached.

There are actually a lot of tell-tale signs that give away what a player plans to serve, and often you see them subconsciously without consciously knowing what it is. For example, there's a top junior at my club I recently played in practice who telegraphed when he was serving deep. I could tell every time, but it took me two games before I figured out what was giving it away—whenever he served deep, he'd set up with his racket slightly farther back and more closed than when he was going to serve short. I beat him three straight, and then told him what had happened. The cure? Set up each time as if you plan to serve the same serve, and only after you are set to serve do you "change" your serving plan to what you really want to serve.

Five-time U.S. Champion Dan Seemiller once told me that he could often tell what an opponent was serving before they served. The subtle clues are often there, you just have to look for them, both consciously and subconsciously. Trust your subconscious when it picks up on something. It usually knows what it's doing.

"I'm so nervous I think I'm gonna die!"

While writing this book, I was coaching 10-year-old Derek Nie at a major tournament. After a long battle against a much higher-rated player, he found himself leading 10-2 in the fifth. He then fell apart, missing easy shots, and lost four in a row. I was about to call a time-out but he beat me to it. He walked over and said, "I'm so nervous I think I'm gonna die!" After we finished laughing, I told him to put all his nervousness into a ball, and give me the ball, and I'd keep it on the sideline for him until the match was over. He handed over the ball of nervousness, and won, 11-7. (Later we tossed the ball of nervousness in the trash.) Often the best coaching isn't tactical but psychological.

Covering Up the Weak Spots Against Fast Hitter/Blockers

Here is an unconventional tactic I and some players I coach have used for years against fast hitters and blockers, especially in fast exchanges with junior players. Typically these players hit hard, quick shots over and over to the wide backhand, middle, and wide forehand. The tactic assumes you have a decent forehand and backhand, and can keep the ball in play pretty well, and can attack with your forehand against a quick shot if you see it coming and know where it's going to go.

As soon as you get into a fast rally, stand toward your backhand side with your feet in a slight forehand position, but rotated to the left so you are facing the table in a backhand position. By rotating at the waist or taking a short step with the left foot, you should be able to cover the wide backhand and middle with your backhand, using the incoming ball's speed to rebound it back. Watch the opponent until you see him about to go to your forehand. Immediately step over to the wide forehand and counter-attack. (This is where having your feet in a slight forehand position helps.) The key is you don't try to cover the entire forehand side with the forehand; you anticipate that it'll go to the wide corner and move there immediately to counter-attack. If the ball comes to your middle forehand, where you'd normally be comfortable, you'll have difficulty since you are anticipating it going to the wide forehand, since that's where top players and up-and-coming juniors are trained to go. What this strategy effectively does is move the middle weakness into the middle forehand, where few strong players will place the ball. Since your opponent is probably hitting down the line with his backhand, an aggressive counter-attack to his wide forehand usually wins the point.

Since I coach at the Maryland Table Tennis Center, where we have lots and lots of up-and-coming juniors who are extremely fast, I use this tactic in practice matches on an almost daily basis, to great success. I usually just counter-hit the crosscourt winner, but sometimes I loop it. It works either way. (Beware—if you use this tactic against a junior I'm coaching, I'll tell him to put the ball to your middle forehand. Hah!)

Sudden Chops—Conventional Becomes Unconventional

One of the great rivalries of USA Table Tennis was between Dan Seemiller and Eric Boggan, from the late 1970s to the late 1980s. Eric had overall better results overseas, beating more top players (though Dan was more consistent in mowing down "weaker" players), but head-to-head they met at numerous USA Nationals Men's Singles Finals. In the end, Dan won five titles, Eric two, despite Eric being "favored" (by rating and international ranking) to win perhaps two of the ones Dan won, particularly in 1982 and 1983 when Dan won close finals. The difference? Chopping.

Dan was primarily a one-winged forehand looper with a good backhand block, while Eric was one of the best blocker/counter-drivers in the world. Eric would go to his wide forehand and then come back to Dan's backhand, and there was no way Dan could compete backhand to

Table Tennis Tactics for Thinkers

backhand with Eric. So what did Dan do? He devoted 20-25 minutes a day to chopping. In the past, that would have been a conventional tactic, but not in the modern era of sponge and looping. But Eric was a blocker with a relatively weaker loop—and the strategy worked as Dan got out of those fast exchanges by backhand chopping. Against Dan's chops, Eric would sometimes attack, often weakly or erratically, or he'd push, giving Dan the chance to loop.

Down-the-Line Chopping

In a hardbat match (i.e. no sponge), I played a player with a much stronger backhand than mine, but who was slow on his feet. He took every ball off the bounce aggressively to wide angles, running me all over the table relentlessly. My usually reliable forehand started to fall apart. In desperation, I tried chopping, but the opponent kept hitting backhands off these shots, over and over to my weaker backhand. Then a light bulb went off in my head. The rest of the match, all I did was chop every ball as wide as possible to the opponent's wide, wide forehand. He was afraid to go to my forehand, where I would smash, and so rally after rally was his forehand drive down the line to my backhand chop. The opponent fell apart and I came from behind to win.

This was a case where I retired my "A" game (my forehand hitting) as well as my "B" game (backhand chopping all over the table) and won with my "C" game (chopping to one spot with little variation) by forcing my opponent to use his "D" game (his forehand).

Just Smash Everything

Way back in 1987 I was playing a match against a lefty 2300 looper. The guy was super consistent, and nothing seemed to work. I blocked, I smashed, I looped and counterlooped, and he held me under ten. About a year before I had become the full-time manager for the resident table tennis training program at the Olympic Training Center in Colorado Springs, and so was essentially a full-time practice partner/assistant coach, and my level had dropped a lot. And so my confidence level was approaching zero. Between games 13-year-old future Olympian Todd Sweeris came over and said, "Larry, you're getting killed. Just smash everything. You have nothing to lose." He was right. So I decided that no matter what, every time he looped, I'd go for a forehand smash. Lo and behold, with my tactics thus simplified, my game came together, and everything landed. I won two straight.

Just to be clear, this wasn't a matter of mindlessly smashing everything. It was a matter of playing tactically (mostly with lots of serve and receive variations) so that the opponent's opening loop wouldn't be too strong, and *then* mindlessly smashing everything.

The Deathly Down the Line

Before the USA National Cadet Team Trials one year I was watching videos of the top seed and trying to figure out how my player could beat him. There are zillions of possibilities, but finding those two or three is always the tricky part. In this case, I found two.

First, the kid had really good serves that went either very long or slightly long ("half-long" serves). He ate up opponents who returned these serves soft. Against opponents who looped them he'd switch to a shorter serve that wasn't nearly as effective. It takes a certain level to be able to effectively loop these tricky long and half-long serves, but the player I'd be coaching wasn't going to win if he couldn't. So we knew he absolutely had to loop these serves, including the slightly long ones.

Second, the kid often seemed to jump all over his opponents returns off his serves and aggressive angles—then I realized it was because most opponents returned his serves and aggressive angled shots crosscourt, and the kid always set up for the crosscourt return. When an opponent did go down the line, he often looked awkward and made soft returns.

So the player I was coaching—Tong Tong Gong—practiced looping both half-long serves and aggressive angle shots down the line. When he played the kid in the Trials, the tactics worked, and my player not only pulled off the upset, but went on to make the USA National Cadet Team.

Naah, Just Go Crosscourt (and Push Short at End)

At the U.S. Open one year, I coached Nathan Hsu (a top USA junior) against a Canadian. Nathan has a great backhand loop, and the opponent had trouble when Nathan moved it around. The problem was Nathan kept missing. Between games, with Nathan down 1-2 in games, I was telling him where to place it, but he looked sort of glum. I asked why, and he said he didn't have any confidence in his backhand loop anymore, that it was spraying all over the court. So we changed strategies, and simplified things: just keep backhand looping right into the opponent's wide backhand until he got an easy shot to put away. There wasn't a whole lot the opponent could do with this shot,

Nathan Hsu dominating with the backhand loop. Photo by Hans Hsu

Table Tennis Tactics for Thinkers

even though he mostly knew it was coming, and when he did make a weaker return, that's when Nathan could end the point to the middle or wide forehand, with either his forehand or backhand. The key was that Nathan got his nice backhand loop back, and went back to dominating with it.

This worked well, and Nathan won the fourth 11-6. The Canadian almost always served short, often no-spin, but when Nathan pushed short, the Canadian dominated with a nice flip. So Nathan had been flipping most of the Canadian's short serves, forcing wide-open topspin points that he was very good at. But at 2-2 in the fifth, Nathan flipped two balls and the opponent made strong loops off each to take a 4-2 lead. I realized the Canadian was literally serving short and then stepping back to loop. Nathan won the next two points on his serve (4-4), and then I did something that is usually considered a no-no in coaching—I called a time-out when my player had the "momentum," having won the last two points. But it was important. I told Nathan to push the next two serves short to the forehand, that if they were no-spin, to chop down on them softly, just keep it short. He looked skeptical, but this time I was pretty certain. And sure enough, the opponent was practically caught on his heels, and even though Nathan didn't push that low, the opponent wasn't ready, made a weak push, and Nathan won the point. The next point was almost a replay. The rest of the game the opponent stayed close to the table after his serve, ready to flip if Nathan pushed short, and so Nathan went back to flipping the serves, avoiding the opponent's dangerous flip. From down 2-4 in the fifth, Nathan won 11-5.

Immediately afterwards Nathan's mom came rushing over to ask what I'd told Nathan to do. I was relieved—what if Nathan hadn't executed well, and the advice had backfired? But this was one of those times where things went right—as they will more often than not if you play smart tactics.

No-Spin to the Middle to the Rescue!

I was coaching a match when a player from another match asked if I could coach him in his match. I told him I'd come over when I was finished with the match I was coaching. By the time I got over there, he was between games after losing the first two of the best of five to a lower-ranked player. I asked him what was happening. He said when he served the least bit long, the opponent looped his serve. When he served short backspin to the backhand or forehand, the opponent either dropped it short or quick-pushed at a wide angle. The player I was coaching had a powerful forehand attack, but was weaker on the backhand, and wanted to follow his serves with his forehand. The angled receives and short pushes were stopping this.

I suggested serving no-spin to the middle. When you serve short to the backhand, you give the opponent an extreme angle into your backhand. When you serve short to the forehand, you give him an extreme angle into your forehand. (And guarding that angle leaves you open on the backhand side.) And there's nothing easier to push short than a short backspin serve—while a short no-spin ball can be tricky to push short.

His eyes went wide for a second, and then he said, "Why didn't I think of that?" He went back out, served short no-spin to the middle at least 60% the rest of the way, and won three straight. (Ironically, he almost lost the match toward the end by over-using the short no-spin serve, allowing the opponent to get used to it. You always want to vary your serves.)

Afterwards we were discussing the match, and he made the observation that it's so easy to think of the obvious things on the sidelines, but when out there playing they are so easy to miss. So true.

Make It Up As You Go

I can't finish this section without mentioning Jan-Ove Waldner of Sweden, considered by many to be the greatest player ever. He was the master at messing up an opponent—nobody felt comfortable playing him. How much of this was planned and how much of it did he make up as he went along? He wasn't so much a tactician as a strategist, who strategically developed so many tactical

The Master—Jan-Ove Waldner
Photo by Diego Schaaf

tools that he had more weapons in his bag than anyone else. In matches, he'd just experiment until he found the ones that worked. He'd throw both convention and unconventional tactics at opponents, with changes of direction, pace, spin, and every sort of misdirection imaginable. The coach of the Chinese National Team once said that it was impossible to coach against Waldner because you never knew which Waldner you would be playing.

The moral is that if things aren't working, experiment until you find something that does work. Normally this will mean a conventional tactic, but sometimes it'll be decidedly unconventional. The moral also is to develop your tactical toolbox so you'll have these weapons on demand.

CHAPTER EIGHT

Table Tennis Tactics for Thinkers

Service Tactics

What is your goal when you serve? That is the primary question you must ask yourself when considering service tactics.

Serves are one of the most under-practiced aspects of the game, and yet they are often the quickest way to improve and to develop the tactical weapons needed to win. Not only does your serve start off half the rallies, but a good serve sets you up to attack, and if you do this enough, you improve your attack as well.

Remember in the chapter on Strategic Thinking I talked about how you needed to develop an overpowering strength? (If your overpowering strength happens to be serve or receive, then focus on the strongest shot in your game that your serve sets up.) The primary purpose of your service game should be to get that overpowering strength into play. But what is that strength?

Two-time World Cup Women's Singles Champion Guo Yan
Photo by Diego Schaaf

For many players, the answer is both easy and hard. It's easy because they know what they want to do: serve and loop, the most common goal at the higher levels. It's difficult because you can't effectively use the same serve over and over or your opponent will adjust. So even these players have to develop a repertoire of serves that set them up to do what they want to do.

So what do you want to do with your serve? There are two categories of serves, which I will call set-up serves and trick serves.

- **Set-up serves** are designed to set you up for whatever you do best, such as looping, hitting, blocking, or whatever else you do well, or want to learn to do well. For example, a looper might serve straight backspin so that he'll get a pushed return he can loop. A hitter might serve side-top so he can get a slightly popped up return he can hit. The purpose of a set-up serve isn't to win the point outright, though that often happens as opponents try to return it so you can't do what you want to do. Set-up serves are usually short serves (including half-long serves), but can also be deep serves.
- **Trick serves** *are* designed to win the point outright, either with a

miss or an easy pop-up. The problem with a trick serve is that they are often all or nothing; either they win the point outright by catching the opponent off guard, or the opponent attacks it effectively, putting the server on the defensive.

2009 World Men's Singles Champion Wang Hao of China . . . eyeing the ball as he serves
Photo by Diego Schaaf

A serve can be both a set-up serve and a trick serve. For example, a short sidespin-topspin serve might be a set-up serve, but if it really looks like backspin, it can also be a trick serve that gets missed over and over.

Regardless of what type of serve you are doing, don't telegraph it. You need to be able to pull off all types of serves with the same basic motions. Even if your opponent doesn't notice this consciously, he will likely subconsciously react to the various motions used for each serve, and even the motions before the serve. One way to avoid telegraphing your serve intentions before you serve is to set up each time as if you were doing the same serve each time (both mentally and physically), and then change to whatever serve you had planned.

You can actually take this the other way, and intentionally "telegraph" a serve, but instead do some other serve. For example, many players who toss the ball high when serving (high-toss serves) don't have good control over it, and so the serve goes long. If you do a high-toss serve that goes long, the next time you do it, your opponent will likely expect it to go long, so you can cross him up with a high-toss short serve. But make sure to practice this because it's not a weapon if you can't execute it in a match.

Learn to put lots of spin on the ball. This is a book on tactics, not technique, so we won't really be going into how to do that here. (See TableTennisCoaching.com.) Suffice to say that to get great spin on your serves, you need a grippy surface; contact near the tip (the fastest moving part of the racket); and most important, lots of racket speed (accelerate into the ball) while just grazing the ball. (If you graze it finely enough, it'll tend to go short, even if your racket is moving very fast at contact. If all your serves go long, you probably aren't grazing the ball finely enough, though it helps to have the first bounce on your side near the net.)

Service Depth

Service depth is extremely important. You want your serves to

Table Tennis Tactics for Thinkers

either be short (including half-long serves that might go slightly long) or very deep (so it bounces near the end line on the opponent's side of the table). Anything in between simply isn't as effective, and is more easily attacked. And yet, many players serve so that the ball bounces in the middle of the table (depth-wise), and so the receiver doesn't have to move in or move out, and can easily attack the serve. Players get away with this at the beginning and often at the intermediate level, and often it becomes a bad habit they never break. Learn to control the depth of your serves, and make sure your serves are either short (including those half-long serves) or very deep.

Serve Variety

Many players develop a small but effective set of serves, and find success with this. It's generally best to focus on one or two service motions, and develop all sorts of tricky variations with these motions, such as different spins, speeds, placements, and depth. Many players, however, have few variations of the serves they have, or have only one main motion. They are limiting themselves with a lack of variety.

While it is important to develop a small set of highly effective serves that you can use over and over, it's also important to have enough variety in your serves that you can most likely find one that the opponent has trouble with.

For example, many players develop very nice forehand pendulum serves, the most popular serve in high-level table tennis. But since so many players do this serve, many opponents are good at receiving them, while having trouble with other serves. I've seen many players who have trouble with a specific serve, such as a backhand-type sidespin serve short to the forehand. (This has the opposite sidespin as a forehand pendulum serve, and can also be done with a reverse forehand pendulum serve or a tomahawk serve.) And then, when I coach against this type of player, I find that the player I'm coaching can't do this type of sidespin, or can't even serve short to the forehand! They may be able to do a regular forehand pendulum serve short to the forehand, but it's the other type of sidespin

2011 Men's World Champion and 2012 Olympic Gold Medalist Zhang Jike of China doing an intricate reverse forehand pendulum serve. Photo by Diego Schaaf

short to the forehand that many players have trouble with.

Another example would be fast and deep serves. Many players have difficulty with certain types of these, such as fast and dead to the middle (elbow). And yet many players can't do these simple serves, and so are giving away many points, games, and winnable matches. Fast sidespins to the wide backhand give many players trouble, and yet few bother to learn these serves. And then there are the all-out forehand loopers who forehand loop every deep serve to the backhand—and woe be the server who can't cross up this player with a fast serve down the line to the forehand!

The list goes on and on, and yet the principle is simple. Learn to serve short and long (including fast) to all parts of the table with all varieties of spin and you'll have it all covered—topspin, sidespin, backspin, no-spin, and if you high-toss serve, don't forget corkscrewspin. While you don't need to be an expert on every serve, you should be at least proficient at all these variations so you can pull out the needed ones on demand.

Don't robotically limit yourself to one serve that seems to work. I once coached a player after he lost a close first game. His tomahawk serve to the forehand was giving his opponent fits, so I told him to use that serve. He then went out and served *nothing* but that serve! The first few times the opponent had trouble, but then he got used to it, and began to loop it over and over. Rather than think, my player kept using the same serve, often walking about and grumbling between points. After losing the game badly (this was when matches were two out of three to 21), he came to me and exclaimed with great indignation, "*You told me to use that serve!*" Moral: Vary your serves.

Serve Location

There's a simple way of thinking of all the placements and depths you can use when serving. Roughly speaking, you can serve to the forehand, the middle, or backhand; you can serve short, half-long, or long. This gives you nine variations; find out which ones work for you and against specific opponents.

There are really more variations, of course. For example, serving long to the forehand corner is not the same as serving long and outside the forehand corner. Serving short to the extreme forehand (where the receiver has to really reach in for the ball) is not the same as serving short to the middle forehand (where if the receiver doesn't move some to his left, he may be stuck with an awkward forehand over the table). The more you play and think about these things, the more you will learn how to take advantage of all the possible placements.

Table Tennis Tactics for Thinkers

Where to serve from?

Most top players serve mostly from the backhand corner. This allows them to follow up the serve with their forehand, usually with a loop. This is probably what most players should do, though you should vary this sometimes to throw the opponent off. You can also follow the serve with a backhand loop, or some other attack.

In particular, if you want to serve short to the forehand, you might want to serve from a little more over the table, perhaps

World #1 woman Ding Ning of China serving from her backhand corner. Photo by Diego Schaaf

even from the middle or the forehand side. This gives you a better angle into the forehand. (This is especially effective if you serve so the ball breaks away from the server, i.e. a backhand-type sidespin serve.) This forces the receiver to use his forehand to receive, which some players do not like to do, especially against short serves.

Some players with strong backhands like to serve more from the middle or even from the forehand side. They often serve and follow with the backhand, usually a backhand loop. They may serve and prepare for the backhand loop, knowing that if the serve is returned to the forehand, they can just rotate their shoulders and loop the forehand without moving much. Or they might serve sidespin-topspin and follow mostly with a forehand or backhand hit.

Set-Up Serves

These should be the foundation of your service game. They include short serves, half-long serves, and some long serves.

The most basic set-up serve is a short backspin serve, which is often pushed back long, usually to the backhand, setting the server up to forehand or backhand loop. In fact, against most intermediate players, you can serve short backspin to the backhand, turn your back on the table, go for a stroll, perhaps attend the World Championships or the ITTF Museum, take a short tour of the galaxy, and when you return, there'll be a predictable deep push return to your backhand ready for you to loop. (A critiquer told me this description was too "campy," but I've used this in lectures on tactics at training camps for years. It gets the point across.) It's predictable, and is what keeps many players at the intermediate level. And yet it's also an effective return against many players, if done properly. (See the chapter on Pushing.) Develop your game so you can attack this ball with a forehand or backhand loop, since this alone will put you well on the path to high-level table tennis. We're going to spend much of this section assuming you have a good loop, and that when serving, your primary goal is to set up your loop. Later we'll look at other styles and how they should serve—but it's rather simple: you want to serve to set up what you do well, which usually means some sort of attack, most often a loop.

The advantages of short backspin serves are many. By serving it short, your opponent can't loop it. If it's low and heavy, it's very hard to flip. So most returns are passive pushes that, in theory, you can attack.

Look to see how your opponent pushes your serves. Are his pushes heavy? Does he vary the spin? Are they low? Deep? Angled? Quick? Does he change directions at the last second? If the answer to all these is yes, then he has a good push, and you might have trouble attacking his push, except perhaps with a slower, more consistent loop than usual. (Of course, world-class players would still rip these, but their opponent would be able to handle their rips. They are supernatural beings, right?)

However, if his returns are deficient in any of these seven aspects, than you can take advantage of it. If they aren't heavy, you can loop through the ball with great power, since you don't have to provide much lift. If they are not varied, you can get into a rhythm and make the same loop over and over. If they aren't low, you have more clearance to loop or even smash them. If they aren't deep (but not short pushes), then they are much easier to loop aggressively than longer ones. If they aren't angled, then you don't have to move as much to get to the shot, and you are more likely able to use your stronger side, often (but not always) the forehand, and you don't have to go much out of position to do so. If they aren't quick, then you have more time to prepare and are more likely to attack with your stronger side, or with either side consistently since you aren't rushed. If they never change direction at the last second, you can move into position early.

The problems with serving short backspin over and over are also many. First, it becomes repetitive, and so your opponent gets used to it, and so not only will he make few mistakes against it, but his returns will get better and better. Second, opponents can push it quick at a wide angle, usually to your backhand, which can be difficult to attack, especially if you are primarily a forehand attacker. This becomes even more difficult to handle if they can hide their direction until the last second, or change directions at the last second. Third, opponents can push it very heavy or vary the backspin, both of which can be difficult for many players to handle. Fourth, opponents can push it short, stopping your loop

Table Tennis Tactics for Thinkers

completely. And fifth, opponents can flip the serve, taking the initiative unless you have the mobility and strokes to attack their flip. *Varying your serve makes it more difficult for your opponent to do any of these things.*

Often the best way to vary your backspin serve is to use the same motion but serve no-spin, which often leads to a popped-up return. More on this later.

Trick Serves

Trick serves are serves that are designed to win the point outright, either with a miss or an easy pop-up. We've covered some of them above, especially with the deep serves. Develop your own trick serves that you can pull out several times a game for "free" points.

2012 European Top 12 Champion Dimitrij Ovtcharov of Germany has tricky serves.
Photo by Diego Schaaf

As noted earlier, a serve can be both a set-up serve and a trick serve. For example, a short, no-spin serve with a big spin motion ("heavy no-spin") is a good set-up serve, but can also be a trick serve, especially at the intermediate level, where players pop them up over and over. A good set-up serve puts pressure on an opponent to the point that they can essentially be trick serves that win the point outright. The distinction between a set-up serve and a trick serve is not always clear.

There are two types of trick serves: ones that are only effective when used as a surprise to catch the opponent off guard (and can be effective at all levels as long as they are used sparingly), and ones that can be used over and over again and still be effective (though normally only against lower-level players, and even they will eventually get used to them). An example of the former (a surprise serve) would be a fast and deep serve that catches the opponent off guard. (A fast no-spin serve to the opponent's elbow is the best example of this.) An example of the latter might be a deep tomahawk serve to the forehand, which breaks away from the opponent, and can cause havoc at the beginning and intermediate levels even if used over and over—though of course any serve that's over-used loses its effectiveness.

If you do have a trick serve that opponents miss or pop up over and over, that's great. However, too much reliance on this can strategically hold you back. The same trick serve that your peers mess up against might be returned more easily by stronger players, including the ones you hope to learn to beat. For example, if you have a side-top serve that many opponents push back and so pop up, stronger players, especially after they see the serve a few times, might just flip, drive, or loop it, and suddenly your serve is a disadvantage. So instead of relying on winning off the trick serve over and over, develop your set-up serves, ones that will consistently allow you to attack. Then you can use the trick serve as a highly effective variation that even stronger players might never adjust to.

Jan-Ove Waldner, one of the greatest servers of all time. Photo by Diego Schaaf

In other words, don't get into the habit of trying to win with trick serves because you are afraid to serve and attack under pressure. Focus on serve and attack (i.e. set-up serves) and use trick serves sparingly and tactically.

Many players do not use their trick serves effectively. Many only pull them out at the end of a close game, when if they had used them earlier, it might not be a close game. Also, you don't really know which trick serves are effective until you try them out on an opponent. So I recommend trying out your trick serves early in a match, see what works, then hold back on them for a time, then come back to them, either at the end of a close game, or better still, in the middle of a close game to make sure the game doesn't stay close. You don't want to overuse these serves and let your opponent get used to them, but often players under-use the serves that give the opponent the most trouble.

You need to find a balance between set-up serves and trick serves. The higher the level, the more the balance tends toward set-up serves, since tricks serves become less effective—but by using them less often, they become even more effective when they are used.

Table Tennis Tactics for Thinkers

Short Serves

How do you serve short and force the opponent to give you lots of balls to attack? By varying your short serves to both force mistakes and to take away the receiver's most effective receives. Let's look at your options. Using the many variations listed below, you should be able to develop your serves strategically so you can use them tactically to set up your loops and drives.

1. **Vary the placement of your backspin serve.** If you keep serving to the backhand, the opponent will get used to it. Make him return with both forehand and backhand by serving sometimes to both sides.
2. **Serve to the middle.** Many players serve over and over into the backhand or forehand, which gives the opponent an extreme angle. If you serve to the backhand, the receiver can angle his return into your backhand, usually taking out your forehand attack. If you serve short to the forehand, there is the threat of an angled push to the wide forehand. Servers often get caught by that, or else they position themselves to cover the wide forehand, thereby leaving their backhand side open. Instead, why not serve to the middle? This means there are no extreme angles to cover, and in general, less ground to cover. While players often go for extreme angles from their corners, few have the control to do so from the middle. And so the returns tend to come inside the corners, which are easier to attack from either side.
3. **Serve very, very low.** This is one of the most under-learned skills. If you watch top players, you'll see that their short serves are very low to the net. Watch intermediate players, and see how much higher their serves cross the net. A low serve bounces low, forcing the receiver to hit up more. This leads to more mistakes and higher returns, cuts off the potential angles, and makes it harder to flip.
4. **Serve "heavy no-spin."** If you use a spin motion, but contact the ball near the handle, you can fake heavy spin (especially backspin) and get a no-spin serve. Opponents will misread this over and over, popping up their pushes, and going off the end when they flip. It's tricky pushing a no-spin serve short—very easy to pop up—and opponents won't be able to push it as heavy as they could against a backspin serve. (Against backspin, the ball rebounds off the racket with the reverse spin. Against no-spin, the receiver has to generate all the spin himself.) At the world-class level, this is one of the most popular serves, and even more so in doubles. Mixing in short no-spin serves is the easiest way to deal with an opponent who pushes your short backspin serves short.

5. **Vary the backspin with sidespin-backspin.** The sidespin (jumping both on the table and off their racket) will cause the receiver to lose some control, and he'll make more mistakes.
6. **Server extra-heavy backspin.** After varying your sidespin-backspin and backspin serves with the same motion, throw a straight heavy backspin serve at the opponent. Since you are no longer trying to disguise the motion (by rotating the racket about to fake sidespin), you can get a heavier backspin. The receiver will no doubt read it as backspin, but after facing all the earlier less-spinny backspins, will often misread the degree of backspin and make mistakes.
7. **Mix in sidespin and sidespin-topspin serves.** If your opponent is making effective pushes, and doesn't see the change in spin, he'll pop the ball up or off the end or side. Plus he'll have more serve variation to worry about, also leading to a loss of control and more mistakes against your other serves.
8. **Serve sidespin in both directions with good placement.** It's difficult for opponents to adjust to both. Favor serves where the ball breaks away from the receiver. A short serve to the forehand that breaks away from the server (i.e. backhand-type service spin) is awkward to return, since the ball is both breaking away (forcing the receiver to move or reach), and because the receiver has to angle his paddle to his right, and is difficult for many to return down the line. And so you narrow down where the return might be. Similarly, a short serve to the backhand that breaks away (i.e. forehand pendulum-type service spin) is also awkward to return down the line, and so you again generally narrow down where the return will be.
9. **Deceptive follow-through.** Have a big follow through to your short serve in the opposite direction of the actual spin you served. For example, if you serve sidespin or side-top, follow through down as if it were a backspin serve.
10. **Serve half-long serves.** These are short serves that, given the chance, the second bounce would be near the end line. By doing this, you give a serve that is difficult or impossible to loop, but maximizes the distance from the net and your side of the table from where your opponent makes contact. This takes away the extreme angles, makes it difficult to push short, and gives you more time to respond to the receiver's shot. A short serve that goes too short is actually easier to make an effective return against for most players. (More on half-long serves later on.)

Table Tennis Tactics for Thinkers

11. **Deep Serves.** Throw in some deep serves for variation, especially fast & deep. If you give your opponent a steady diet of short serves, he can hang in over the table. A deep serve will often catch him outright, and force him to guard against it, thereby costing him some control against short serves.
12. **Throw in some "surprise" serves.** We will cover this more shortly. This gives the receiver still more things to think about and prepare for, leading to still more mistakes.

Let's suppose you are *not* a looper, and are *not* looking to serve and loop. This is where it is important to know your game—remember the statement, "If you couldn't write a book about your game, either you don't know your game, or you have no game." Look through that book in your mind, and figure out just what it is you *do* want to do when you serve.

For example, Dave Sakai, a top U.S. senior player, has one of the best backhand counter-drives in the USA. Much of his game is based on getting into backhand-to-backhand exchanges and blocking. It would be dumb tactics for him to focus on serve and loop over and over, which would take out the best part of his game. Instead, his best serves are short topspin and sidespin-topspin, usually to the opponent's backhand. There isn't much you can do with this serve except hit it back with a backhand drive, and if the serve is to the backhand, there's no angle into Dave's forehand. And so over and over you either get into a backhand-to-backhand rally with him, or you go down the line and give him an easy forehand. Dave rode this backhand—and the tactics that took advantage of it—right into the U.S. Table Tennis Hall of Fame.

Another example would be an all-out hitter, such as a pips-out penholder. Because of his pips, he probably can't loop against backspin as well as an inverted player. So he might serve varied sidespin and topspin serves, both short and long, looking for chances to serve and smash. Or he might serve and loop with the pips, and then smash.

Short Sidespin-Topspin Serves

Since beginners and many intermediate players can't serve short sidespin or topspin, many players automatically assume any short serve is backspin, and so push it. If you can serve varied short sidespin, topspin, or side-top, that alone will allow you to dominate against many intermediate players. Learn to hide the spin—see section coming up on deception—and you'll get a lot of misses and easy returns.

Against stronger players, you won't get as many easy returns, but they will often be predictable. Since very few players can drop this type of serve short, you know it's coming long, and so you can serve and loop over and over. Some players will chop down on this serve and so push it back low, giving you a backspin ball you can loop. Most, however, will do a flip, which you can also attack. (If they are attacking it hard, then you probably aren't serving very low or the serve is too easy to read.) At the higher levels, players often serve short sidespin-topspin, and loop the return, even if it is flipped.

Here the geometry of the table becomes important. If you serve short to the forehand, many players will not be able to flip down the line, especially against a sidespin that curves away (such as a reverse pendulum, tomahawk, or backhand serve), and so you know the return will probably be toward your forehand. If you serve short to the backhand with a forehand pendulum spin, many players will not be able to take it down the line effectively, and so you know the return will probably go toward your backhand side. However, in both these cases, you are giving the receiver a potentially wide angle to play into.

A solution to this is to serve side-top serves to the middle of the table. (Here we mean the middle of the table literally, not the receiver's elbow.) These are difficult to return at wide angles, and so are often easier to follow up than with short serves to the corners. But this all depends on the opponent, so experiment and see what works. Personally, my favorite "go-to" serve and attack serve is a forehand pendulum side-top serve short and low to the middle, which is difficult to angle or return short, and so I usually can follow with my forehand.

Half-Long Serves

Half-long serves (also called tweeny serves) are serves that, given the chance, the second bounce would hit right near the receiver's end line, or sometimes barely long. Many players use short serves that are too short, where, given the chance, the second bounce would be well inside the end line (and the ball might actually bounce more than two times). This means the contact point for the receiver is closer to the net than it would be for a half-long serve. By being closer to the net at contact, the receiver can rush you more, get better angles, drop the ball short much more easily, plus there's no indecision on whether the serve is long (and loopable) or short. At the higher levels, half-long serves are the dominant serve. (The main advantage of serving extra short is that it brings the receiver in over the table, leaving him vulnerable to the next ball.) Also, a very short ball to the forehand can be awkward to return for some players.

Most of the tactics for half-long serves are similar as for those given for short serves. The main difference is that by their very nature, some half-long serves go a bit long, and so sometimes the receiver can loop the serve. (At the highest levels, servers have such control that they can control this,

Table Tennis Tactics for Thinkers

thereby varying whether the second bounce is just short or just long.) Or the receiver can sometimes go over the table to loop the serve, especially with the backhand (where you can wrist-loop the ball a bit more easily than on the forehand side, i.e. a "banana flip," or the rarer and more difficult "strawberry flip." If the serve is low and the ball barely goes long, then most of these loops will be soft, and higher-level players jump all over these returns, usually loop-killing them, though they may also smash or quick-block them effectively.

    The key is to find out early how the receiver will return these serves. If he pushes, it will likely go long, with little angle—or does the player have the touch to keep it short, as some top players can? What type of angles can he get? If he attacks, how fast and spinny are the attacks? Can you stop the attack by making the serve just a touch shorter?

    Many players have great difficulty with a half-long serve that goes barely long. They want to loop the serve, but the table is somewhat in the way. While some players are very good against these slightly-long serves—forcing you to serve shorter—many are not, and you should take advantage of this.

    One problem with half-long serves is that there is a tendency to serve them slightly longer in the pressure-packed situation of a tournament or league match. If you practice them so that the second bounce is right at the end line, often at key times under pressure they go long. So it's important to really practice these serves to develop depth control. Different conditions also affect this. Faster tables, faster floors (a table on cement plays faster than one on wood, for example, though some don't believe this), thinner air (i.e. high altitude) will all make your serve bounce longer, so take these things into consideration. Strategically, you might want to practice serving so the second bounce is a few inches shorter than where you'd want it in a tournament—just in case.

    If you watch top players, every now and then you'll see a player absolutely rip the serve with a loop kill. The majority of the time this was against a half-long serve that went too long. The difference between an effective half-long serve and one that is easily looped is often only a few inches. So be careful with these serves.

Long Spin Serves

    These are deep, spinny serves that break as they approach the receiver. You want the first bounce to be deep, with the ball breaking dramatically as it hits the table. They should have lots of sidespin and/or corkscrewspin.

    The main principle to remember is that, in general, opponents will have more trouble returning a serve that spins away from them than one that spins into them. For example, when a righty serves a forehand pendulum serve to another righty (so that the ball breaks to the server's right, the receiver's left), if the ball is served to the wide backhand, the ball spins away from the receiver, and is usually harder to receive than the same serve to the forehand, where it breaks into the receiver. Similarly, a backhand or tomahawk serve to the forehand is generally more difficult to receive than one to the backhand, since it also breaks away from the receiver (to the server's left, the receiver's right). There are three reasons for this.

First, a receiver has to move or reach for a serve that breaks away. This makes it trickier to control as he may be hitting on the move, making it harder to control.

Second, while the receiver may set up with his racket at the right height to receive the serve, when the ball breaks away and he moves or reaches for it there is a tendency to lower the racket. This means he will likely lift the ball too much, and either go off the end or receive soft and high.

Third, to counter the incoming spin the receiver has to aim to the left to receive a ball breaking away on the backhand side, and to the right to receive a ball breaking away on the forehand side. In both cases it's more natural to aim the other way, especially on the forehand side. So countering a sidespin that breaks away is usually more awkward.

Here's a simple way of visualizing this third reason. Imagine a forehand pendulum serve short to your forehand. To counteract the spin, you have to aim to the left, i.e. a normal crosscourt forehand, which is not difficult for most players. In fact, if you wanted to place this ball crosscourt you would want to aim to the left of the table, which isn't that difficult with a little practice. Now imagine a backhand or tomahawk serve short to your forehand side, so the ball is breaking away from you. To counteract the spin, you have to aim to the right, down the line—see how awkward that can be? If you wanted to take it down the line, you'd have to aim to the right of the table, even more awkward. Even advanced players often have trouble with this.

There are always exceptions. Some players are good against balls that break away, and are awful against ones that break into them. Or perhaps you simply are better at one type of sidespin serve, and the opponent will have trouble with it on both sides (especially if you vary the placement), while having little trouble when you use your other, less effective sidespin serve. Some players are very good at receiving forehand pendulum serves with their backhand, even though the ball breaks away from them, because they see this serve so often. So experiment—but do so with the knowledge that sidespin serves are usually more effective when placed properly. (And if you haven't yet developed these spin serves, there's no time like *now* to start learning them.)

Table Tennis Tactics for Thinkers

For variation, you should do these serves both ways, for example using a reverse pendulum serve from the backhand side into the receiver's backhand, where it breaks into the receiver. Or you can serve it more to the middle so that it breaks away from the receiver, into the forehand side. You should learn to serve both sidespins to all parts of the table.

Deep spin serves in general (but especially to the forehand) are less effective at the higher levels since they are usually looped, but there are many that mix in deep spin serves to the backhand. If the receiver doesn't have a good backhand loop, he will likely have problems with this serve. If the receiver has a good forehand loop and fast footwork, then he may loop it with his forehand, but this does put him out of position, and so the server can either quick-block to the forehand, or (if the receiver moves to cover the forehand too quickly) to the backhand. Since the receiver will miss some of these deep, spinny serves, all the server has to do is roughly break even when the receiver successfully loops the serve—but that's a calculation you will have to make. Some are very good at this type of tactic.

If the receiver returns these serves passively, whether with backspin or topspin, then a deep spin serve can be an effective set-up serve. In fact, if the receiver is passive against these serves, you can serve long backspin, and then have lots of time to set up to loop the receiver's push, where he will have no angle and will not be able to rush you. However, most long, spinny serves are designed more to win the point outright (via a miss or easy pop-up) than as a set-up serve.

Fast & Deep Serves

The problem with long serves is that they are often easy to loop. (This assumes your opponent has a good loop—if not, long serves usually become more effective.) Serving short is one way to stop that. Another way is to simply serve with enough speed that the receiver doesn't have time to loop. This means you can serve fast to the corners or to the middle, and many opponents will not be able to attack it effectively. However, many will be able to, and others will return these serves with a forehand or backhand drive. So long, fast serves are mostly "surprise" serves, where you catch the opponent off guard. The key is they must be fast so the opponent doesn't have time to respond properly. (You can also serve deep with spin, as covered in previous section.)

It takes more timing to do a fast & deep serve with great speed then other serves. So even if you use these serves only occasionally, you need to practice them far more than the proportion of times you use the serves. If you don't, when the score is close and the time comes to catch the receiver off guard with a fast & deep serve, will you really be able to pull it off consistently at full speed? (By the way, calling the serve "fast & deep" is redundant, since a fast serve is always deep, but that's the conventional terminology.)

The contact point should be a bit behind the table so that the first bounce can be near your own end line, which gives the serve the maximum amount of table to drop and hit the other side. Other than that, doing a fast serve is more a matter of timing and practice than technique.

There is a new serve that's come out recently, a "hyperbolic serve," which is a super-heavy topspin serve that travels at seemingly hyperbolic speeds. It's the fastest serve I've ever seen—the extra topspin pulling the ball down allows the extra speed. It's often done with a forehand motion but where you hit the ball with the backhand side of the racket by angling the forehand side up, and snapping the racket into the ball at full speed while still grazing the ball. If you want to see this, go to youtube.com and put in "hyperbolic serve table tennis." I think the serve can probably be done just as fast with a more standard forehand or backhand topspin serve, but remember that you have to exaggerate the topspin to be able to serve extremely fast and keep it on the table. This serve isn't common, and it may never be, but here's a chance to stay ahead of the curve—why not be the first in your club to develop this serve?

Fifteen Important Fast and Deep Serves

When you serve fast and deep, you want to aim at one of three main targets: to the wide forehand, wide backhand, or at the receiver's elbow. It's also best to have at least two variations to each location so they can't adjust, ideally with a fast sidespin or side-topspin serve, and a fast no-spin serve. (No-spin serves don't jump off the receiver's paddle as fast, so opponents have to stroke the ball more, which is problematic when you rush them by serving fast no-spin.) So players should develop at least six variations of their fast & deep serves, or even more. You can do it with sidespin left, sidespin right, side-top left, side-top right, and no-spin, and can do all of these to the wide forehand, wide backhand, and middle. That's fifteen variations, and that's just to start, since you can vary the degree of each type of spin, as well as the motion used for the serve.

No, you don't need to perfect all fifteen, but you should try them all out, and decide which ones work for you. At the very, very minimum, have these three—a fast down the line serve, a fast no-spin serve to the opponent's elbow, and a breaking sidespin serve to the opponent's backhand that breaks away from him.

Fast Serves to the Forehand

A fast, down-the-line serve from the backhand corner (most often done with a forehand pendulum service motion) is a valuable serve. It's

Table Tennis Tactics for Thinkers

great at catching righty forehand loopers off guard as they look to loop your serve from the backhand corner. It's also sometimes effective against more neutral players, as they aren't used to fast serves to the forehand and so can be erratic against it. It's even effective against lefties, who are often guarding against serves wide to their forehand, and so are vulnerable to this sudden serve to their wide backhand. Against lefties, however, you'd normally look to ace them by going crosscourt to their forehands, though you are less likely to get an ace as players generally guard the crosscourt angle. (Lefty servers, this serve is effective for you as well—a righty is rarely used to a lefty serving fast down the line.) So develop this serve or you will be handicapping yourself against some players.

If you aren't sure how to do the serve, ask a coach or top player to demonstrate, or go to Youtube and do a search for "table tennis fast serve." But the key is to fake as if you are serving crosscourt, then at the last second change directions and serve fast down the line.

Pick and choose when to use this serve. Often you can tell by the receiver's stance and body language if he's looking to step around. Even if he's not stepping around, if a receiver looks a bit flat-footed, he's probably vulnerable to this serve.

Once you can do the serve effectively, it's time to make it even more effective. Here are two ways you can do that. First, you can use spin, either sidespin either way or extra topspin. If you do, make sure to put more power into the serve so that you don't sacrifice much speed for spin. Extra topspin pulls the ball down and allows you to serve even faster, if you can generate enough power for both topspin and speed while controlling it.

Second, contact the ball with the racket still aimed at the righty receiver's backhand, but hit it down the line with sort of a slapping sidespin motion (your racket going from right to left at contact). This is my favorite. Typically the first time I go down the line, I do it the "easy" way, changing the racket direction at the last second. Now they are watching for that last second racket change (at least subconsciously), so I don't give it to them. By keeping the racket aimed to their backhand, you catch them moving to cover that shot, and their forehand side is open.

Once you've done a fast down-the-line serve, the rest of the match the opponent is guarding against it, and guess what? All your other serves become a bit more effective.

Fast no-spin to the middle

At the intermediate level, this is probably the single most effective serve there is. Even advanced players have difficulty with it. It is often my own "go to" serve in a close match. It is probably the best example of a serve designed for one purpose—to win the point outright. I've often marveled at how few players use this serve. It's easier to learn than a spin serve, and will absolutely devastate many players. We're talking free points—so why don't more players develop this serve?

To do it, simply serve a fast serve but contact the ball with a *light* backspin. After two bounces on the table, this light backspin has become no-spin. Since most players are used to fast serves having topspin, they automatically return it with a slightly closed racket—and so go into the net. If they try to loop the serve, they also misread it as topspin, and go into the net. (Surprisingly, it's often looped off the end as the receiver recognizes the serve and over-compensates.) Even if they read it and realize they have to lift the ball some because the ball is dead, they are too rushed to do this, and so mis-hit. So the serve is often effective even right into a player's forehand or backhand.

But now let's raise the ante and serve at the receiver's elbow. Now he has to make a snap decision on whether to receive forehand or backhand. Then he has to move to the ball (which gives the added benefit that he opens up a corner for you to attack on the next shot). With having to make the forehand or backhand decision, having to move to the ball, and the serve coming at him fast, he's rushed, and rarely will take a full swing. But because the ball is dead, he can't rely on the ball rebounding off his racket like most fast serves, and so he *needs* a full swing! Since players have so much trouble taking a full swing in these conditions, and with all the variables mentioned above that can go wrong, players miss this serve over and over.

It's mostly effective against a two-winged player. If the receiver is looking to attack the serve with his forehand, he's probably going to have less trouble looping this serve. (Instead, he'll be vulnerable to a fast serve to the corners.) But if, like most players, the receiver is set up to receive forehand or backhand, depending on where you serve, this serve may give him indigestion.

Short to Forehand, Long to Backhand

One way to turn your opponent into a pretzel is with one of the most common serving combos in table tennis: short serves to the forehand, and long, breaking serves to the backhand.

Short serves to the forehand are usually more awkward to handle than short ones to the backhand. This is because the wrist is freer on the backhand side to adjust the racket angle, and also because contact is made in front of you, right in front of your eyes, instead of to the side with a forehand receive. Long serves to the backhand are usually trickier to handle than long ones to the forehand. This is because most players loop better on the forehand side, and because you have a bigger hitting zone on that side than on the backhand side, where a breaking serve can be awkward to handle.

Serving short to the forehand or long to the backhand also maximizes the amount of table the receiver has to cover. Suppose you serve very short and wide to the forehand, so the receiver has to contact the ball one foot from the net near the sideline. Suppose you serve long to the backhand, so the receiver contacts the ball about a foot past the end line behind the backhand corner. Then the distance between these two contact points is about 6.7 feet. (The same is true, of course, if you serve short to the backhand or long to the forehand.) If you instead serve short and long to the forehand (or to the backhand), then the distance is about five feet. That's over 20 inches of extra movement for the receiver. It's even more if you serve wide to the backhand, and perhaps break it even wider with sidespin, so the receiver has to take the ball from outside the backhand corner. The contact points between a short serve to the forehand and a deep breaking serve to the wide backhand can be over seven feet apart.

So why not combine these two into a deadly duo?

You can do this with forehand or backhand serves. Make sure to start out the same, with the same motion until just before contact. Then either serve very low and short to the forehand, or a long, breaking serve into the backhand.

Short serves are often best where the second bounce on the far side of the table, if allowed, would be near the end line. However, in this case, it's better to serve very short to maximize how much distance the receiver has to reach to get to the serve. Make him cover the full seven feet.

The receiver also has to prepare for the deep serve into the backhand. By making it break, it makes the receiver reach even more. (This is especially true if you can break it away from the receiver, such as a forehand pendulum serve if both players are righties.) It's often effective to focus on deep spin serves, but not too fast. A fast serve to the backhand can often be more easily backhand countered, using your own speed against you.

So the receiver has to be ready both for the quick step in to reach the short serve to the forehand, while also covering that deep, breaking serve into the backhand. This is not an easy task, and leads to many mistakes. On top of that, it also makes it almost impossible for a receiver to forehand loop the serve from the backhand side.

So twist your opponent into a pretzel as he tries to cover these two diagonally opposed serves that the human body was never designed for. Make him cover the full seven feet as you turn him into a cooked pretzel.

Serve Deception

There are a number of ways to trick your opponent into misreading your serve. Always remember that while having spinny serves is important, a less spinny serve that is misread is more effective than a spinny serve that is not. Technically, learning deceptive serves isn't tactics; it's just another tool to develop that you can use tactically. But they are so tactically important that I'm going to go over four ways of doing this. To really learn these serves, work with a coach or top player, and watch how the top players do it.

1. Sheer Quantity of Spin

The more spin you put on your serve, the harder it will be for your opponent to read the degree of spin. If you can spin the heck out of the ball when serving, you will put tremendous pressure on the opponent.

It's not just the reading of the spin that gives your opponent problems. He's also used to using certain racket angles against spin. When he sees a ball that's spinier than he's used to, he's likely going to use one of the angles he is more used to using against less spinny serves, and so will not get the angle correctly. (This is also why players block spinny loops off the end over and over, even when they *know* how spinny it is—they want to close their racket more, but it goes against their natural reactions. Blame it on the subconscious, which isn't *always* your friend.)

Super spinny serves can be especially effective when you challenge your opponent by serving them deep with sidespin. The spin makes the ball break dramatically, forcing the opponent to move or reach for it, plus he has to compensate for how the spinning ball will bounce off his racket, and do all this while hitting the ball from farther away than he is used to.

Here's a tip that will greatly enhance your spin. Just before contact, imagine your arm hits a pole between the wrist and elbow, near the wrist. Imagine your wrist, hand, and racket whipping about that pole with great speed, like a tetherball shooting about the pole as it runs out of string. Or just imagine your racket is the tip of a whip, and really whip it about. (In both cases, accelerate the racket through contact.) All this extra racket speed means extra spin, as long as you graze the ball.

2. Semicircular Motion

If you contact the ball with your racket moving in a straight line, you may get great spin, but it'll be obvious what spin it is. If, however, you instead move your racket through a semicircular motion, then to read the spin, the receiver has to figure out at what point the racket contacted the ball.

Table Tennis Tactics for Thinkers

For example, consider a forehand pendulum serve, the most popular serve in table tennis. With this serve, the racket moves from right to left. If you do this in a straight line, the spin is obvious. Instead, have it go through a semicircular motion, starting down, then sideways, and then up. In service lectures I often do this motion without the ball and ask the players what spin it is. Invariably some say backspin, some sidespin, some topspin. The correct answer, of course, is you don't know since I didn't show them at what point in the serve contact was made. It's a trick question.

If you hit the ball on the downswing, it's backspin. At the part where the racket continues down but starts to move left, you get sidespin-backspin. When it moves sideways, sidespin. As it begins to move up but is still moving sideways, sidespin-topspin. As it goes straight up, topspin. Learn to do this very fast, as the top players do, often with a very tight motion, and watch the receiver struggle to figure out the spin.

If you want to double the receiver's confusion, try a forehand pendulum/reverse pendulum serve. The first half of this is a regular forehand pendulum serve, with the racket going through a semicircular motion from right to left. The second half of this serve is a regular reverse forehand pendulum serve, with the racket now going left to right. Do this in one continuous motion, with the racket going right to left and then left to right, contacting the ball right about the time you are switching directions, and let the receiver try to figure out where contact was made. (Serves like this take a lot of practice, but they pay off in dividends.)

3. Exaggerate the Opposite Motion

If you serve backspin, you follow through down, right? And if you serve topspin, you follow through up, right?

Wrong! At least, you shouldn't. Instead, right after contact, try changing the direction of your racket and exaggerate the *opposite* motion. Combined with the regular semi-circular motion explained previously, this can create havoc for the poor receiver.

Logically, if you always follow through downward on topspin serves, and upward on backspin serves, your opponent will pick up on this, right? Actually, not very often. Since returning serves (and most other table tennis strokes) is done instinctively, the receiver's instinctive reaction to a downward motion is to read backspin, and for an upward motion to read topspin. So in most cases you can get away with this, though you should vary your follow-through just in case.

So when you serve side-backspin, follow-through up and to the side; when you serve side-topspin, follow through down and to the side. You'll be amazed at the confusion and havoc this will create.

4. No-Spin Combos

You can also fool your opponent by faking spin, but instead serving a very low no-spin ball. The very threat of spin makes this serve effective as the opponent busily tries to figure out if it's topspin, sidespin, backspin, or some combination, when it is none of these. Surprisingly, few players at the intermediate level serve with no-spin, and so few are used to this type of serve. It's at the advanced levels (and, of course, beginning level, where they can't put spin on the ball) that no-spin serves become common, as players fake all sorts of spin but serve no-spin, resulting in all sorts of mistakes. At the higher levels, it's sometimes the most common serve in singles and even more so in doubles.

And yes, when you have a big spin motion, but serve no-spin, it is called "heavy no-spin." It's my favorite table tennis term.

How do you serve a heavy no-spin serve? Use the exact same motion as a spin serve, but instead of contacting the ball near the fast-moving racket tip, contact the ball near the handle, which is moving much more slowly. At contact, you might also pull back slightly so as to produce a truly no-spin ball. Make sure to really exaggerate the spin motion on this serve—you have to really sell it.

Learn to serve it very low. A no-spin serve that goes even slightly high often gets hammered. You want all your serves to be low, but you can get away with a slightly high spin serve much more than a slightly high no-spin serve.

The most common version is where you fake backspin but serve no-spin. Over and over opponents will push this back high, or attack it off the end. Often they read it at the last second, and overreact, and so push or attack it into the net. Or they read the no-spin, but are so used to spin making the ball jump off their paddle that they don't compensate for the deader ball, and so go into the net.

When dealing with an opponent who can push your short backspin serves back short, mixing in short no-spin serves is often the best answer. Opponents are often are so used to returning backspin that an actual no-spin serve throws them off. They are tricky to push short, and the returns tend to pop up.

Opponent's Positioning

Be aware of your opponent's receive position—especially pay attention to his feet and grip. For example, is he favoring one side, such as the forehand, with his right foot slightly back or with a forehand grip? If so, he may be looking to play his forehand from the backhand side, and might be leaving the forehand side open, so you might serve fast there. You probably don't want to serve long to the backhand, since he looks like he's itching to step around. (But test him on this—he may not be fast enough to step around

Table Tennis Tactics for Thinkers

or be able to still cover the wide forehand on the next shot.) If he has a good forehand loop, you probably want to serve short to stop his loop.

On the other hand, if he's in a neutral or backhand position, with his feet parallel to the table or with a backhand grip, you get to choose whether he's going to receive forehand or backhand, so generally serve to the weaker side. (As noted in the rallying tactics chapter, sometimes you want to go to the strong side first, and then come back to the weak side.) If he strongly favors the backhand, then you may have to serve wide to the forehand to make him receive forehand, with his transition point between the two well to his forehand side. Against this type of backhand player you might even want to serve from your forehand court so you have an angle into his forehand, or the reverse if one of you is a lefty.

Is the receiver too close to the table? Perhaps jam him with a deep serve. Is he too far from the table? Serve short, especially to the forehand where he probably has to reach more over the table, and make him move in. Is he one of those players who starts off the table, but moves in as you serve? Since his momentum is forward, he might be vulnerable to a deep serve that jams him.

Forehand or Backhand Serves?

The various variations of the forehand pendulum serve dominate at the higher levels. With this serve you can serve sidespin both ways, rotate the body into the ball for great spin, and distract the opponent from seeing contact by doing so very close to the body as the body vigorously rotates about. (Many players also illegally hide contact with this serve, unfortunately, unless an opponent or umpire calls them on it.) Most top players learn this serve.

Most players can only sidespin one way with the backhand serve (racket moving from left to right), though some have developed reverse backhand serves, with the racket moving the other direction—but it's generally not as spinny or deceptive. However, there are advantages to the backhand serve. It's often easier to control the height, allowing you to serve very low to the net. It's a quicker motion, which messes up some

Five-time U.S. Men's Singles Champion Dan Seemiller had one of the best backhand serves in the world.
Photo by John Oros

opponents. Because it's less often used, opponents aren't as used to it. Plus the backhand serve has one big advantage—you can see your opponent more easily as you are serving. Some players can actually change their serve in mid-motion based on what they see the opponent doing during the serve.

Holding Back on Serves

Suppose you have a tricky serve that gives your opponent all sorts of problems. But suppose it's also one of those serves that he can get used to, and only works by either surprise or by the opponent's not being used to it. Should you hold back on this serve for key points in the match?

To start with, you won't really know if the serve is effective unless you actually try it out against an opponent. Sometimes you may know from previous matches. Either way, you should use it early on to establish whether the serve is effective. If the serve is not effective, then you know not to use it later on. If it is effective, you get to use it early in a game, and then come back to it several more times, including near the end if necessary. If you do need to come back to it again near the end of a close game, imagine where you'd be if you hadn't used the serve early on, perhaps more than once?

The idea behind holding back on a serve is that 1) if you use it too often, the opponent will get used to it, and so 2) hold back on it until you reach a key point. The thinking is that if you use it early in a game, and that games ends up not being close, then you've "wasted" that serve.

There is logic behind the above, and yet many players way overdo this, holding back on their best serves—i.e. some of their best weapons—except when it's close. This is like a looper not looping until it's close, or a hitter waiting until it's close before hitting.

If you have a serve that really bothers an opponent, use it regularly in rotation with your other serves, and put yourself in a position where you use the serve at the end of games to win that game, not just when you are down (and where you might "waste" the serve anyway if your comeback falls short). If you are in a competitive match, and can win one "free" game on the strength of one serve, use it! And don't kid yourself into thinking that your opponent will magically become strong against this serve as long as you use it somewhat sparingly and with some variations. His returns may become more effective, but that's true of any shot you may throw at him.

If you do have one serve that really gives the opponent trouble, try to use variations of it to keep him guessing throughout. The more you vary it, the harder it will be for the opponent to get used to it, and so you can use the serve more often.

It's better to use your winning shots (and serves) and win than to hold back on them and hope to come back and win with them at the end.

Table Tennis Tactics for Thinkers

The Ten-Point Plan to Serving Success

Serving is both the simplest and most complex of shots. You are in control, but there are a huge variety of intricate possibilities. It's your front-line shot, so you want to make the most of it. How can you do that? How can you be sure you are getting the most out of your serves? Here are ten principles that should help you develop your serving game. Read them, and then get a bucket of balls and practice.

1. **Serve Legally:** Many top players have horror stories of being faulted at a key time—don't let this happen to you. The service rules are simple to follow. If your serve is borderline (which is sometimes an advantage), that's okay, but be ready to serve very legal if you are warned or faulted.
2. **Serve with a Plan:** Too many players just grab the ball and serve. Serve with a plan as to what you will do with the next shot. If you like looping against backspin, you should probably favor serving backspin serves, hoping to force a push return. If you like to counter-drive or hit, you might favor serving topspin.
3. **Maximize Spin:** Serving is not a passive shot. You must accelerate your racket to full speed, and then just graze the ball for maximum spin. Strive for as much spin as you can on each spin serve, and you will find your serves getting better and better. Faced with great spin, your opponent will be on the defensive right from the start.
4. **Vary Your Spin:** Don't get into the habit of serving the same way over and over. Mix up your serves—use all variations of topspin, backspin, sidespin, perhaps corkscrewspin and no-spin.
5. **Disguise Your Spin:** An obvious backspin, sidespin, or topspin serve is not going to fool many players, but if you can disguise the spin somewhat, it will be far more effective. Your racket should travel in a semi-circular fashion, so that during the serve it goes down, sideways, and then up (or up, sideways, and then down). Use a fast motion so your opponent can't pick up whether you contacted the ball on the downward, sideways, or upward motion of the stroke. You should mostly follow-through in the opposite direction of the spin, i.e. follow-through down for a topspin serve, up for a backspin serve. Even if this seems predictable, most players won't adjust well since their subconscious reacts to deceptive motion. You might also sometimes contact the ball near the handle of the racket, and serve no-spin. If your opponent thinks there is more spin on the ball than there is, you've fooled him, and he's going to make a poor return.

6. **Speed:** A fast deep serve is only effective if it is truly fast. Don't chicken out—learn to serve fastballs, both with or without spin. It's not as hard as it looks, but it can give an opponent fits. Especially try fast no-spin serves, especially to the opponent's elbow, or serves into the backhand that break away from the receiver. And don't forget to sometimes serve fast to an opponent's forehand.
7. **Low bounce:** Too many players let their serves bounce high, giving an easy attack to the opponent. A low serve not only is harder to attack, but it forces the opponent to lift up some, which can lead to pop-ups. To make the ball bounce low, contact the ball as low to the table as possible.
8. **Direction:** There are three directions you should mostly be aiming your serve: wide to the forehand, wide to the backhand, and to an opponent's elbow (middle). Serve mostly to the opponent's weaker side, but if he steps around and uses the other side (usually the forehand from the backhand side), a sudden fast and deep serve to the other side will often win a quick point—and make the opponent think twice about stepping around. A fast, deep serve to an opponent's middle will also cause some trouble if the opponent doesn't make a quick decision as to whether to use the forehand or backhand. Also, serves to the middle cut off the wide angles on the returns.
9. **Depth:** Deep serves should be very deep, with the first bounce landing close to the end line. Short serves should be able to bounce twice on the opponent's side of the table, given the chance, which stops your opponent from looping. A third option is to serve so that the second bounce would be right near the end line, so that the table gets in the way, yet the serve is relatively deep—a half-long or tweeny serve. Your opponent then has to decide whether the serve is long or short, and the table may cramp his stroke. This also makes it difficult to return the serve short, and so often sets the server up for an easy attack.
10. **Follow-up:** Don't just stand there after serving—follow your plan! Get into a ready position, but don't over-commit. Be ready to attack if given the shot—or to use whatever arsenal of shots you have, if necessary. But the whole advantage of serving is to set you up for your best shot or type of rally, so make sure to use that advantage.

Table Tennis Tactics for Thinkers

CHAPTER NINE
Receive Tactics

What is your goal when you receive? That is the primary question you must ask yourself when considering receive tactics. This is no different than thinking about serve tactics except that when you serve, you have complete control over which serve you use, and you can spend time between points making that decision. When receiving, you can only think about what receives you will use against given serves.

2010-2011 USA Women's Singles Champion Ariel Hsing, ready to receive. Photo by Diego Schaaf

Receive is one of the most under-practiced aspects of the game, with serves a close second. Every rally starts with a serve and a receive, and yet players rarely take the time to practice and develop these techniques. Receive is probably the most difficult part of the game to master, and it's doubly hard when players only practice it in actual games. Instead, find a practice partner and take turns practicing your serve and receive.

Returning serves must become instinctive, i.e. your subconscious must control it. Remember what was said on this in the chapter on Tactical Thinking: "You may seem to have a lot of time against a slow incoming serve, but you don't have time to consciously recognize the spin, speed, direction, and dept of the serve, and then decide what shot you should respond with. It has to be instinctive, i.e. subconscious." The only way to do this is practice.

Most players are either overly aggressive or overly passive when they receive. It's important to find the middle range. However, it is even more important to understand that it is consistency, placement, and variation that are most important.

Flip kills and loop kills are exciting ways to return serves. They are also quick ways to lose the point via missing. Always remember that all you have to do is break even on your opponent's serve, and you'll probably win on your serve. So you don't need to hit a winner off the serve. Just return it in such a way that your opponent can't hit a winner—which normally means catching him at least slightly off-guard. To do this takes good placement, variation, and hiding the direction and shot selection until the last second.

If you don't place the ball well, your opponent may jump all over your return. Few players can cover the entire table with a strong third-ball attack, especially if you don't telegraph your direction early in the shot, so it's important to figure out what part of the table your opponent will have the most trouble with, and go there. A well-placed passive return is often more effective than a strong return hit right at an opponent's strength.

Without good variation, of course, your returns are predictable. Mix in loops, flips, pushes, drives, and do them at different speeds, spins, depths, as well as varying the placement. Aim one way, then at the last second go the other way so your opponent can never know where you are going until you contact the ball. If your opponent looks likes he's looking for a push return, give him anything but that.

A key component of receiving is not to think as the server serves, just respond and do what you have practiced doing. The server has a huge number of options, far too many to try to consciously respond to.

You can make conscious tactical decisions on how you want to return certain serves, especially the ones you are seeing most often, and your subconscious will get the message. If you keep telling yourself that when you see a short backspin serve you should push it short, your subconscious will get the message.

One way to develop your receive game is to work on your own serves. When you master a serve, you better understand it, and see how others return it. Then it becomes easier for you to return it. That's why the best servers are often the best receivers as well—many top players are serve & receive specialists.

What is your primary goal in returning serve? It's the same as with any other tactic. To mess up your opponent.

Reading the Serve

If you can't read the serve, you have a serious problem. The specifics of this are outside the scope of this book (see TableTennisCoaching.com), but here are a few general things, and then some tactical ways to read a serve. (Also see the section "Reading Spin" in the chapter "All About Spin.")

Ignore all racket motion except right at contact. No matter what the racket is doing, it's not creating spin if it's not in contact with the ball. A good server will use different racket motions both before and after contact to get you to misread the serve, so don't fall into that trap. To read spin, all you have to do is see the direction and speed of the racket at contact, and how fine the grazing motion. See how easy that was?

You can also read spin by the way the ball travels through the air and how it bounces on the table.

Sometimes you can read spin by the general motion the server uses. Even if you can't see contact, many players have slightly different motions

Table Tennis Tactics for Thinkers

for different spins. You can subliminally read this, and connect, say, a backspin serve with one motion, a sidespin-topspin serve with another. If you watch closely, you should be able to figure out what exactly he is doing differently.

There are other clues. If the opponent does a high-toss serve, can he control it enough to keep it short? If not, then you know a long serve is coming, and you can get ready to attack it. Does he get more or less spin on the high-toss serve? Top players generally get more, but many players get less.

Sometimes the clues are obvious, if you observe them. Remember the example earlier of the player who always stuck his tongue out when he was about to serve a fast, deep serve, or the one who had his racket more closed and farther back when he was about to serve long? I once played someone who, when he did his pendulum serve, kept his wrist locked when he was about to do a fast, deep serve, so I could anticipate it. The funny thing is when I first saw this, I could tell he was doing something different in his motion when he served fast and deep, and took advantage of it, but it wasn't until later in the match that I realized exactly what it was that gave it away.

Three Ways to Receive

There are three basic philosophies you can adopt when receiving, or some combination of these three. You can use **passive receives**, where the goal is to make no mistakes, but the opponent gets to attack if he chooses; you can use **disarming receives**, where your goal is to disarm your opponent so you can get into a neutral rally, thereby taking away their service advantage; or you can use **aggressive receives**, where you take the initiative, but will often make mistakes in doing so. All three ways are effective if used in the right circumstances.

- **Passive Receives**

Passive receives usually mean a well-placed long push against backspin, or a deep but soft topspin. Against sidespin or topspin, you'd go for a steady flip, drive, or loop. Even though the receive is passive, you still want to place the ball as well as possible so the server doesn't have an easy attack. You might want to put it to the opponent's weaker side. Or, if he has a big forehand and likes to play it from the backhand side, but has a weaker backhand, you might intentionally go to the forehand so you can come back to the weaker backhand.

This type of receive is best against players who do not have strong attacks, and so there's no purpose in forcing an attack against their serves. It's also effective if the server has very good serves but an attack that you think you can handle, and so the goal is not to lose to those serves.

The downside of this type of receive is that the server is in control, and if he has a good attack, he should be able to dominate the rallies when he serves. Far too many players are too passive when receiving. While receive is mostly about control, you want to do something with the receive to make things difficult for a server with a good attack.

- **Disarming Receives**

    Now the goal is to neutralize the opponent's serve, so that you can play even on his serve, and win on your own serve. This is the most common type of receive at the higher levels, and while you need to sometimes be aggressive, if you are able to easily attack the opponent's serve, then you are probably just a better player or the opponent has weak serves. So most often, neutralizing the opponent's serve is all you want or need to do, since you can then win on your own serve. (Hopefully he won't neutralize your serve!)

    Against a short serve, there are several ways to do this. A simple backhand or forehand flip to the server's wide backhand will often force a neutral backhand-to-backhand exchange. A flip to the wide forehand may allow you to block back to the backhand, again forcing a neutral backhand exchange, with the server also forced to hit his backhand on the move. An aggressive push (against a backspin or no-spin serve) to the wide backhand will often take away the server's attack, or force him to attack weakly or from out of position. (Make sure the push is effective—see chapter on Pushing.) At the higher levels, the most common disarming receive against a short backspin or no-spin serve is a short push, which mostly stops the server from looping while bringing him over the table, where he may get jammed on the next shot.

- **Aggressive Receives**

    Against a weak serve, the receiver should play aggressively, take the initiative, and try to dominate the point. Examples include a short serve that pops up slightly, a serve that goes long that the receiver is ready for, and almost any serve where the receiver reads the serve well early on and is comfortable attacking. A player should always be looking for such serves and be ready to pounce on them.

    Top players often are very aggressive when receiving, especially against long serves. Against short serves, they often favor short pushes or aggressive but consistent flips. Many see and copy the aggressive flips, but don't notice the consistency. An aggressive but inconsistent flip is just another efficient way to lose.

Table Tennis Tactics for Thinkers

Long and Short Serves

It's best to divide all serves into two types: long and short serves. Against the long serves, you should mostly attack. Against the short serves you should focus on control, consistency, and variation, using flips, and both long and short pushes.

Attack the Deep Serve

Against a short serve, you can take the ball quickly and rush the opponent, you can go for angles, and you can drop the ball short. So have a number of ways to mess up an opponent without actually attacking the serve. This is where you can get really creative.

Against a deep serve, you don't have these options. You can't rush the opponent as well with a quick shot, go for extreme angles, and you can't return it short. If you return the deep serve passively, you are giving your opponent lots of time to set up his best shot. So don't.

Instead, get in the habit of attacking deep serves. (There are tactical exceptions, such as when playing a passive defensive player who won't attack even if you return his serve passively, if your own game is primarily defensive, or when you return a deep serve defensively as a variation.) Ideally you should loop all deep serves. If you make mistakes at first (you will), then that's the best reason to keep attacking them—to learn to attack them. The more you do it, the better you'll get at it, and your level will go up. It's an example of strategic development.

The key is to practice attacking them, generally by looping, both in games and in practice. I've seen many players lose a match because they couldn't return serves effectively—and later they'd be off practicing their strokes rather than practicing return of serve. If you have trouble attacking a deep serve (or any other serve return), find someone who can do the serves that give you trouble, and practice against them, either in practice sessions or matches.

You don't have to go for a big loop against deep serves. A consistent, aggressive loop is all that is needed. You can loop soft and spinny as well, as long as your loop lands deep on the opponent's side.

Having said all this about attacking deep serves, there are some matches where you might want to push most backspin serves back, even if they are long. If you have a good push, and the opponent isn't an overly strong looper, it might be the tactical thing to do, at least in that match. Strategically, however, you should learn to attack most deep serves.

Against deep serves, since you *know* you are going to (mostly) attack, much of the indecision is taken out of the matter. You still have to read the serve early (not only its depth, but also its spin, speed, and direction), and you have to decide how to loop it (forehand or backhand), how fast or spinny, and where (wide backhand, wide forehand, or at elbow). Base these tactical decisions on your own strengths and weaknesses, and your opponent's.

Loop the deep serves to one of the three spots you should always attack—wide corners and elbow. Keep your loops mostly deep, though a loop that lands short is a good variation against some players. It's not easy controlling your loop's depth when also trying to deal with the service spin and other factors, so if you start looping off, don't worry so much about depth; get the loop on the table.

It's sometimes a good idea to shorten your loop stroke when looping a serve. This will lead to a less powerful loop, but will increase your control and consistency. At the higher levels, however, this may not work as the opponent will jump all over your loop if it's too soft, though a somewhat soft but spinny loop that goes deep on the table is often effective. At the higher levels, players may use a full stroke and essentially overpower the service spin with their own looping topspin, which pulls the ball down so fast as to make up for any minor misreading of the spin.

You might also find that there are some types of serves you can loop better than others. For example, many players (including me) find it easier to forehand loop a pendulum serve, where the spin makes the ball break into the player, than a serve that breaks away. So you can be more aggressive against some deep serves than others. On the other hand, if you are too aggressive off one type of serve, and your shots are hitting, you may never see that serve again—so I sometimes hold back a bit, and focus on good, consistent loops that might not scare the server from using the serve I want him to use.

Returning Long Serves With the Backhand

This gives lots of players trouble, so let's give this an entire section.

The key is that you have to *do something* when returning any long serve or you give the opponent a big opening. And that usually means attacking it. Against a long serve to the backhand, that means either backhand looping or hitting/punching a strong backhand. A player with good footwork may step around and

Timo Boll backhand loops from close to the table, perhaps off a serve that just went off the end.
Photo by Diego Schaaf

Table Tennis Tactics for Thinkers

loop with the forehand, but most can't do that on a regular basis unless they are very fast or they anticipate the serve. If the serve is fast, you can use the speed against the opponent with a punch block or regular backhand. If you have trouble attacking the serve, try shortening your stroke.

You want to place the ball, usually wide to the corners, or (if the opponent isn't looking to attack with the forehand) a strong shot to the elbow. Shots to the middle backhand or middle forehand put little pressure on the server, and are often ripped. Ideally, return it outside the wide backhand corner, which makes it difficult for an opponent to step around and use a forehand, and also makes a backhand down-the-line attack difficult.

You want to hide the direction. For example, if you aim your backhand crosscourt to the wide backhand, then at the last second change and go to the wide forehand, you can catch an opponent off guard. If you aim to the wide forehand, many opponents will move to cover that, and then you can do a simple return to the backhand.

You want depth. Even a weak topspin ball that goes deep can be effective if it either has topspin or is to a wide angle. Against some players who hang back to counterloop, a shorter, softer, spinnier topspin return is sometimes more effective, but don't overdo it or they'll get used to it.

A sudden chop, chop-block, or sidespin block can also be effective, but only if you can control it, and usually only as a variation. If you can deaden the ball with a chop-block or sidespin block, many opponents will have great difficulty. If the serve has sidespin, try sidespin blocking it back, using the opponent's own spin against him. (Go with the spin, not against it, i.e. against a forehand pendulum serve, your racket should go right to left for a sidespin block.)

Lastly, variation is important. If your opponent knows what you are going to do, things get pretty easy for him. Even if you are going to loop all deep serves (as most advanced players should), you should vary the placement, depth, speed, and spin.

Returning Short Serves

If you have read the spin correctly, it is usually easy to return short serves, especially those to the backhand, though of course returning them *effectively* is another matter. But a short serve to the forehand can be awkward because the table gets in the way, and it's tricky aiming to the right to compensate for sidespin that pulls the ball to the left. You may need to practice this a lot.

The proper racket angle is essential to controlling the spins you will encounter. Unfortunately, experience is the real teacher here and that's why receiving is usually the hardest part of the game to master. Ask a good player or coach at your club to practice his serves against you. It will benefit him while you learn without the pressures of a real match.

When receiving, you should always be looking for chances to take the initiative. Don't keep pushing long if your opponent attacks the pushes effectively. Flip or push short instead, or learn to push long more effectively.

Most importantly, vary the way you receive short serves. An effective receive makes the rally go the way you want it. As always, look to mess up your opponent.

Against a short serve, you can push long, push short, or flip. Let's look at each.

- **Long Push Receive**
You generally don't want to push a serve unless it has backspin or no-spin, and unless you have a good flip, you will most often push against short backspin. When you push long, make sure the push is quick & fast, heavy or varied, low, deep, angled, and with disguised placement that you can change at the last second. If you do all but one of these things, a good player will take advantage of the one you don't do. Often players lose match after match because of this without realizing it. (See chapter on Pushing.)

A good heavy push (a "stiff push") will give most players difficulty, especially if kept low, deep, and angled. Only a high-level player can really rip this ball. Test out your opponent and see what he does against a stiff push. If he can loop it consistently, then you probably don't want to push long to him too often.

Against some players, you might want to push at their elbow to make them decide whether to attack with their forehand or backhand, to make them move to attack, and to get them out of position. If you do this, push somewhat aggressively, quick off the bounce and with some pace. You want to rush the opponent into making mistakes. If you learn to push the ball a little quicker off the bounce than most players, your opponent will likely have difficulty adjusting, and will often rush his shot and make mistakes.

To really mess up your opponent, aim one way, but at the last second push the other way. This means either aiming at the wide backhand and going to the wide forehand at the last second or the reverse.

Against a sidespin or topspin serve, and probably most no-spin serves, you should normally flip. However, you can push against sidespin or topspin by chopping down on the ball to keep it low, which is basically a chop-block, which is half push, half block. Think of it as a push with a

Table Tennis Tactics for Thinkers

closed racket. If you use a normal push, it will pop up. You shouldn't overuse the chop-block, but against some players it is effective if they can't attack it effectively. Against a player who jumps all over your topspin returns, a chop-block can take them out of their game. It can be placed short or long, but to keep it short takes a lot of touch—but many top players can do this to stop the server from attacking.

Pushing long can be effective if done well and not overdone. Too many players either don't do it effectively, or they overuse it. At the higher levels, a long push is a variation, and rarely the primary receive option.

- **Short Push Receive**

Against a short serve, a short push often is the best way to stop the server from looping. It is mostly done against short backspin serves, though you can also push short against no-spin, and if you have nice touch, against short sidespin and even topspin serves. In general, however, I'd recommend flipping most sidespin and topspin serves.

To push short, you should contact the ball just after it bounces and with a soft motion and light touch, and return it as low as you can. Don't just pat the ball back; give the ball some backspin with a light grazing motion. The backspin will not only make it harder for the opponent to attack the serve, but it will also slow the ball down when it hits the table, making it easier to push short. The backspin also makes the ball travel more in a line, making it easier to keep the ball low. It's also easier to have a soft touch if you graze the ball since the ball then leaves your racket slower.

2009 USA Men's Singles Champion Michael Landers drops the ball short.
Photo by Diego Schaaf

The ideal short push isn't too short; given the chance, its second bounce would be near the server's end line. This makes it difficult for him to loop, flip, or push short, and will often be returned with a long push you can attack. If you drop the ball too short, it is easy to pop the ball up slightly (an easy flip kill for the opponent), plus it's usually easier for the opponent to handle effectively than a slightly longer short push. He can drop it back short; he can flip it more easily, since he's closer to his target (your side of the table); he can hit quick off the bounce, thereby rushing you; and he can angle the ball, since the ball is so close to the net.

Of course, all this is easier said than done. Except at the advanced levels, most players struggle to push short, not to mention varying the shortness! But against a predictably straight backspin serve that goes short (i.e. a server without much variation), even intermediate players can begin to control their depth.

The easiest place to push short is either at the part of the net closest to you (i.e. your shot travels perpendicular to the net, and your target is closest), or at a corner (since this gives you more table to keep the ball short on). So normally this is where you might push. However, you should learn to maneuver your pushes around the net. Learn to make last second changes of direction, and drop the ball directly at the net, to the left, or to the right. Figure out which side gives your opponent the most trouble, and favor dropping the ball there. For example, if your opponent has a nice backhand attack against a short ball, but is awkward with this ball on the forehand side, drop the ball to his forehand side. (This is most often the case.)

The problem with the short receive is that with all the varied service spins possible, it is easy to pop the ball up, and a ball that pops up near the net is one of the easiest balls to put away. And so many players shy away from pushing short, and focus on pushing long or flipping, thereby making a strategic mistake that limits their tactical options. A strong player who knows you are going to flip or push long knows that your ball is going long, and so can hang back and attack, probably looping all of your returns. The only way to stop this is with a short push.

One way to handle this is to only use the short push against obvious short backspin serves. Many players do not have much service variety, and others are simply predictable or do not disguise their serves well. So against a server with lots of short, tricky serves, you might temporarily "retire" the short receive, but use it against those with simpler serves when you see short backspin.

Some players figure that they don't need to push short until they reach the higher levels, and then they'll learn to do it. Unfortunately, the lack of a short push not only makes it more difficult to reach the higher levels, but once they do reach that level, they are years behind in their receive development, and so they are stuck without one of the most valuable tactical tools for receiving. So start strategically working on that short push *now*.

Table Tennis Tactics for Thinkers

- **Flip Receive**

A flip is how you attack a short ball. (In Europe, it's called a flick.) On the backhand side, often it's not much different than a normal backhand, though you normally shorten the stroke. (It's quite different if you use a banana or strawberry flip—see below!) On the forehand, it's quite different than a normal forehand, as you step in with your right foot (which would normally be back on normal forehands), and stroke the ball with forearm and sometimes wrist.

You should flip most topspin and sidespin serves, and probably most no-spin serves as well. It's a little trickier for most to flip backspin, but any short backspin serve can be flipped; learn to do so. Even if you won't flip backspin much, you want to establish it as a threat the server has to watch for, and you want to be ready to attack a backspin serve that pops up slightly.

USA Team Member Adam Hugh flips a short ball with his forehand. Photo by Diego Schaaf

You should flip with some topspin to control the shot. At the higher levels, players are now almost looping short balls, creating spin with their forearm and wrist snap, especially on the backhand side. Since it is easier to do this on the backhand side, many top players are now doing what many lower-level players have been doing for many years—often to the chagrin of coaches—which is to attack short serves to the forehand with their backhands. It would seem that doing this would take the receiver out of position, leaving him open on his backhand side, but if you move back quickly, it's not a major problem. Some of the best players get back so fast they can follow with a forehand from their backhand side. This is one of the biggest changes in recent years at the higher levels.

Most lower-level players who had done this before did so because they found it tricky to attack short balls with their forehand, especially against backhand sidespin type serves, where you have to aim to the right to compensate for the sidespin. At the higher levels, they do it because of the extra topspin they can create with the backhand over the table (compared to the forehand over the table), and also because it's also easier for them against backhand-type sidespin serves, just as it is for lower-level players. Many top players who receive backhand against short serves to the forehand only do so against this type of sidespin. (However, for players who use banana flips, it's often the opposite.)

Another advantage of the backhand receive against short serves to the forehand is that players are not used to it. Few things are more disconcerting to a server than having your short serve to the forehand flipped with a backhand to your own wide forehand! It's hard to guard against this shot since you also have to guard against the flip down the line to your backhand, and compared to the forehand flip, the backhand flip is easier to change directions at the last second.

I recommend learning both ways. Against a forehand pendulum-type sidespin serve, for example, it's relatively easy to flip with the forehand, and you don't have to go out of position to do so. It's also often easier to flip kill with the forehand against a slightly high serve. If you can backhand receive over the table with a lot of topspin, then that should become one of your tactical weapons, as it is for most top players these days.

Make sure to place your flips to a wide corner or at the elbow, and to hide your direction until the last second, often changing directions at the last second. Then step back quickly to continue the rally.

Placement of the flips depends on the opponent's style. If the server is mostly a forehand player who has quick feet and is looking to follow up his serve with a forehand from all parts of the table, you might want to flip to the wide forehand, catching him going the wrong way, and setting yourself up to return his shot to his backhand, which makes the server move to hit his weaker shot and may take the opponent's strong forehand out of the rest of the rally.

If the server is more two-winged and ready to attack from either side, then either flip to his weaker side; to the side crosscourt from your strong side (since most flips are returned crosscourt); or at his elbow (forcing him to quickly decide which shot to use and to move to make the shot, and taking him out of position and so opening up a corner for your next shot).

Banana and Strawberry flips—I've mentioned these terms earlier and it's quite possible you are dying to know what I'm talking about if you haven't already checked the glossary. These are relatively

World and Olympic Men's Champion Zhang Jike of China demonstrates a banana flip. His wrist is turned way back, with the racket approaching the ball over the table from the side.
Photo by Diego Schaaf

Table Tennis Tactics for Thinkers

advanced shots, especially the strawberry flip—in fact, while most world-class players now have proficient banana flips, few do strawberry flips. I only recently learned about this shot from U.S. Men's Coach and former German star Stefan Feth, who was known for this shot in Europe. If for no other reason, you should learn these shots because of their cool names.

A banana flip is a wristy backhand return of a short ball, especially one with backspin (usually a serve) that's sort of a mini-loop, with topspin and sidespin, with racket moving from right to left (for a righty). It's especially effective against a forehand pendulum serve sidespin, where you can go with and add to the spin, just as a looper goes with and adds to the spin when looping against backspin. In both cases, you get tremendous spin.

The rarer and more difficult strawberry flip is also a wristy backhand return of a short ball, especially one with backspin (usually a serve) that's also sort of a mini-loop, with topspin and sidespin, with racket moving from left to right (for a righty). It's especially effective against a backhand sidespin-type sidespin, where you can go with and add to the spin. This is a relatively rare shot, meaning the surprise factor if you learn it is high. It's also tricky to learn. Some players do a soft version of this, where they return the ball with sidespin, but without any pace and only moderate spin. As done by a master such as Feth, it comes out as a sidespin-topspin drive, similar to a hooking forehand loop. However, I don't think you can really visualize this shot without seeing it, but it's good to know about—and perhaps a top player or coach can demonstrate. (Most won't, and many won't even know what it is. It's a new term and technique. See, you are ahead of the curve!)

What's the advantage of banana and strawberry flips, as opposed to a regular flip? They have lots of topspin and sidespin, so the ball jumps on the far side, messing up the opponent. Plus the topspin pulls the ball down so it becomes a more consistent shot than a regular flip, which has only light topspin.

Where do these flips get their names? The banana flip is named for the motion the racket goes through as it moves from right to left, curving toward the opponent. The strawberry flip was named by Feth since he needed a different fruit to differentiate it from the banana flip. Seriously. (He could have called it a reverse banana flip, since the racket also goes through the banana motion in reverse, but that wouldn't have been as fun, would it?)

Sometimes Go With the Spin

When receiving a sidespin serve, you probably either aim the opposite way to make up for the sidespin, or simply hit through it (with a drive or loop), and basically overpower the sidespin. However, there's a third way, mostly used by top players. That's to "go with the spin."

Imagine an opponent's forehand pendulum serve (righty vs. righty), with his racket tip down. With this type of sidespin, the near side of the ball is rotating to your left. Why not contact the ball with a right-to-left "swiping" motion, and return the server's own sidespin? (Do the reverse for a sidespin going the other way.) This is a great way to mess up your opponent! This is basically a softer version of the banana and strawberry flips, where the focus is returning the opponent's spin rather than adding to it, with a soft, controlled receive.

What to Do with Problem Serves

Everybody has at least one serve that gives him trouble. It might be a certain sidespin, or a deep serve, a short serve, a no-spin serve, an angled serve, etc. (For example, you can almost divide players into two groups—those who have fits with forehand tomahawk serves to the forehand, and those that loop them with ease. Which are you? See following section on this.) The question is what to do against these problem serves?

The obvious answer is to learn how to return them. (Strategic development!) If you do this, your level will go up—and relative to your new level, you will find other serves that give you trouble. So you should learn how to return each serve—but at the same time, you have to know what to do with problem serves when you see them in a match.

First, focus on control. Place the ball, usually at a wide angle and deep. Often this alone will solve the problem. You don't need to dominate on an opponent's serve (though it helps); you need to break even, and dominate on *your* serve.

If you are still having trouble, analyze the problem. If you keep popping the ball up, or hitting it wide, adjust. If you keep making the same mistake, and don't adjust your return, you'll keep making the same mistake.

Against some serves, you might try a "scare tactic." If there's a single serve that really bothers you, attack it one time. Loop it or flip it aggressively! Scare the server. (This doesn't mean swinging wildly; it means attacking aggressively but with the intent of the ball hitting the table.) Even if you miss it, often the server will be scared from using it again, at least very often. If he does keep using it, then you'll just have to figure out how to return that serve because you're up against a smart opponent.

I have far more difficulty looping a deep serve that breaks away from me, like a deep backhand serve or tomahawk serve. I have little trouble looping ones that break into me, such as a regular forehand pendulum serve. Guess which one I tend to be more aggressive with the first (or perhaps the second) time I see it? The last thing I want to do is be too soft against a serve that breaks away from me, which is practically telling the opponent to keep giving me that serve since I have trouble with it.

Table Tennis Tactics for Thinkers

Conversely, is there a serve that you are very good at receiving? One that you can really loop or flip aggressively, for example? Don't go overboard attacking this serve too much early in a game or you'll never see it again. Consider slowing down your attack of this serve, being consistent with good placement, and slowly building up a lead. Instead of one-shot winners, return the serve to take the initiative—play the percentages.

The Tomahawk Serve or a Lefty's Forehand Pendulum Serve

So many players have trouble with these notorious serves to the forehand that it deserves a section of its own. Since the two serves come out about the same, I'm only going to talk about returning tomahawk serves, but everything applies equally to a lefty's forehand pendulum serve.

At the lower levels, deep spin serves to the forehand can be effective, especially the tomahawk serve, which is the bane of many intermediate players. Why do so many players have trouble with this type of serve? For the very reasons mentioned earlier. As the ball is coming to the receiver, the receiver has to move to the ball. Suppose he does so with the racket at the right height and angle to make a good return. But then something happens—the ball curves away, and the player often reaches for it. This lowers the racket, and so now the racket is too low, leading to a lifting motion, and a ball hit off the end. And lo and behold, players hit this serve off the end over and over. The serve is also tricky to return because the spin makes the ball go to the receiver's left, and so he has to aim right, which is tricky for some on the forehand side. How do you return it? Don't lower the racket more than necessary as you move to the ball, and hit toward the inside part of the ball, so you aim toward the right to compensate for the spin. You also have to anticipate the ball's curving away from you or you'll forever being lunging at it at the last second. You can also simply overpower the serve and its spin with your own aggressive loop, which is what top players do.

The tomahawk serve of Austria's Daniel Habesohn. Photo by Diego Schaaf

Larry Hodges

CHAPTER TEN
Rallying Tactics

Rallying is intricately linked to serve and receive. A smart tactical player uses his serve and receive to set up the type of rally he wants. So in discussing rallying tactics for various shots and styles, we'll be revisiting serve and receive tactics.

We've already discussed many general rallying tactics in the chapter on Conventional Tactics. Now it's time to go more in depth.

Kalinikos Kreanga of Greece
Photo by Diego Schaaf

There are an incredible number of playing styles—no two players play exactly alike. For example, let's look at loopers. Some are one-winged loopers, who race all over the place to loop with their forehands. Others are two-winged, able to loop from both sides. Others loop on the forehand while hitting on the backhand. Some loop close to the table, some from off the table, and others somewhere in between. Some loop with great speed, others with great spin, some with both. Some are extremely consistent, others are more hit and miss. There is no way of systematically covering every tactic for every type of looper, or for any other style.

Instead, we will talk about general rallying tactics in this chapter. Then, in the following chapters, we will get into specific tactics both for and against various styles of play. At each step, using your own strategic and tactical thinking, it is your job to decide what fits your game. (Remember WEAR, from the chapter Your Tactical Game? Watch, Experiment, Analyze, Remember? Of course, you should have been doing this already in the chapters on Serve and Receive.)

When to Respond

You should develop the habit of watching how an opponent hits the ball. Does he ever change directions at the last instant? Or does he commit early on to a direction, with the stroke and racket position showing where the shot is going? Most players stroke the ball in such a way that you can see where they are hitting the ball by the time they start their forward swing (or even before), but most players don't react to the ball direction until after the ball has been hit, losing vital time. Learn as early in a match

Table Tennis Tactics for Thinkers

as possible when an opponent has committed to a direction for each major shot, and learn to react and move at that time. Then let your subconscious take over as you just respond to the opponent's shot. You'll find that this is how top players can seemingly return smash after smash against weaker players while a top player's first smash (better disguised) usually wins on the first shot.

There really are two key points in the swing. The first is when the opponent has committed to the placement, but you don't know where yet. Normally you would not respond to this, but sometimes, against a predictable opponent (which means most players), you can *consciously* anticipate. For example, if you serve a deep breaking serve to an opponent's backhand, most likely he'll return it to your backhand. So you might anticipate this, and at the instant when you figure the opponent has committed his direction—but hasn't actually telegraphed the direction—you might anticipate his return by stepping over to attack with your forehand. (Just make sure you don't try to consciously control your shot; let your subconscious take over for that.) Don't overdo this, but it's a definite tactical advantage if you can do this sometimes.

The second important point in the swing is when the opponent has telegraphed where his placement will be. You should learn to observe this so you can move the instant you can see the direction. Many players don't move until the opponent has hit the ball, but for the large majority of players, you can see where they are going by the time they start their forward swing, and if you don't react to that, you are losing valuable time. At the higher levels, many players learn to hide their direction longer and to even fake one way and go another, so against players like that learn when they have *really* committed. The more you observe this, the more your subconscious will learn as well, and the faster it will respond.

The shoulders are usually the giveaway for where a player is going on the forehand. Many players line their shoulders up early to hit crosscourt or down the line, and it's like they have a big sign across their shoulders saying where the shot is going. When you first learn the forehand, this is okay, but as you advance, learn a little subtlety and deception. For example, from the forehand side, rotate the shoulders way back as if you are going down the line, then at the last second whip about and go crosscourt. Or set up to go crosscourt, and at the last second rotate the shoulders back more so you can go down the line. (Sound familiar? We talked about this earlier in the chapter on Conventional Tactics, and we'll be talking about it more in this chapter.) Or simply bring your arm and wrist back at the last second and go inside-out down the line. (This last tactic is especially effective when looping or hitting a forehand from the backhand side, where you aim down the line but at the last second go crosscourt.) These are easier shown then explained—have a top player or coach show you how to do these shots. Once learned, you'll be shocked at how your subconscious automatically does these shots at just the right tactical times.

General Rallying Tactics

Much of this was covered in the chapter on Conventional Tactics, and rallying tactics for specific styles will be covered in upcoming chapters. Your greatest weapons in a rally are any of the following—so strategically develop these weapons for your tactical toolbox.

- Your best rally shot, the one that scares your opponents
- Quickness
- Speed
- Spin
- Depth (mostly deep on the table)
- Placement (wide angles, elbow)
- Variety
- Misdirection
- Consistency

Now let's cover some general tactics that come up regularly for nearly all styles.

Playing the Weaker Side

It's obvious that you want to go to the opponent's weaker side as often as possible. However, if you overdo that, he might move over and play his stronger shot from that side—and he gets to choose when to do this. For example, if your opponent has a weak backhand and you keep playing there, he may step around and attack with his forehand—and since he gets to choose when to do this, it'll probably be a strong shot. Worse, he's now in a forehand dominant position, and will probably get another forehand shot, especially since he's just hit a strong shot, which will likely force a weaker return from you.

At the lower levels, and against slower players, you can go to the weaker side over and over. However, as shown here (and explained in the Beginning Tactics chapter), it's not always a great strategy. Instead, consider playing to the opponent's stronger side (aggressively when possible), and then coming back to the weaker side. This allows *you* to choose which ball the opponent gets to use his strong side against, as well as making him move to hit from his weaker side.

Table Tennis Tactics for Thinkers

Sometimes the "stronger side" is only strong against balls that can be attacked. If you attack the stronger side, sometimes that side turns into the weaker side. For example, many players have strong forehand attacks and backhand blocks, but are not very good if you attack their forehand, where their defense might not be so good.

The Value of Down the Line

Crosscourt. It's so much easier to hit that way. Most often you get to hit the ball back the way it's coming, and it's easier to hit that way than re-directing it down the line. You've probably hit so many crosscourt forehand-to-forehand and backhand-to-backhand shots that it's second nature to you. And you've got fifteen and a half more inches of table than when hitting down the line.

But guess what? Your opponent also likes those crosscourt shots, and he's probably already setting up for it. Watch that split second of absolute horror on his face as he realizes you are going down the line—or at least a look of apprehension—and you'll know the value of down-the-line shots. There may be less table to aim for, but it means the opponent has less time to react.

So when you warm up, practice your down-the-line shots. It's a big table out there; use both sides of it.

Sometimes Hit to the Same Spot Twice

You want to keep moving the ball around to make the opponent move. However, sometimes you want to go to the same spot twice. Here are a few good examples.

You've just blocked the ball to the opponent's wide forehand. The opponent had to go out of position, but made a somewhat aggressive topspin return from his wide forehand. After the shot, he began to move back to cover his wide backhand. Most players try to take advantage of the opponent being out of position by going back to the backhand. This will often work, but it's often better to go right back to the forehand. The opponent is moving in the wrong direction, and likely will have trouble covering this shot a second time in a row. Even if he does, he probably won't have time to get to the shot and put much power on it.

You also want to use this tactic when moving a player in and out. Suppose you're playing a chopper (though this applies to any off-table player, such as lobbers and fishers). You've made a good attacking shot, but the chopper chopped it back. You then did a drop shot, the chopper ran in and pushed it back, and then quickly stepped back for your next attack. Do you attack again? If the opponent is too close to the table, or if his push was weak, then yes. However, if the opponent is stepping back to prepare for your next attack, why not do a second drop shot, and catch him going the wrong way? Most likely you'll not only get a relatively weak return from a lunging opponent, but your opponent will probably now be jammed at the table, unable to get into position to chop your next ball. Easy point!

Suppose you've smacked a strong shot right at the opponent's playing elbow—usually a player's weakest spot. The opponent manages to make a return, but not a particularly strong one. You get ready to attack his weak return. Why not go right back to his middle? If you go to the corners, you might give the opponent an easy forehand or backhand. By going to the middle, you may catch him again. Since his previous shot was weak, he's unlikely to be looking to counter-attack from the middle since he'll more likely be in a defensive position.

Against some opponents, what works once will work over and over. (In other words, your opponent is not a thinker, at least at the table.) Against other opponents, you have to mix things up. This means knowing when to change directions and when to go right back to the same spot.

Placement of Backhand Attack

Many players automatically attack crosscourt with their backhand to their opponent's backhand. When attacking with the forehand, these same players don't hesitate to move their attacks around, probably because they figure they have more power with their forehand, and so can get away with attacking an opponent's normally stronger forehand side.

These players forget that their backhand attacks are usually quicker than their forehand attacks and that this very quickness gives opponent's trouble counter-attacking with their forehands. Even when backhand looping, the swing on the backhand is normally shorter, and so harder to read where it is going.

When a player attacks with his backhand to an opponent's backhand, he is probably using the worst possible placement. An opponent's backhand is the very shot that is probably quick enough to handle a quick backhand attack!

Instead, look for chances to attack with your backhand to the opponent's slower forehand side or into the opponent's middle (elbow). Going down the line to an opponent's forehand means the opponent not only has to react to a quick backhand, but to the shorter down-the-line distance. Going to the middle means the opponent has to decide whether to use a forehand or backhand while being rushed. Either of your placements puts you in the driver's seat.

Table Tennis Tactics for Thinkers

Misdirection

It's a huge advantage if you can aim one way, then go the other, thereby faking your opponent out of his socks. Remember, the goal of tactics is to mess up your opponent!

Many players telegraph the direction of their attacking shots. Often, the opponent isn't sure how he knows where you are going, he just senses it. That's because when he sees the same stroke pattern resulting in the ball going one way, and another stroke pattern going the other way, it becomes habit to react to it—even if he isn't sure specifically what in your stroke is different. (When you recognize a person's face, do you consciously see the distinct features that make this person's face unique?) So try to keep your shots identical as long as possible before using misdirection.

On the backhand side, this is relatively easy, especially when blocking. You should normally be facing the direction you hit your backhand. Suppose you line up to hit one way, but at the last second rotate your shoulders and aim the other way? The opponent will likely already be reacting to the way you set up the shot, and the last-second change will mess him up.

Here's another way to hit a deceptive backhand down the line. Aim your backhand crosscourt with a normal backhand stroke. At the last instant, just before contact, push your wrist forward, but let the racket fall behind. Your racket will now be aimed to the opponent's forehand but your opponent will probably have already reacted to a crosscourt backhand. This is especially effective when blocking loops. (When you first learn this you should turn your shoulders some so you are facing the direction you block. As you get proficient you can get away with just the wrist turn, thereby making it harder for the opponent to pick up on the change of direction.)

Forehand Deception with Shoulder Rotation

Whether you are hitting or looping, you should normally line up your shoulders when you backswing on the forehand so that the shoulders roughly aim in the direction you are hitting towards. This maximizes your hitting zone and allows you to stroke naturally through the ball. If you don't rotate the shoulders back enough, you'll have an abbreviated stroke, costing you control and power. (The reverse is less often a problem, but if you do rotate the shoulders back too much, then the stroke becomes too long and cumbersome to control, as well as taking too long in a fast rally.)

So a top priority in developing the forehand is proper shoulder rotation. But once the shot is developed and the shoulder rotation natural, you can use this very shoulder rotation to deceive an opponent.

Imagine lining up to hit or loop a forehand crosscourt from your forehand side. You line the shoulders up during the backswing, and are about to start the forward swing. Your opponent sees your shoulder rotation, sees that they are lined up to hit crosscourt, and instinctively moves to react to a crosscourt shot since most players hit the ball wherever their shoulders line up to hit. Then, at the last second before starting your forward swing, you rotate the shoulders back a bit more, line them up for a down-the-line shot, take the ball a little later, and then hit down the line. Instant free point.

The key is that instant of "hesitation" where you have stopped your backswing with the shoulders lined up crosscourt, where you let the opponent react, and then the final extra bit of shoulder rotation before going down the line. The timing is surprisingly easy as long as you focus on lining up the shoulders properly for whatever direction you are going.

The shot can also be done with the forehand from the backhand side, where you aim down the line and at the last second go crosscourt. In both cases you are faking to the left (for a righty), but going to the right.

The alternate version is to line up your shoulders to go down the line from the forehand side, and simply rotate the shoulders forward more during the forward swing so that you hit crosscourt, taking the ball a little sooner than if you were to go down the line. Or from the backhand side, line up the shoulders to go crosscourt and go down the line. In these two cases, you are faking to the right (for a righty), but hitting to the left.

When doing these deceptive shots, note that some opponents automatically cover the wide crosscourt angle no matter how you line up your shoulders. Against this type of player you should mostly fake crosscourt before going down the line. Some might be so ingrained to cover the crosscourt angle that no deception is needed, just go down the line. But when/if they adjust to that, then you can fake the down the line and go crosscourt. One consequence of the tendency for some opponents to cover the wide crosscourt angle is that it is sometimes less effective to fake down the line and then go crosscourt, since the opponent might be ready for that.

There are other ways of misdirecting an opponent with your forehand. Another way is to learn to hit inside-out, where your shoulders aim left but your arm and wrist twist back at the last second and you go to the right, often with sidespin. However, that takes great timing, and while many top players master the shot (especially when looping, where they have extra topspin to pull the shot down if it isn't timed perfectly), the simple last-second shoulder rotation allows you to get almost the same misdirection without developing the difficult timing of that inside-out shot.

Table Tennis Tactics for Thinkers

Changing the Pace

A major strength of some players is an ability to change the pace, thereby throwing an opponent's timing off. If you rarely change the pace, you are helping your opponent's timing. Many players try to change the pace, but do so unsuccessfully—often because they don't really understand the purpose of doing so.

Here is a simple way of looking at it. Against aggressive players, you primarily change the pace to win the point outright via the aggressive player's misses. Against control players, you change the pace primarily to force a weak shot for you to attack. There is some overlap, of course, especially when you change the pace against an attacker and force him into making an uncomfortable soft return that you can attack.

How do you change the pace? Usually by blocking softer and shorter on the table (especially when the opponent is off the table), or by looping slower and spinier than usual. Make sure the soft shot goes to the side where the opponent has the most trouble attacking a shorter, slower ball. Try not to telegraph your shot—ideally start your stroke as if you were hitting it harder, then soften the shot.

Rally Down Faster and Quicker Players

When faced with a faster or quicker opponent, many players try to match them in speed, and end up losing because of too many unforced errors. Instead, ask yourself if it is realistic to play at the opponent's pace. You might decide you can do so for perhaps the first shot in a rally, but not afterwards. For most rallies, you might have to take perhaps a half step backwards to give yourself more time. Or you might decide you really can pick up your pace and match your opponent.

If you can't play consistently at your opponent's pace, instead learn to out-rally him, using his own pace against him. If your opponent hits the ball hard, you don't need to create your own speed; just meet the incoming ball, and let it bounce back. (You can do this blocking off the bounce, or by counter-hitting at the top of the bounce or perhaps a half-step back.) Since you don't need to create much speed on your own, you can shorten your stroke, and just keep the ball in play and out-rally your fast but frustrated opponent. Make sure to move the ball around and keep it deep!

Where to Place Your Putaways

Where should you put your putaway shots? Whether they are smashes or loop kills, there are basically three options. You could think of the three options as the wide forehand, the wide backhand, and the middle, and those are your three options. But there's another way of looking at it.

Option One: The easiest spot. This usually would be the longest diagonal. This gives the most table to aim for, and so is the safest and most consistent. The down side—it's also the spot most opponents will expect you to aim for, and so is the most likely to be returned. At the beginning/intermediate level, you should aim most putaways to the safest spot since it's probably not coming back.

Option Two: Aim one way, go the other. Often this means aiming for the longest diagonal, and then, as the opponent moves to cover that spot, going the other way, usually down the line. This is riskier as you both have less table to go for and you are setting up to go one way, then have to change at the last second, but it's also going to make it very difficult for the opponent to return this shot. It's only at the higher levels that opponents can react and cover both corners.

Option Three: The opponent's middle. This is the transition spot between forehand and backhand. At all levels this is probably the most difficult spot to respond to. There are players who can almost relentlessly return shot after shot at the corners, but go at their middle and they fall apart. This is the most common spot top players aim at. The down side—it means you don't get the long diagonal to aim for, plus it's a moving target, depending on where the opponent is. Also, a forehand-oriented player who is off the table may counter-attack that ball with his forehand—but if he does, he's probably moving early. This means he is leaving his wide forehand open, which is where you would go in this case.

(For more on putaways, and in particular against off-table topspin defenders, see the chapter on Fishers and Lobbers.)

Develop an Overpowering Strength

This has come up already, but it's important to strategically develop overpowering strengths that you can use in a rally. (Some top players make serve or receive their "overpowering strength," but you need something to follow those shots up.) What is your overpowering strength, the "big tool" in your tactical toolbox? Forehand or backhand loops or smashes? Or something else—it doesn't have to be a putaway shot. Quick, aggressive blocks? Steady looping or counter-hitting? Chopping? Just make sure it is *something*.

I said that your overpowering rallying strength didn't have to be a putaway shot. However, develop one. If you can't consistently put the ball away when the opponent gives you the chance (often because of whatever your "overpowering strength" is, if it's not a putaway itself), you are at a huge disadvantage.

Table Tennis Tactics for Thinkers

Playing Lefties

The problem with playing lefties is two-fold: first, their shots come out differently than righties, and second, your natural ball placement to a righty is usually wrong against a lefty. In both cases, the key is to play against lefties until you both understand the differences and are comfortable playing them.

A righty often spends a lot of time blocking against righty crosscourt loops to his forehand (both in practice and in games), and so develops a good forehand block. Often lefties have weak forehand blocks, since they are usually playing their forehands against a righty's backhand. Lefties also tend to develop good backhands, since righties tend to play into it and because a good lefty backhand that can hit to all parts of the table can be tricky to play against for a righty. When playing a lefty, find out quickly if they have either of these two common traits.

A lefty's hooking sidespin loop can also give a righty trouble, but this is mostly because they aren't used to it, and is usually easy to adjust to. It's not hard to adjust to the lefty's loop on the backhand, where it breaks away from the player, since the backhand block is easy to maneuver about. On the forehand side, the lefty loop breaks into the righty, and this is usually easier to adjust to than one that breaks away. In both cases, it's just a matter of getting used to it by playing lefties with hooking sidespin loops. Most problems with returning a lefty's loop are temporary.

Three shots from a lefty that most commonly mess up a righty are: 1) down the line backhands; 2) aggressive crosscourt backhands to the wide forehand; and 3) their serves, especially forehand serves into your forehand that break away. It's just a matter of getting used to these shots.

1) **Down the line backhands**. Lefties are often used to playing their backhand down the line to a righty (to avoid going to the righty's forehand), while a righty might not be as used to this, and may be erratic or the ball may wander out over the table, allowing the lefty opponent to use their forehand to put the ball away. (Of course, sometimes the lefty's backhand is stronger, in which case you'd be playing more to the forehand, but that can be risky since it's almost always easier to end the point with the forehand.) So practice your backhand down the line regularly, since it's valuable not only against lefties but against righties as well.

2) **Crosscourt backhands**. Righties are not always used to a lefty's quick, crosscourt backhand to the forehand, so find chances to practice against lefties who do this. You can do the same shot to a lefty, but he may be more used to it since he probably plays righties regularly.

3) **Lefty forehand serves**. One trick for returning a lefty's forehand serve that breaks into your forehand is to aim the ball down the line to the lefty's forehand. The lefty has to be ready to cover that shot, and so at the last minute you can take the ball crosscourt into their backhand. (This is assuming they are stronger on the forehand; if the reverse, you may do the reverse.) If you wait until the last second and then lunge for the ball as it breaks away, you're probably going to miss. Besides losing control by lunging instead of stepping, you probably lower your racket as you lunge, and will likely lift the ball too much and go long. (See the discussion on returning the tomahawk serve and lefty pendulum serve in the chapter on Receive.)

Use what a lefty does effectively against you right back at them. Serve breaking serves into their forehand just as they do to you, often serving them short or breaking them outside the forehand corner, making them tricky to return effectively. (Though here the lefty has an advantage—he's probably more used to a righty doing that to him than you are used to a lefty doing it to you.) If the lefty starts to cover that shot, perhaps by standing more toward his forehand side when receiving, a sudden fast down-the-line serve to the backhand will likely mess him up and set you up for more breaking serves to their forehand.

Assuming you are comfortable against a lefty's shots, then the key becomes tactical. Where do you want to play your shots? For example, against a righty, you might play steady shots to the backhand, knowing the opponent can't put his backhand through you (in most cases)—but now that same shot goes into a lefty's forehand, where he may have more power. Or you might play quick shots to a righty's forehand, if your backhand is quicker than the opponent's forehand—but now that shot goes into a lefty's backhand, which not only may be as quick or quicker than your backhand, but also gives him that wide angle into your forehand.

So you may want to rethink your basic ball placement shots—but also use the reverse. Against a lefty, now you can hit quick, aggressive backhands crosscourt into their wide forehand; now you can lock them up on their backhands with your forehand into their backhand. Plus now you can use your own forehand pendulum serve that breaks into their forehand.

So there are really three basic keys to playing a lefty—the aforementioned getting used to their shots, and your own ball placements, which are really two things—learning (instinctively) what shots you do against righties that you don't want to do against lefties, and learning (also instinctively) what shots you normally don't do against righties that work against lefties.

Table Tennis Tactics for Thinkers

Slippery Floors

Many of you have had the experience of playing on a slippery floor. It isn't fun to rally on—you can barely move. But if you do get stuck playing on such a floor, there's a solution. Bring a small towel with you (or use paper towels), and wet it so it is damp but not dripping wet. (Too wet and you'll just make things worse.) Put it next to the table. Then step on it every chance you can. Try it out, and you'll see how much grippier your shoes will be for the next few points.

It's also important to have good playing shoes so you can move on all surfaces, and also learn to put your weight on the front inside part of the foot. This not only allows quicker movement, but concentrates your weight into a smaller area, thereby giving better traction. (This last section isn't exactly tactics, but you lose much of your rallying tactical toolbox if you can't move!)

CHAPTER ELEVEN
Different Grips

There are two major grips in table tennis—shakehand and penhold—and a third that is common enough that it merits mention, the Seemiller or American grip. Each of these grips has its own variations, and each variation has its strengths and weaknesses. It is important to know the general strengths of each grip. However, it's more important to play each grip as the player plays it. For example, penholders often have weaker backhands, but many do not, and if you go into a match against a penholder assuming he'll have a weak backhand, you may not find out until it is too late that he is stronger on the backhand. But knowing the general strengths and weaknesses of each grip gives you a tactical advantage going into the match since you can't test everything without risking a lot of points.

Shakehands Grip

There are three major variants of the shakehand grip: neutral, forehand, and backhand grips. With a neutral grip, the wrist lines up with the racket. With a forehand grip, the top of the racket rotates some to the left; with a backhand grip, the top of the racket rotates some to the right. Generally, the descriptions describe the grip—the forehand grip favors the backhand, while the backhand grip favors the backhand. But there are exceptions. For example, while a backhand grip usually leads to a better backhand block and backhand loop, often a forehand grip gives a better backhand smash. In general, don't worry too much about the specific version of the grip; every player is different, so find out what your opponent's strengths and weaknesses are, regardless of the grip. Sometimes a player adjusts his grip to strengthen a weak part of his game, and that part might still be a relative weakness, even with the adjusted grip. A player with a weak forehand loop might go to a forehand grip to strengthen the shot, but it might still be a weakness.

Some players use variations of the normal grips. For example, some shakehanders have their index finger more out on the backhand side, sometimes almost straight up, like 1967 Men's World Champion Nobuhiko Hasegawa. This sometimes makes it difficult to hit shots to the right. The finger can also get in the way on the backhand.

Shakehand players are generally strong from the corners, but weaker in the middle. Far too often players play to the corners against a shakehander, when it is the transitional point at the elbow that most shakehanders have difficulty covering. (Of course, the wider you go to the corners the more problems a shakehander will likely have since he has to move more.)

Table Tennis Tactics for Thinkers

The shakehands grip is the most common grip, but since it is the grip most players are familiar with, and since it's the most all-around grip (i.e. no great strengths or weaknesses), there's less to write about tactically.

Penhold Grip

Like the shakehand grip, there are variants of the penhold grip, more than for shakehanders. Many of these variations involve the intricate positioning of the fingers on the back of the racket. Others involve how the racket is tilted in relation to the hand—if it is rotated to the right, it's a backhand grip; if it is rotated to the left, it's a forehand grip, and of course in between is a neutral grip. Most modern penholders tend to use a forehand grip as this is also the best grip for the reverse penhold backhand.

**Penholder Xu Xin of China rips one.
Photo by Diego Schaaf**

A big advantage for penholders is that their wrist is generally freer on most shots, especially on serves and against short balls. Shakehanders can make up for this on the serve by adjusting their grip, but penholders normally have some advantage on short balls.

Most penholders have strong forehands—that is at least a small advantage of the grip, since the racket is more naturally held down, making it slightly easier to attack with topspin. But this is a relatively minor advantage, as many top shakehanders have forehands that are just as strong. I've always thought that the reason so many penholders have great forehands has less to do with the grip and more to do with covering for a weak backhand, especially with a conventional penhold backhand. It also had a lot to do with tradition, as it became traditional for penholders to focus on all-out forehand attack. There's no special tactics for playing against a penhold forehand; play it just like any other forehand. (One style unique to the penhold grip is the pips-out penholder, which will be covered in the chapter on Blockers, Counter-Drivers, and Hitters.)

A conventional penhold backhand is often more cramped and limited than a shakehands backhand. However, there are three types of penhold backhands, and this is probably the first thing you should note about penhold opponents.

Reverse penhold backhand. Until the mid- or late-1990s, nearly all coaches would say it was bad technique to use the back of the racket for the penhold backhand. And then came an explosion of top players from China who did exactly that! This is now considered the normal penhold backhand, and gives penholders a backhand attack that can be as strong as a shakehanders. Most modern players with reverse penhold backhands return everything with the reverse side, but some attack that way, but block conventionally. This style can be weak in the middle, like a shakehander.

Conventional Chinese penhold backhand, where the player mostly blocks. With this style, there is little middle weakness, and blocking is usually strong, but it's more difficult to attack with the backhand, and it can be tricky closing the racket against deep, spinny loops. You still might go to the middle against this backhand, but mostly to cut off the extreme angles. It's difficult to win a battle of angles with a conventional penhold backhand, which often specializes in quick angled blocking.

Reverse penhold backhand of China's Wang Hao, 2009 World Men's Singles Champion. Photo by Diego Schaaf

Korean penhold backhand (also called Japanese penhold grip), with the racket brought to the side and swung almost like a second forehand. This style can be scary until you realize that they have a bigger weakness in the middle than a shakehander, plus it can be difficult blocking this way. Some players use conventional penhold blocking backhands and

Conventional penhold backhand of USA's David Zhuang, 6-time U.S. Men's Singles Champion. Photo by John Oros

Conventional penhold backhand smash of former Japanese star Hiroshi Takahashi. Photo by Mal Anderson

Table Tennis Tactics for Thinkers

smash with this style. Few top players use this technique anymore.

Seemiller or American Grip

This grip was named for and popularized by five-time U.S. Men's Singles Champion Dan Seemiller, who was ranked in the top thirty in the world in the late 1970s. He was followed by Eric Boggan, who reached top twenty in the world. No other U.S.-trained player has come close to these rankings in the sponge era (since the 1950s). Four of the five U.S. team members at the 1983 World Championships used this grip—Dan Seemiller, his brother Rick Seemiller, Eric Boggan, and 1983 Pan Am Men's Singles Gold Medalist Brian Masters. (All four are in the U.S. Table Tennis Hall of Fame.) The grip is sometimes called the American grip, but is more commonly called the Seemiller grip.

The Seemiller backhand of USA's Dan Seemiller, 5-time U.S. Men's Singles Champion - the grip is named after him!
Photo by John Oros

The grip is sort of a variation of the shakehands grip, with the top of the racket rotated to the left so that the index finger curls around the side of the racket. The forehand is played about the same, but on the backhand the arm rotates about so that the same side is used on the forehand and backhand. Despite its promising start, the grip never came close to the popularity of shakehands or penhold, and in recent years fewer and fewer players use the grip. However, you will face these players in tournaments (especially in the northeast U.S.) and need to be ready.

Like shakehands and penhold, the Seemiller grip also has its backhand and forehand variations, except here it is more extreme. If the top of the racket is rotated to the left, it is a backhand grip, as used by Eric Boggan and Brian Masters, which weakens the forehand loop. If the racket is rotated to the right (almost becoming a regular shakehands grip), it is a forehand grip, as used by Dan and Rick Seemiller, which weakens the backhand.

The Seemiller grip has four major advantages. It is probably the best grip for blocking, especially on the backhand. There is very little weakness in the middle—in fact, the grip is at its best there. It gives a very natural wrist snap on forehand loops against backspin. And since only one side of the racket is used, and because the racket is easy to flip with this grip, it allows a player to have an off-surface on selected shots, usually antispin, though some use long pips. A player with this grip can flip to use that side as a variation, and then flip back to the regular surface, usually inverted. (All four of the U.S. team members mentioned above used antispin on the reverse side, inverted on the other.)

The disadvantages are that the wrist can make it difficult to play the corners (and so players with this grip often have trouble with players who play to the wide corners); it limits the backhand mostly to close-to-the-table blocking and hitting, with a very limited backhand loop; and it can be difficult to counterloop with this grip.

Because of the lack of a strong backhand loop, deep serves and pushes to the backhand can give this grip problems, unless the player has very fast footwork and can play the forehand from the backhand over and over. (Others, like Eric Boggan, learned to hit backspin serves with his antispin side, and then flipped back to inverted for the next shot.)

Some players with the Seemiller grip can be absolute walls on the backhand, and it makes no sense trying to overpower that side—but if you attack the forehand side first (and perhaps force them a step off the table) and then come back to the backhand, then the backhand wall might crumble. The grip is weaker from off the table, and like most shots, is less consistent when you have to move.

Most players with the Seemiller grip use the off surface to return serves, especially short ones. Some have the ability to quickly judge the depth of the incoming serve, and use anti against short serves, inverted to loop or otherwise attack long serves. If they use the anti to return most serves, serve deep, and you should get a relatively weak return or an erratic anti attack. Often a deep serve to the forehand is especially effective. If they try to flip the racket based on the depth of your serve, mix in short spinny serves and fast, long serves, and watch them struggle to flip their racket appropriately—it's not easy! It is very important not to telegraph your serves—players like this are very good at picking up small cues, so try to use the exact same motion for both short and long serves, at least until contact.

Table Tennis Tactics for Thinkers

CHAPTER TWELVE
Pushing

Pushing isn't really a style, but some players do push a lot. Even if you push just once, you want that push to be effective. Often players push just to keep the ball in play. Push with purpose and placement! *Do* something with it.

Japan's Ai Fukuhara carefully pushes a backhand.
Photo by Diego Schaaf

So, what can you do?

Purpose: There are three major things you can do with the push, and each has a purpose. You can push it very heavy or with variable spin, with the purpose to force a mistake or weak return against the heavy or variable backspin. You can push quick and fast to wide angles, with last-second changes of direction, with the purpose to either rush your opponent into a mistake or weak return which you can attack, or to take away his attack by keeping the ball away from his strong side, usually the forehand. Or you can push short (so that the second bounce, given the chance, would bounce on the table), with the purpose of making it difficult or impossible for your opponent to attack effectively.

Placement: Many players don't pay attention to placement, they just get the ball back, and give the opponent his best shot. A push that lands six to twelve inches inside the backhand corner is relatively easy to loop, forehand or backhand. A player with a strong forehand loop and decent footwork can use his forehand without going that far out of position to do so. A push that goes right over the corner, angling away, or even outside the backhand corner, is a different story—it takes very fast footwork to use the forehand against that ball, and if your opponent does, he's way out of position. Often he'll be rushed, and either make a mistake, a weak shot, or (often underestimated) his shot will be easy to read since a rushed player isn't very deceptive, and so his loop is easy to jab-block or counterloop away. (At the North American Team Championships in November, 2010, I coached Tong Tong Gong, a top cadet player then rated about 2200, to an upset over a 2350 player, with a major part of the strategy quick pushes to the very wide backhand. The opponent often stepped around and ripped them with his powerful forehand, but because he was rushed, his normally deceptive loop's placement was easy to read, and so Tong Tong was able to block them back to the wide forehand over and over for winners.)

The other option is pushing to the wide forehand. If your racket is aiming toward the opponent's backhand until the last second, and then you change and quick push to the forehand, your opponent's going to have a hard time reacting. If he does attack it, you can now just block to his backhand, taking his forehand out of the equation while making him move to play his often-weaker backhand.

When and How to Push

The push is probably the most over-used and under-used shot in table tennis. This may sound contradictory, but it really isn't. Most players either push too much or too little.

Many players push because they feel uncomfortable attacking the incoming ball. Others don't push because they feel they should attack every ball. Both of these are poor reasons to push or not push.

Instead of pushing because of what you can or cannot do, push more based on what your opponent can or cannot do. For example, if your opponent has an excellent loop against backspin, you should attack first whenever possible. Pushing simply arms your opponent.

On the other hand, if your opponent doesn't attack backspin well, why force your attack, and make mistakes? Instead, pick your shots.

Don't push because you have to; push because you choose to for tactical reasons. This means that you should learn to attack against any given ball, but then choose tactically whether to push or attack. And make sure to practice your own defense (or counter-attack) against your opponents' loops.

I do recommend favoring attacking whenever possible, especially in practice. Why? Because, although it won't always be the best tactic, you will improve faster as a player by doing so—think strategic development. The problem, of course, is that if you don't push much in practice matches, how can you perfect the shot so that you can use it in important matches? You need to find a balance.

You also may not want to overdo the use of pushing as a tactic in tournaments. There's a lot more pressure on you in a tournament than in a practice match, and it's a lot easier to push under pressure than to attack. Therefore, you may need to attack more often in tournaments than good tactics would suggest, so that you can strategically *become* more comfortable attacking under pressure.

Usually, the player who tries to attack first in practice and tournaments becomes a stronger player than those who push more often, and don't develop as strong an attack. However, a player who favors attacking but learns to push effectively becomes best of all—but only if they learn to push for tactical reasons, not because they have to.

Table Tennis Tactics for Thinkers

Pushing: Five Out of Six Doesn't Cut It

When you push long, you must do six things. If you do four or five, your push *might* give intermediate players trouble, while advanced players will have little trouble. Most players do several of these things well, and never understand that if they did them all even reasonably well, even advanced players would have difficulty attacking their pushes. What are the six things that top players do when pushing deep to make their pushes effective?

1. Quick and fast
2. Heavy or varied
3. Low
4. Deep
5. Angled
6. Disguised placement

If you do most of these pretty well, you'll give intermediate players trouble. If you do all of them pretty well, you'll give advanced players trouble.

A few notes on this. Angled placement doesn't mean you don't ever push quick to the middle—some players have trouble with that as they have to decide whether to use forehand or backhand, plus they have to go out of position some to do so—but most pushes should be angled to the corners or even outside them. This makes it harder for your opponent to attack (especially if they want to attack with their forehand and you push to their wide backhand), and down-the-line attacks are riskier, so attacks are often predictably crosscourt. Disguised placement means not telegraphing where you are pushing, i.e. able to push to the wide forehand or backhand at the last second, including sometimes faking one direction and going the other way.

The first time I really thought about this as a set of six attributes that went together was while playing a practice match with 13-year-old future USA team member Han Xiao. I liked to serve short backspin and loop with my forehand, but I was struggling to loop his pushes. After losing the match (he was already rated about 2400, the highest-rated of his age in U.S. history at the time), I mentioned how I couldn't serve and loop with any power and consistency. He said that's because Coach Cheng Yinghua (former Chinese team member and four-time USA Men's Singles Champion, and my fellow coach at the Maryland Table Tennis Center) had told him that if he did all of these things with his push, my loop would fall apart. It did. I could handle any five of these things, but not all six.

Larry Hodges

Sidespin Push

Another way to mess up an opponent by pushing is with sidespin, especially with the backhand. If you're right-handed, normally start with your racket a little to the right of the contact point, and brush the ball with a right-to-left motion. The ball will curve to your right, into the opponent's backhand. Five things may now happen.

1. Your opponent will misjudge how far the ball will break into his backhand, and will either get jammed if he uses his forehand or get caught reaching if he uses his backhand.
2. Your opponent may try looping the sidespin push, but thinking it has more backspin instead of sidespin, he will lift too much and loop off the end.
3. Your opponent may push it back, but thinking it has more backspin instead of sidespin, the ball will pop up and off the side.
4. Your opponent will look at you with a strange and quizzical look.
5. You'll laugh your head off as you add the point to your score.

Chinese and USA star Gao Jun is known for her sidespin and other tricky pushes. Penholders tend to push with sidespin more often, but shakehanders can and should do so as well.
Photo by Diego Schaaf

You can also do the reverse, and sidespin push the other way, with the racket moving left to right. If you do this to the forehand side, it'll curve away from your opponent, which may give him trouble. You can also do these sidespin pushes with the forehand, though that's trickier to learn with the shakehands grip. Penholders have a looser wrist when pushing, and may find forehand sidespin pushing easier.

Varying the Spin

A nice, heavy push is usually more effective than one with less backspin. But if you mostly push heavy, then throwing a push with less spin will often mess up your opponent.

The best way to vary the spin is with the timing of your wrist movement. When you push heavy, you use lots of wrist to snap the racket into the ball. If you instead contact the ball before you snap the wrist—and

Table Tennis Tactics for Thinkers

then snap the wrist after contact to fool the opponent—it'll look like a heavy push when in fact it'll have little spin. It'll be a "heavy no-spin push."

You can just pat the ball back without grazing the ball. While this can be effective, at the advanced levels it is usually too obvious. You can also vary the spin by contacting the ball nearer the handle, since that part of the racket is moving more slowly than the racket tip, but that can be tricky to control.

Pushing Short

Especially at the higher levels, a long push is usually attacked with a loop. While there are ways to mess opponents up with a long push, the simplest way to use a push to stop a looper from looping is by pushing short.

It's almost impossible to push short against a deep backspin serve or push, but you should normally attack those deep balls. It's against a short backspin serve or push that you should learn to push back short. Take the ball right off the bounce with a light touch, and push it like a normal push but with a soft touch, keeping the ball very low. Many players make the mistake of just patting the ball back with little backspin, but to be effective and to control the height better, you need to put backspin on the ball with a light grazing motion. (The backspin makes the ball travel more in a line, which makes it easier to keep low, plus if you graze the ball, it comes off your paddle softer, making it easier to push short.) Keep the ball low; slightly high short pushes are easy to smash or flip kill and also tend to go long.

It's easier to push short either by going to the nearest part of the net (so your shot is perpendicular to the net), since your target is closer, or by going crosscourt, where you have more table. As you develop feel, experiment with last-second changes of direction. Learn to drop the ball short to the left, right, or middle. If you develop a good feel for pushing short and maneuvering around the net, you'll have a valuable weapon in messing up opponents.

Some top players are known for taking control of the point even when receiving. Often they do this by maneuvering around the net with short pushes against serves. Top U.S. players like Ilija Lupulesku, David Zhuang, and Dan Seemiller are especially good at this cat and mouse game, where they are usually the cat as they make last-second changes of direction and drop the ball short and low anywhere by the net. They won 15 U.S. National Men's Singles titles.

When to Learn the Short Push?

At the higher levels, pushing short is extremely important for stopping an opponent from looping. It is especially used when returning short backspin serves. However, until a player reaches a 2000 level or so in U.S. ratings (the equivalent of a "master"), it is usually a low-percentage shot, since it is so easy to make a mistake and pop the ball up or go into the net. But here's the problem: if you wait until you are 2000 level before developing the shot, you will be years behind your competition in developing your short push. So, if you have aspirations to reach a high level, start developing your short push now, even if it means losing a few practice matches. Think strategically.

I've seen players spend 5-10 years developing their looping game, and then spend just a few games trying to push short and then give up on it. This never made sense to me.

Should You Develop Your Forehand Push?

At the lower levels, pushing is often over-used; at the higher levels, spectators often underestimate its value. All top players have excellent pushes. However, advanced players—and even intermediate ones—rarely push against deep backspin to the forehand, unless they are choppers. (And modern choppers usually attack those.) It's simply better for them to forehand loop. (The same can be said on the backhand, if you have a good backhand loop.) So … should you develop your forehand push?

Timothy Wang, 2010 & 2012 U.S. Men's Singles Champion and 2012 Olympian, does a forehand push. Is it long or short? Photo by Diego Schaaf

The answer is yes—but not necessarily against long backspin to the forehand. You need to develop your forehand push mostly against short backspin to the forehand. Against this ball, you can flip, but pushing may be the better bet. You can push short, push quick and long, go for angles, heavy spin, sidespin push, etc.—all sorts of variations. And because you are closer to your opponent, he has less time to react. (At the same time, don't predictably push—learn to attack short balls with a flip.)

The problem is how do you practice your forehand push? If you push forehand to forehand with a partner, then unless both of you are practicing short pushes you'll be practicing pushing against long balls. (This is how you initially learn to push with the forehand.) To develop the

Table Tennis Tactics for Thinkers

forehand short push, make sure your partner is also working on short pushing, and push short, forehand to forehand, or forehand to backhand. (Of course, if you want to develop your short push, you should also practice pushing short with the backhand, so add backhand to backhand to your short push practice list.)

One thing missing here is that often you want to push long against the short push. To practice that, you should do drills where the drill starts with you pushing against a short backspin. For example, your partner serves short to your forehand; you push quick off the bounce to your partner's backhand; he pushes quick to your backhand; and you loop, either forehand or backhand. (Or, alternately, your partner loops off your forehand push, if it's "his" drill—and you still get practice pushing as well as perhaps blocking his loop.) Or you can start a drill by pushing short with your forehand. The goal is to do drills that mimic what happens in a real match.

Meanwhile, a nice drill is to push forehand to forehand (or backhand to backhand) where both players push short—but the first time a player pushes long (by mistake), you loop. This develops your short push, develops your loop, and best of all, develops your judgment on whether a ball is long or short. Another way to do this is if you think your partner's ball is going long, just let it go and see if you are correct. Or you can add flipping to the drill, where either player can flip if the short push pops up, as well as loop if it goes long.

A Trick to Beat a Tricky Pusher

Some players have very accurate pushes, and will push very wide to your backhand over and over—until they see you stepping around, or even hedging that way. That's when they push to your wide forehand, and catch you off guard. So here's a simple trick: Serve backspin to the pusher's backhand. Then take a step to your left with your left leg (for right-handers). As the pusher is about to push, step back into position. You'll be amazed at how many pushes you'll get right into your forehand, where you are now ready and waiting. The pusher saw your fake "step around," and changed directions—but you were one step ahead of him. I've used this trick for years.

Whenever I think of this tactic, I think of the Hokey Pokey: "You put your left foot out, you put your left foot in, opponent pushes to your forehand, and you loop a winner in. You do the Hokey Pokey as you celebrate the win, that's what it's all about!"

Larry Hodges

CHAPTER THIRTEEN
Loopers

Loopers dominate the game at all levels from intermediate to world-class. Modern inverted sponges allow them to loop so easily and with so much spin that other styles rarely compete at the higher levels. The few styles that occasionally survive at the higher levels that do not focus on looping are focused primarily on stopping the opponent's loop.

Serving tactics: Loopers should mostly use short or half-long serves. Be careful with the half-longs—if they go too long, the receiver may get an easy loop. However, if the serve only barely goes long, the loop is often weak (since the table is in the way), so be ready to pounce on that ball with a putaway counterloop.

The loop that won three World Men's Singles titles: China's Wang Liqin. Photo by Diego Schaaf

One of the favorite service combinations for loopers is backspin and no-spin. The backspin serves are often pushed long, so the server can serve and loop. The danger is that the receiver may push short, which stops the loop, plus they can be pushed aggressively to wide angles with heavy backspin (see chapter on Pushing). To combat this, the server should also serve "heavy no-spin" serves, where he makes it look like backspin but serves no-spin. If the receiver tries to push this short, it will often pop up, giving the server an easy putaway. If the receiver pushes it long (most will except at the higher levels), it will tend to pop up a little, with less backspin, and so is an easier loop than against a push against a backspin serve.

Short sidespin-topspin serves are effective if the receiver doesn't flip them aggressively. (If he does, make sure you are serving low and remember to vary your spin.) They are almost always returned long, so you can loop. However, you'll either need to be able to loop from both wings

Table Tennis Tactics for Thinkers

or have good footwork to get your forehand on the ball. Use the service tactics discussed in the chapter on Serving Tactics to try to cut off parts of the table by using sidespin and placement.

Don't be afraid to throw other serves at the opponent, even if they don't really match your game. For example, a deep serve will often get attacked, taking away your loop. On the other hand, if used only occasionally as a surprise serve, you might get some "free" points from it, as well as weak returns that you can loop. If your opponent is predictable and returns most "surprise" serves crosscourt—as most do—then you can anticipate that and be ready to loop even against an aggressive return.

Receive tactics: Loopers are at their best against long serves, which they can loop. A looper's main questions here are whether to loop forehand or backhand, placement, depth, and how fast and spinny. Of all these aspects, depth may be the most important. If you loop deep, you can get away with a relatively soft loop against most players.

Against short serves, since you want to loop, you probably don't want the opponent to loop first. So loopers should generally avoid pushing long too often, unless the opponent can't take advantage of it. Of course, this is easier said than done, since pushing long is the easiest way to return short backspin serves, but pushing long too much is also one of the primary reasons many intermediate players stay intermediate. However, a good, aggressive push to the server's weaker side often will be pushed or attacked weakly, giving the looper a ball to loop.

Loopers need to be able to push short against short serves, along with flipping. By pushing short, the server is faced with a ball he can't loop, and may not be as ready for. There's a good chance he'll push it long, giving the looper a chance to loop. At the least, a good short push stops the server's attack, and it becomes an even battle over who will make the first effective attack.

An aggressive flip, if well placed, will often set up the loop. By placing it to the server's weaker side, or catching him in the middle or going the wrong way, you can force a ball that can be easily looped.

Rallying tactics: Once in a rally, a looper wants to either loop a winner (if the shot is there), or keep looping, with the intent of forcing a ball that he can loop for a winner. Some loopers just loop steady over and over until the opponent misses, but strategically even these players should learn to pounce on any weak returns with a putaway loop.

Keep the ball deep on the table. This cuts down on the angles your opponent can use against you, it jams him, it forces the opponent to hit his shot from farther out (so often a weaker shot), and it gives you more time to respond to his shot. Starting at the intermediate level, when players begin to learn depth control, learn to loop deep on the table.

There are times you want to loop shorter on the table. Slow players sometimes can't respond quickly enough to a loop that lands short. If the opponent backs off the table (usually to counterloop, fish, or chop), a shorter loop may catch him off guard, with the ball dropping in front of him.

Place the ball to the three spots—wide corners and opponent's elbow. Why make things easy for the opponent?

Most players are weaker blocking on one side, often the forehand, and most loops should go toward that side or the middle (elbow). Try to get into rallies that let you loop over and over with your forehand (or backhand, if that side's stronger) into the opponent's weaker blocking side and middle. Sometimes this will draw the opponent to that side, allowing you to loop a winner to the open "strong" side.

Another favorite strategy of loopers is to loop over and over with the forehand from the backhand corner, usually into the opponent's deep backhand and middle. When an opening appears, loop kill to either wide angle or the middle.

Most players are weak from the middle due to indecision as to whether to use the forehand or backhand. But others are strong there, especially all-out forehand attackers (who use their forehand over and over, so there's no indecision), backhand-oriented shakehanders and penholders, and those with the Seemiller grip. (Technically, a backhand-oriented shakehander's middle is simply more toward the forehand side, but for some of these players there is often so much overlap between their backhand and forehand coverage that they have little trouble covering the middle, and often they just cover the forehand side with backhand blocks.) If an opponent is strong in the middle, then he's probably weaker on at least one of the wide corners or both. Find the weakness and go there.

If you loop to a corner, the opponent can block back at a wide angle. By going to the middle, you take away the extreme angles. It does give your opponent an angle down both sides, but if you keep your loop deep, he won't be able to get a good angle, and you are more likely to be able to keep looping with your strong side, usually the forehand. This is why it sometimes pays to play the middle even against a player who is strong there, since they can't angle block as well from there, and so you get a return you can attack more easily.

Another thing to take into account is variation. Most players will get into a rhythm against your loop if you always do it the same. Learn to loop at all speeds—fast, medium, and slow. A slow but deep loop is surprisingly hard to block back effectively, especially if you jam him to the backhand where the opponent's body is in the way. In fact, slow loops are usually either attacked hard (and sometimes erratically) or returned weakly and

Table Tennis Tactics for Thinkers

often off the end.

Your distance from the table when looping in a rally should mostly depend on your style, but also on the opponent's. Against an opponent who hits the ball quick or hard, you'll need more time, and so you should back up a little more. However, tactically it is usually best to loop from closer to the table, where your opponent has less time to respond. This makes it much easier to loop a well-placed winner. (Emphasis should be on "well-placed.") Often it's best to start out close to the table looping aggressively, but back up when forced to.

How much to focus on speed versus spin is also a personal choice, based on your style. One advantage of looping with speed—besides the obvious advantage of often being a winner—is that it will always go deep on the table. This puts tremendous pressure on the opponent, who never gets an easy ball. However, speed is hard to control, and only top players can loop with great speed and consistency over and over—and they do so by putting tremendous topspin on the ball, which allows them to control the ball at high speeds. Until you get the right ball to loop for a winner, most loopers should put at least half of their power into topspin.

Strategically, make sure you have developed your forehand loop so that you mostly rotate in a circle during the shot, as if rotating about a pole going through your head, with your weight always somewhere between your legs. This way you'll finish the shot in the same spot and balanced, ready to loop the next ball. If you don't do this, then continuous looping will be more difficult, and that's one less tactical tool you'll have.

Misdirection When Looping

Most blockers develop timing to react to your normal loop, and commit during your stroke to blocking either forehand or backhand. So set up to loop crosscourt from your forehand side, and make no attempt to hide this. Wait a split second longer than usual and watch as your opponent moves to cover the apparent crosscourt loop. Then rotate your shoulders back and go down the line to their open backhand. You can also do this with a forehand from the backhand side, faking down the line, and then going crosscourt to their backhand.

You can also do this the other way, faking down the line from the forehand side and then go crosscourt. Rotate your shoulders well back, making it look like you are going to the right, and at the last second, whip your shoulders about and go to the left. (Lefties, remember to reverse all this.) I've written about this type of misdirection in other chapters, but it's worth reviewing since so few players below the advanced levels do this. And it's so easy!!!

Backhand Loop?

Backhand loops by China's Chen Qi and Ma Long.
Photos by Diego Schaaf

There was a time when you could become a top player with a forehand loop but no backhand loop. Those days are pretty much gone. While there are exceptions, anyone without a backhand loop in these days of super-duper fast and spinny sponge is at a tremendous disadvantage. At the minimum, learn to backhand loop against pushes. That way your opponent can't simply serve short to your forehand and then quick-push to your backhand. You could do a regular drive against backspin, but it's not as effective or as consistent, and unless you hit it very hard (and so less consistently), many opponents will easily counter-attack against it, especially at the advanced levels. You should also learn to backhand loop against deep serves or you will likely have perpetual problems with them.

At the world-class level, the backhand hit is almost gone. Nearly everyone backhand loops over and over, often right off the bounce. If a player does hit, the other loops, the hitter turns into a blocker, and the looper dominates.

Looping a Push

When someone pushes long to you, and you are a looper, you want to loop. You should be in one of four tactical states. We're assuming you can loop both forehand and backhand, or (if no backhand loop) have very fast feet for #4. Which of the below do you use?

Table Tennis Tactics for Thinkers

1. **Loop forehand or backhand, depending on where the push goes.** This means if the ball is to the right of your playing elbow, you forehand loop; if on the backhand side, you backhand loop.
    - *Advantages*: You are ready to loop anything, and you don't have to go out of position.
    - *Disadvantages*: Your opponent chooses if you are going to loop forehand or backhand (and presumably will have you do your weaker shot), and you might have problems deciding which way to go on pushes to the middle, especially quick ones. It also leaves you in a neutral position, so that the opponent can keep going after your weaker side.
2. **Favor forehand, but ready to loop backhand if it's a quick push to the backhand.** This means you are ready to forehand loop most pushes, including ones to the middle and weak ones anywhere, but won't force it against a good push to the backhand, which you'll backhand loop. (Of course some might just push this ball.)
    - *Advantages*: You are ready to forehand loop—presumably your stronger side if you choose this strategy—against most pushes, both strong ones anywhere except to the wide backhand, and weak ones anywhere.
    - *Disadvantages*: Your opponent may take away your forehand loop by quick-pushing to your backhand over and over. You may have a lot of ground to cover if you want to use your forehand from all parts of the table against weak pushes. If you are looking to forehand loop and are forced to backhand loop against a quick push to the backhand, you may not be ready and so may backhand loop weakly or inconsistently.
3. **Favor backhand, but ready to loop forehand if the push goes to the forehand side.** This means you are literally setting up to backhand loop most pushes, including pushes to the middle or even slightly toward the forehand side, but are ready to rotate the shoulders to the forehand side to forehand loop if the push goes there. You are basically telling your opponent, "I'm going to backhand loop, but if you want to give me an easy forehand loop, then go ahead and make my day--push to my forehand."
    - *Advantages*: Allows you to really prepare for your backhand loop, often compensating for having less power on that side. Also allows you to have less ground to cover for forehand loops. Allows you to stay in position for most loops. If your backhand loop is stronger than your forehand loop, allows you to maximize the chances of backhand looping.
    - *Disadvantages*: You'll be doing a lot of backhand loops, often

weaker than the forehand loop. Can be caught off guard with a quick push to the forehand side if you are too quick to set up for a backhand loop. Can have trouble backhand looping pushes that go to the middle if you don't learn to step into position properly for this.

4. **All-out forehand looping.** You basically decide in advance that if it's humanly possible, you are going to forehand loop. (This is how I used to start every rally before my feet slowed down.) You can only do this if your footwork is fast and technically sound. Off the serve, good footwork technique and anticipation can make up for not having super fast feet, especially if you are willing to let the ball drop more and slow loop against pushes to wide corners that you are slow getting to. (Note that the logical alternative to this, all-out backhand looping from all over the table, is rarely done since there's less range on the backhand side. There are some players who do this, but they are few.)

> *Advantages*: You get to use your forehand loop a lot, presumably your stronger shot. Allows you to get into forehand position so you can do a series of forehand loops in a row. Takes the indecision out of the shot since you know what you are going to do.

> *Disadvantages*: You have a lot of ground to cover, and so can get caught out of position, both while trying to make the shot and for the next shot. May make weak or inconsistent shots if you aren't in position quickly enough. Can be exhausting. When you get older, you begin to wish you had strategically developed that backhand loop.

After Looping the Serve or a Push

When you loop pushes and most serves, you are close to the table. If the ball is blocked back quickly, you may need to take a step back to loop the next ball. If you are a truly great athlete and train regularly, you may be able to handle this ball without backing up, taking it at the top of the bounce or even on the rise, as the best players often do. However, it's more likely you'll need to step back to give yourself time for the next shot. It's better to take the ball a little later and make a strong, consistent loop, then to rush a shot closer to the table and mess up. That's playing right into the hands of an opposing blocker.

Once you've looped and your opponent is blocking, there's a little cat and mouse game going on—but who's the cat? He's the one in control, while the mouse is the one scurrying about, struggling to stay alive. The looper wants to attack over and over with strong, deceptive, well-placed loops, forcing the blocker to struggle to keep the ball in play. The blocker

Table Tennis Tactics for Thinkers

wants to play aggressively, with quick, deceptive, well-placed blocks that the looper struggles to respond to and run down. One is balanced and in control, the other is off-balance and struggling to stay in the point. As a looper, your goal is to be the balanced cat in control.

Other Strokes for Loopers

Because a looper often plays off the table, he needs to develop his off-table shots. When attacking, he's mostly looping. But if he's off the table and in trouble, what does he do? Most good loopers are also good at fishing and lobbing. These are mostly last-resort, defensive shots (especially lobbing), but some players have trouble with them, and they keep the looper in the point. And as long as the looper is in the point, he's a threat to find a ball to loop, perhaps off a poorly-placed or weakly-hit smash, and then he's right back in the point. (See the chapter on Fishers and Lobbers.)

Since a looper can't always attack first, he needs to develop ways to defend against the other player's attack. At the higher levels, they most often back up and counterloop (which isn't so defensive) or fish, or something in between. However, most players, including top players, need to block against the other player's loop. The key is to block *effectively*, looking to force either a miss or a weak loop that can be counterlooped.

If you are a looper and want to be a top player, learn to counterloop. It's a standard shot at the higher levels, and pretty much the main rallying shot at the world-class level. It allows a looper to loop even when the other guy is looping. A looper who can't counterloop often finds himself blocking way too much, and at a huge tactical disadvantage against a looper who can counterloop.

Dummy Loops

In this modern game of topspin, many players battle to see who can get more topspin on the ball, with more speed and more consistency. After all, isn't that what tends to win games?

Yet you might want to consider whether you want to join in this escalating topspin battle every single point. Why not throw a changeup at them--a "dummy loop"--and watch them mess up? Go for less spin, and mess up your opponent's consistency!

A dummy loop is a loop that looks like it has a lot of topspin, but is not very spinny. You execute the shot almost like any other loop, except you start with your wrist cocked up, so there's no natural wrist snap, so little whipping action to add to the topspin. By using a full motion, it looks like you've done a normal loop, yet the ball comes out relatively dead, causing havoc for your opponent.

Some players dummy loop by contacting the ball closer to the handle, while contacting the ball near the tip for maximum spin. It's a little trickier this way, but can be even harder for an opponent to see the difference. How many opponents can tell whether your loop contact was near the tip or handle?

A key point of all dummy loops—do the shot with a full swing, with full enthusiasm, as if you were really going for your spinniest loop. If you try to hold back on spin by holding back on the stroke itself, the opponent will see that easily.

It's fun watching an opponent block into the net, and stare at his paddle in disbelief!

Playing Loopers

Loopers come in many varieties. Some like to loop kill the first ball while others will loop ten in a row to win one point. Some run all over the court looping only with the forehand while others loop with both backhand and forehand. Some let the ball drop below table level before lifting it in a sweeping topspin (often slow but spinny) while others practically take the ball as it bounces on the table. And then there are those who combine looping with some other shot such as chopping or hitting. There are very few cut and dried rules for loopers.

A looper tries to loop as early in the rally as possible. Once he loops, he wants to keep looping until the rally is over or he gets an easy kill—which he may loop kill. Your job, when you play a looper, is to stop him from doing these things. You want to mess him up.

A looper generally has five basic weaknesses. Take advantage of all of them.

1. Because he is looking to loop, he is often not ready if you attack first.
2. He will have difficulty looping a short ball that doesn't bounce past the end line after the first bounce. A serve or serve return that lands short will often give him trouble. If he's off the table, a dead block will also give him trouble, even if it wouldn't double bounce.
3. He must take a longer stroke than others, which slows him down and often forces him into mistakes or to move off the table.
4. Because he uses some of his power to put spin on the ball, his loops lose some speed. This especially makes it difficult to loop a winner off deep balls or when moving or even slightly off balance.
5. A loop that lands short is easy to attack (with practice), and a looper can't keep every ball deep.

The most obvious way to beat a looper is to not let him loop. If you

Table Tennis Tactics for Thinkers

attack first, you take away his loop or make him go for a more difficult loop, usually a counterloop (if you loop first), which isn't an easy shot below the elite levels. Use your serve and receive game to set up your attack and put the looper on the defensive.

If your opponent does have a potent counterloop, then vary your first attack to throw him off. Vary the spin, speed, depth, and placement.

If you serve short and push backspin serves back short, you also stop the looper from looping. He may try to flip the ball and loop the next one, but if you keep the ball low as well as short, his flip will often be either erratic or soft.

Serving short is especially important against a looper. It takes a lot of practice to learn to return a serve short, but anyone at even the advanced beginner's stage can learn to serve at least a short backspin.

If a looper does flip or if he serves topspin or sidespin, take advantage of weakness number three, his longer stroke. Attack the topspin serve aggressively and attack his flip quickly and he will be forced to back off the table to have time to loop, taking away much of its effectiveness. And if he's away from the table, he will have difficulty looping winners—not only do you have more time to respond to his shot, but weakness number four comes in. He sacrifices speed for spin. You can simply outlast him if he can't get the ball past you, as long as you can handle his topspin. Keep the ball deep when you rally, and loopers will have trouble looping winners.

Of course, some loopers look like they just got out of a powerlifting meet and if they lose power to spin, it's not noticeable. Against these Herculean players you must be careful not to give an easy shot. Let them try to loop hundred mile per hour zingers against balls that you choose to give them. If they don't hit, you win! If they do, well, work on making stronger or more effective shots yourself so the opponent can't keep ripping loops. You might also use his own speed against him. If you block his powerful loop, it'll probably go back so fast he won't be able to react to it, especially if you place the block well.

Because a looper has a longer stroke, and because he has to range off the table, he is often vulnerable to changes of pace as well as direction. Block one hard, then one soft, move the ball around, and watch him flounder about.

A one-sided looper rushes all over the court trying to use his forehand. Don't make the mistake of going to his backhand over and over. A looper's strongest loop is often his forehand from his backhand corner. Instead, go to his wide forehand first, then come back to the backhand. He'll probably have to return the second shot with his weaker backhand. Attack it.

If the looper seems a little too slow on his feet, go wide to his backhand. He will either have to use his weaker backhand or rush to step around. If he does, a quick block to his wide forehand will often win the point or set you up to end it. Even if it doesn't, a quick return to the wide backhand will make him use his backhand while moving, not an easy shot.

A two-sided looper stands in the middle of the table and loops both backhands and forehands, though he might still step around his backhand to loop kill easy balls with his forehand. The key here is to find his weaker side and play to it, usually the backhand. (Or, of course, just don't let him loop!) Move him in and out—backhand loopers are especially vulnerable to that movement. A hard block followed by a soft one is usually more effective than two hard ones in a row since it breaks the looper's rhythm. Also, note that most two-sided loopers are relatively weak in the middle against a hard block. Unlike a forehand looper, he has to decide which side to loop with. Remember that his middle is roughly where his playing elbow is, and attack it every chance.

A consistent looper just keeps looping until you miss or give him an easy shot. He usually loops from both sides, but not always. You must move him around as much as possible, both side to side and in and out. Although you hope he will miss, don't expect him to. Usually you will have to earn the point either by using your serve and receive to set up your own attack before the looper can loop, or by counter-attacking a weak loop. Force him off the table with your own aggressive attack, whether it be blocking, hitting, or your own looping. If you see a winner, go for it. If not, keep moving him, both in and out and side to side, attacking whenever you can. But beware his topspin. If you make too many mistakes against it, you will lose. This is true against all loopers.

By taking advantage of these weaknesses, you can force mistakes or loops that land short. A loop that lands short is very easy to attack if you don't hesitate. Look for these short balls and attack them with whatever you do best—counterloop, smash, or aggressive blocks.

Table Tennis Tactics for Thinkers

CHAPTER FOURTEEN
Hitters, Blockers, and Counter-Drivers

These are the "flat" styles, players who focus on speed and quickness rather than spin. (They don't really hit the ball flat most of the time, just with far less topspin than a looper.) While looping tends to dominate at the higher levels—though nearly all elite players still

David Zhuang smashes a winner.
Photo by John Oros

use these shots, especially blocking—many loopers struggle against flatter shots since they are so used to playing other loopers. Below the elite level, hitters, blockers, and counter-drivers are just as common as loopers. It's not an absolute thing—loopers also block and hit, blockers and hitters also loop, etc. Regardless of your style of play, you are likely going to need to at least learn to block against opponent's loops (unless you are a chopper), and so should learn to block effectively.

A blocker hits his flat shot quicker off the bounce and not as hard as a hitter, who generally hits the ball at the top of the bounce and focuses on speed. A counter-driver is in between—he focuses on counter-hitting the opponent's attacks, usually at the top of the bounce (but quicker off the bounce against a loop), focusing on strong, steady shots, but also blocking and smashing when needed. Often the three styles are almost indistinguishable, and most who play one of these styles do the other two as well (to some degree), but there are major differences. I'm going to focus on hitters and blockers, with a shorter section on counter-drivers, since they are roughly in between these two styles.

<u>Hitters</u>

Hitters once dominated the world scene, but no longer, not in the age of super inverted sponges. There are few real hitting styles among world-class players, which is dominated by loopers. The problem for hitters is that the basic rallying shot of a looper, a loop, is very hard to hit, and so a hitter playing a looper is quickly turned into a blocker. Even when a hitter does hit, his margin for error is much lower than a looper's, whose heavy topspin keeps the ball on the table.

Below the world-class level, there are plenty of hitters, and unless you are hoping to be world champion or make a living as a player (or somewhere in between), there's nothing wrong with the hitting style.

It's an advantage to hit with short pips instead of inverted. Spin doesn't take on it as well, and so it's easier to hit against spin. However, this makes looping difficult, and when a pips-out player does loop (primarily only against backspin), it's not as spinny. Even for hitters, it's an advantage to be able to loop against backspin, so hitters have to decide whether to go "all in" and use pips-out, or use inverted on at least one side to allow a stronger loop. Pips-out also limits the spin on your serves and pushes.

While essentially all hitters are also blockers, not all blockers are hitters. This is a strategic weakness on the part of some blockers. More on this in the section on blocking.

Hitters rely on speed and (when blocking) quick, aggressive angles to win the point. If you play this way, you want to stay right at the table and control play by being faster and quicker than your opponent. Never give him an easy shot; always keep him rushing to the ball, and end the point quickly with your smash.

In general, there are three types of hitters. There are your pure forehand hitters, often pips-out penholders with quick-blocking backhands. Then there are two-sided hitters, hitting hard from both sides. Lastly, there are hitters who loop to set up their smash. Of course, most hitters combine some attributes from all three of these types.

Serving tactics: Most hitters use more variety on their serves than loopers. Their goal is to get a ball they can smash, or at least hit hard. Unlike a looper, who is quite happy with low, passive returns he can loop, a hitter wants the ball up higher, and so has to find ways to trick his opponent, even if this means serving long more often and risking the receiver looping.

Hitters serve more topspin and sidespin-topspin than loopers, since they are often trying to get a higher return, not a low push. They should do this both short and long, while mixing in fast, deep serves. They should constantly change the placement, depth, spin, and speed of their serves.

While a low, heavy, deep push can give the hitter trouble, a good hitter can easily hit or smash a push if it isn't low, heavy, and deep. (Many players are especially surprised at how easy it is to smash against a low, heavy push that doesn't go deep.) So hitters should keep mixing up their serves, never allowing an opponent to get into a rhythm where they can push effectively.

One of the most effective serving strategies for a hitter is to serve a long, breaking forehand pendulum sidespin serve from the backhand

Table Tennis Tactics for Thinkers

corner to the opponent's wide backhand. Even if the opponent backhand loops the ball—many won't—he'll be reaching for the ball, and will often make a weak loop. Many players will return this with a regular backhand. Since this type of serve is very difficult to return down the line, the hitter can cheat toward his backhand side and look to smash a forehand off the return, or he can simply backhand smash. By constantly varying the spin on this serve—from pure sidespin to sidespin-topspin (or corkscrewspin), as well as some fast, dead balls (more often to the middle, but also sometimes to the wide backhand) or breaking serves that go the other way as a variation—the receiver will have difficulty adjusting. Many hitters thrive on this long serve and smash tactic, though it won't work as often at higher levels, where opponents are more likely to loop it effectively, either backhand or forehand.

Many hitters use a loop to set up their smash. In this case, they should use the same tactics a looper would use to set up their loop, which in turn sets up their smash. See the section on serving tactics for loopers in the chapter on Loopers.

Receive tactics: Speed and quickness are a hitter's strengths, and since he rarely can smash the serve, he should use quickness when receiving. Against short serves, a hitter should use all the weapons—short and long pushes, and flips. In fact, most hitters welcome short serves, since it allows them to rush the opponent with quick, angled receives. Attack the corners and the server's elbow, and look to follow any effective receive with a smash or hit.

Against long serves, a hitter has to hit or loop. Looping effectively isn't always easy for a hitter, especially if he has pips, but it's usually the best option against deep backspin serves. Against other deep serves, he should probably hit, although if he has a decent loop, he may use that to return serves whenever possible to set up his smash.

Rallying tactics: Once into the rally, a hitter should be hitting as aggressively as possible while still keeping the ball on the table. (Though he should throw in occasional softer shots, such as a dead or sidespin block to mix up the pace and mess up the opponent.) He could hit from both sides, or perhaps play a blocking backhand while smashing the forehand, or (if he has good footwork) try to cover as much of the table as possible with the forehand, smashing every chance. Some hitters favor the backhand, hitting all-out from that side, even from the forehand side. (Viktor Barna won Men's Singles at the World's five times that way, though that was in the 1930s during the hardbat days. That style doesn't work very well at the higher levels in the modern game.)

When a hitter does hit with anything less than a smash, whether against backspin or topspin, he should generally do so right off the bounce, rushing the opponent. His weapons are speed, quickness, and deceptive placement.

Since hitters play fast and quick, opponents are especially vulnerable to shots to their elbow, since they have to react to the shot, choose whether to play forehand or backhand, and then move to make the shot. (This works both ways—hitters are close to the table, and so have little time to react, and so often are weak in the middle.)

The goal of every shot by a hitter should be to either end the point, or to force a weaker ball that he can smash to end the point. Even a counter-hitting style, a player who counter-hits from both wings but doesn't force the smash, should be looking to smash as often as possible.

A hitter's game is all about percentages. Assuming your opponent can't return your smash, if you smash every point, all you have to do is make 51% of your smashes and you win. Since some smashes will come back, and since you won't be smashing every shot or every point, you will need to up that percentage quite a bit. Get an instinct for what shots you can smash, and don't be afraid to take the shot when it's there—or to *not* take the shot if it's not, instead using another effective shot that may set you up for the next ball.

It's difficult being a hitter against a high-level looper. So don't go into the match strategically lacking. Arm yourself with a full arsenal of shots. Learn to loop, at least against backspin, focus on receives that take away the looper's loop (such as pushing short, or quick and aggressive), and develop your blocking game so you can block your opponent's loop while looking for chances to hit or smash.

There are two common tactical mistakes hitters tend to make. Some are too tentative and don't let themselves go for the shot. A hitter must be somewhat reckless, or he will find himself constantly trying to decide whether to smash. He doesn't have time to do that! A hitter must accept the fact that he will sometimes go for a seemingly dumb shot so as to make sure he doesn't let an opportunity to smash go by. (The better the hitter gets, the less often this happens.) He cannot be a hesitant hitter; he must be decisive. He will find to his surprise that many of these "dumb" shots will actually go in. As he improves, he will go for fewer and fewer dumb shots.

The other common mistake is just the opposite—trying to hit too much. A hitter should hit right from the start of the rally, but he does have to use some judgment. Rather than hit the first ball for a winner every time, why not loop or hit an aggressive drive first and smash the next ball, which might be easier?

A hitter should find out which side an opponent is weaker on (which to a hitter often means softer) and go to that side over and over,

Table Tennis Tactics for Thinkers

always looking for a ball to put away. He should go to the strong side only when he can make a strong shot or when the opponent is out of position. Because a hitter strives to be faster than his opponent, he can get away with going to the weaker side over and over, since the opponent won't have time to respond and perhaps move to use his stronger side.

If a hitter mostly likes to hit with one side, he has to be especially reckless. The longer the rally goes on, the more shots he will have to make with his weaker side and the more likely he will make a mistake. Since he's mostly hitting from one side, there's less indecision; he *knows* he's looking to hit his forehand (or backhand). When he sees the shot, there should be no hesitation; take the shot.

A two-sided hitter can be more picky and play longer rallies. He is a threat to hit from both sides, and although he should end the point as quickly as possible, he is under less pressure to do so. He can hit strong drives (instead of smashing) knowing that there is no worry about a return to his weaker side, since he doesn't have one.

A hitter with a good loop has a tremendous advantage if he is able to get both shots going. He should loop the ball as deep and spinny as he can, but not too fast. A slower, spinnier loop will set up the smash more while a faster one usually is blocked back faster, giving the hitter little time to get into position to smash.

Playing Hitters

A hitter may be the most mentally demanding style to play against. No matter what you do, it seems they are able to find balls to hit or smash. Yet keep in mind that a hitter's smashes often miss. Don't be intimidated—it's the quickest way to get passive and lose, and hitters thrive on it. A hitter simply cannot win if he doesn't get enough good balls to hit, so he wants you to be passive so he can pick a shot to smash. It's up to you to deprive him of that.

The key to beating a hitter is versatility. A hitter may only be able to beat you one way; you can beat him a dozen ways. Find the way that works. You might force him to go backhand to backhand with you, or loop everything, or keep everything deep, or just mix up the spins (topspins, backspins, sidespins) and watch him miss. You can keep changing until you find something that works; he often can't. Take advantage of it. Above all, use your loop against him, if you have one. Turn the hitter into either a blocker or a wild hitter who keeps missing against your loops.

Never let a hitter get into a groove. If he does, the match is probably over. After all, he's mastered the fastest shot in the game and if you can't stop him from using it, you are going to lose. Keep him out of the groove by constantly changing your shots, making him hit different types of balls over and over.

A smash has a much smaller margin for error than just about any other shot. Keep that in mind at all times. Right after a hitter hits five winners in a row he might miss five in a row, so never give up.

A hitter likes to start off the point with a quick serve and smash. Often he will serve fast and deep, trying to catch you off guard and giving him an easy winner. Be ready for it. Attack the serve (focus on placement—wide corners or middle) and the hitter will get very uncomfortable. Often he will still smash, but as long as he must go for risky smashes you are in control. Watch to see if he steps around his backhand corner too much to use his forehand. If so, return his fast serve wide to his forehand with a quick drive or block. Disguise the shot, aiming to his backhand before changing directions at the last second.

Because he doesn't usually have a strong loop, a hitter is often vulnerable against long serves. Test him out and find which ones work best. Especially effective are fast, dead serves to the middle and wide backhand, and breaking serves to the backhand. Short side-top serves aren't usually too effective as the hitter just hits them, but short backspin and no-spin serves—keep them low against a hitter!—are highly effective in setting up your own attack, especially by looping, which you use to turn the hitter into a blocker.

You can throw a hitter off by moving him around. Just like a looper, he is often strongest hitting forehands out of his backhand corner. In general, you should either try to pin him on his backhand or you should go side to side, making him hit as many moving backhands and forehands as possible. Because he stands closer to the table, a hitter often cannot react to a quick block to the wide forehand after stepping around the backhand to hit a forehand. Of course, the problem here is that his forehand shot from the backhand corner may already have been a winner, or at least strong enough to keep you from making a strong return. (And if he does get to that wide forehand ball—watch out!)

Since a hitter wants to hit everything, if you attack first (especially with loops), they are forced to either go for low percentage hitting, or to abandon their hitting game and become a blocker. The best defense is often a good offense. Deep, spinny loops to the backhand are especially effective against hitters. Many hitters are very good at smashing soft loops with their forehand, but not so much on the backhand side. It's trickier for them to hit them with their backhands, with the smaller hitting zone because the body is in the way. Many hitters will often step around their backhands to smash them with their forehands. To stop this, mix in faster loops to their forehand side, forcing them to watch for those, thereby slowing them down from stepping around.

Table Tennis Tactics for Thinkers

An **all-out forehand hitter** may have few shots to set up his smash. But he makes up for it in the simplicity of his game. He has often grooved his one winning shot so much that no one thing you do compares to it. You should start many rallies by going to his forehand side, often serving or pushing there short and low, and then come back to his backhand. Off his serve look to go quick to his forehand side since he's often already moving to hit his forehand from the backhand side. Keep moving him side to side with wide angles, and make sure to hide your direction or he'll anticipate your shot and have an easy forehand. You should rarely go to the middle, which just gives them an easy forehand.

Deep, heavy pushes to the corners can give him trouble. If you push to his backhand and he attacks with his forehand, he has little time to cover the wide forehand, and if he does move there quickly, he's probably moved too quickly and left his backhand side open. If he does get to the forehand shot, you go right back to his backhand. If you push to his wide forehand, after he attacks with his forehand, you go right back to his backhand. In theory, it's easy to play an all-out forehand hitter. (In practice, it's not so easy.)

I was an all-out forehand hitter when I first started playing way back in 1976 before I learned to loop effectively a few years later. It's still how I play in hardbat events, where I've won a lot of titles. It's fun and simple, since I know I'm always looking to hit the forehand. While the tactics are often simple, you have to choose them carefully, and there's a lot more subtlety than people realize as you vary the quickness, speed, and placement of your hitting. I still play this way against some opponents, but I'm pretty much all-around now with my normal inverted sponge game—looping, hitting, blocking, fishing & lobbing, even chopping sometimes. I sometimes miss the simple days of all-out forehand hitting.

A **two-sided hitter** can hit from both sides (though they usually hit harder on the forehand side), so moving him around pays off less. However, like a two-sided looper, he is often weak in the middle where he must decide which side to hit with. But only go there aggressively. A weak shot to the middle gives a hitter an easy forehand smash.

Because they play so fast, a hitter is also often awkward against aggressive down-the-line shots. But beware the wide angle return you may get back, and be ready to cover it.

Find a two-sided hitter's weak side and go there (and to the middle) until you find an opening to the other side. Combat his speed with your own drives, and try to be more consistent than him. Try to play into his weaker hitting side—but he can do the same to you. Remember the tactic of going to the strong side first, and then coming back to the weak side, forcing the hitter to move and hit with his weak side.

Since a two-sided hitter is trying to hit from both sides, they often are erratic since they don't have time to set up their shots on both sides. They often hit hard, but usually cannot all-out smash until an easy ball comes, since they are trying to do so much on both sides. Also, most two-sided hitters are slower on their feet, since they don't need to step around as much. Try to take advantage of this whenever they move out of position. Two-sided hitters are also often weak against backspin since they usually specialize in standing in the middle of the table and hitting topspin.

A **looper/hitter** uses the loop to set up his smash. Usually he will loop backspin and smash topspin. Because he only needs to smash against one type of spin, his smash is often more consistent. And unlike an all-out hitter, he has a loop to set up his smash.

The basic weakness of a hitter/looper is that he is trying to do too many aggressive shots. It is very hard to learn to both hit and loop well, and even harder to get both in a groove at the same time. Looping is basically a lifting shot while hitting is a forward shot, and trying to perfect both modes at the same time can create havoc with their timing. This leads to many missed shots. Only the fact that he only smashes one type of ball (topspin) saves him.

Push heavy to the corners to force the hitter to move and lift the ball. Then quick-block their loops, forcing them to make a quick adjustment from lifting to hitting. Many have great difficulty with this if you rush them and keep the ball deep.

Many looper/hitters loop softly and then smash. Attack the soft loop. If you just block it passively, you are playing right into his game. From the hitter's point of view, a slow loop has more spin than the fast loop and forces more setups while also giving him more time to get into position for the smash. Make him loop more aggressively by attacking the slow loop. He will have less time to respond to the next shot, he will make more mistakes on the loop, and he will have to concentrate more on the loop and less on the smash, leading to more missed smashes. There is nothing a hitter/looper hates more than someone who can attack his loop.

Pips-out penholders are a special type of hitter. Usually they have strong forehand smashes, but mostly block on the backhand, and often play as all-out forehand hitters. (This changes if they have a reverse penhold backhand or a Korean-style backhand, which give stronger backhands but usually weaker blocks and a weaker middle.) Try to pin them down on the backhand side, but beware their blocks, which often come back dead, or even with backspin or sidespin. Rather than go after the backhand over and over, look for chances to challenge their forehand and middle with strong

Table Tennis Tactics for Thinkers

attacks (especially loops), while challenging the backhand with deep, spinny loops, which penholders often have trouble blocking on the backhand. Often a pips-out penholder has a very dead backhand block, or they may chop- or sidespin block. If you have trouble with these shots, don't avoid them; play into them until you are comfortable. Keep the ball deep to jam them, take away the angles, and to give yourself more time to react. Don't take them on in a quickness battle (unless you are a blocker); beat them with stronger rallying shots. Because of the pips, they can't loop strongly, so challenge them with various deep serves. The very depth of your serves will give you time to set up your attack.

**Pips-out penholder Gao Jun smashes a winner.
Photo by Diego Schaaf**

Blockers

The goal of a blocker is to rush the opponent into making mistakes. He does this by blocking the ball quick off the bounce at wide angles and at the opponent's elbow. He can do so focusing on steadiness, aggressiveness, or constant changing of pace.

A blocker may block nearly every ball quickly to the opponent's weaker side, exploiting it to the fullest, or block side to side, making the opponent move about and hit on the run, or he may go after the opponent's middle over and over. A blocker has to be ready to smash when a weak ball comes or all an opponent has to do is keep the ball in play. He has to anticipate weak returns so as to have time to smash, or even designate one side (usually the forehand) as the side to smash whenever possible. Many players combine a backhand blocking/forehand smashing (or looping) game. A quick backhand block will often set up the forehand.

Serving tactics: Many blockers fail to take advantage of their serve. While a serve and block strategy might work, a little strategic development (and lots of practice) might allow them to serve and attack. From the blocker's point of view, this may not seem the best thing to do tactically—after all, isn't blocking what the blocker does best? But imagine the opponent who has to withstand your serve and attack, and who loses a number of points in doing so, and finally gets the initiative—only to find you perfectly comfortable blocking against their attack. The key is that when serving, you have a tactical advantage in taking the attack, and if you do not do so, you are giving up some of that advantage. You don't need to make your attack your strength, but learn to jump on any weak returns of your serve. If you don't get a weak return, do a steady opening attack, or just push, and then start blocking aggressively.

Most blockers should serve more sidespin-topspin serves, both long and short, since this gets them right into a fast topspin rally where they can block all over the court. However, as noted above, a blocker should try to develop a serve and attack if possible (and so serve more backspin and perhaps no-spin), and force the opponent to fight for the attack—only for him to find that he then has to go through your blocking game.

Some blockers prefer to serve backspin, and then push at wide angles until the opponent moves wide to attack, leaving part of court open. This especially happens if a forehand looper loops from his backhand side. This allows the blocker to block quickly and aggressively to the open court, often for an outright winner. (If the looper moves quickly to cover that wide forehand, then the blocker goes to the now-open backhand side.) Or the blocker can push and block to the middle against a two-winged looper, forcing the looper to decide which side to loop with, and to go out of position to do so. Ideally, the blocker can serve backspin and look for a ball to attack; if he doesn't find one, he can then push and let the opponent attack.

By serving fast topspin, the blocker forces the opponent off the table and gets right into a fast blocking rally. By serving short topspin or sidespin, the blocker brings the opponent in, making him vulnerable to a fast, quick block. Blockers should use both tactics.

Receive tactics: Unlike many players whose games revolve around attacking, a blocker can get away more often with pushing long. For many blockers, this is all they do against backspin serves, and even some sidespin or topspin serves, which they chop down on with a chop-block to keep it low. By keeping the ball to a wide angle with a strong push, the opponent has a relatively difficult attack. (See the chapter on Pushing Tactics for ways to push more effectively.)

Against topspin or sidespin serves, a blocker should do what he does best—quick block, either to a corner or to the opponent's elbow.

Table Tennis Tactics for Thinkers

Rallying tactics:

There are generally three types of blockers: aggressive blockers, steady blockers, and change-of-pace blockers. A blocker should learn all three, but probably favor one of them.

Aggressive blockers should attack the wide corners and opponent's elbow with nearly every shot. Their

Ma Long's backhand block.
Photo by Diego Schaaf

goal is to put so much pressure on the opponent that he finally misses or makes a weak return the blocker can put away. Many blockers use their backhand blocking to set up their forehand smash or loop-kill. (A good blocker who can smash effectively from both sides can be rather scary, but there aren't too many of them.)

Steady blockers are just that. Since their blocks are not as aggressive, blocking to the opponent's elbow isn't as effective, so they should focus mostly on wide angles. However, sometimes this can backfire as an angled block can be attacked right back at a wide angle. So a steady blocker might sometimes want to go to the middle to cut off the angled return. This pulls the opponent out of position so he has to move more on the next shot, causing more mistakes. In general, a steady blocker wants to focus on the opponent's weaker side, and go there over and over. Sometimes this means going to the strong side first, and the rest of the rally going after the weak side.

A change-of-pace blocker wants to throw off the opponent's rhythm by changing the pace and depth of his blocks by mixing in aggressive and dead blocks. Often a faster block is easier to attack then one that dies more over the table, putting the table partly in the way and throwing off the opponent's timing. However, too many dead blocks lose their effectiveness, so a change-of-pace blocker needs to complement his dead blocks with aggressive ones. (The exception might be a long pips blocker, but that'll be covered in the chapter on Non-Inverted Surfaces.)

Some blockers change the pace with sidespin blocks, especially pips-out players and penholders with conventional backhands. It not only changes the pace, but the sidespin gives the opponent difficulty. It's important for blockers to learn this technique; otherwise, they are missing an important tool in their tactical toolbox. Most often you sidespin block by moving the racket from right to left at contact, most often into the opponent's wide backhand where it breaks away from him. Some sidespin block the other way by moving the racket from left to right at contact, often blocking this one into the wide forehand, where it breaks away from the opponent.

A blocker who can't put the ball away effectively has a huge handicap. Imagine blocking someone all over the court, forcing the weak ball, and not being able to hit a winner! Most blockers develop at least an efficient smash for when they do get such a weak ball, but many do not develop a good attack otherwise (a strategic mistake), relying instead on quick, steady blocking to win the point, which limits their tactical options. A hitter/blocker, however, would end the point quickly as soon as he saw a ball to smash. There are also many looper-blockers, especially ones who loop on the forehand but mostly block on the backhand, which can be a pretty successful way to play, such as three-time World Men's Singles Champion Guo Yuehua (1981, 83, 85), considered by many the greatest player ever, though his one-winged penhold looping style might not match up well these days against modern two-winged loopers.

Some blockers with good attacks are a master of the "I'll give you one chance to attack" strategy. This means they are willing to push long to a corner one time, challenging the opponent to go out of position to attack it. The opponent doesn't get to pick his shot; the blocker only gives him one chance. If the opponent doesn't attack, and instead pushes it back, the blocker takes the attack.

Conventional attacking players, especially loopers, often do not develop their blocking game even though they use it in matches. This is a handicap; if you are going to block in a game, you need to develop the shot to the fullest, including all of the methods outlined here.

One common weakness of blockers, including other styles who also block, is the lack of a **forehand down-the-line block**. When players loop to the forehand, it is almost invariably blocked crosscourt, even at the higher levels. This can be effective since you do have a wide angle to the forehand, and about 15.5 more inches going crosscourt than down the line. But going crosscourt is so common that players are used to this—but they are often absolutely frozen by an unexpected down-the-line block. The down-the-line forehand block is not a hard shot to do, it's just one that few bother learning. This is partly because they warm up crosscourt so much, and because, deep down, they are trying to play it safe, and go where there's more room and with the more natural block. Instead, learn to tilt the racket tip back so as to angle your forehand block down the line, and watch the awkward returns of your opponent!

Table Tennis Tactics for Thinkers

Chop and Sidespin Blocks

These are some of the more "tactical" shots, and so deserv a section of their own.

What is a chop or sidespin block? It is a block with backspin or sidespin. Since long pips and (usually) hardbat automatically returns topspin as backspin, chop-blocks are the norm for those surfaces. But with inverted (as well short pips to a lesser degree), a topspin ball is normally catapulted back with some topspin.

But what if the inverted or pips-out blocker were to chop down on the ball at contact, thereby returning the incoming topspin as backspin? That is a chop-block, and it can cause havoc with an opponent's timing.

Many players thrive in fast topspin rallies, using an opponent's fast topspin balls to loop, counter-hit, or block back everything aggressively. A sudden chop-block against a topspin ball can completely throw off their timing. Instead of a fast ball jumping out into their hitting zone, the ball dies in front of them, and there's no topspin for them to counter against. The shot is especially effective against loopers who back up from the table a lot, since they are often uncomfortable looping closer to the table, and this brings them out of their comfort zone.

To do a chop-block, simply chop down lightly as you block the incoming topspin (usually against a loop), holding the racket loosely and slightly more closed than usual. Your shot should go out low and soft, almost like a push. Place the ball to the corners to force the opponent to use his weaker (or more awkward against a soft ball) stroke, or to the middle to cut off angles. The shot is usually done on the backhand side, but can be done on the forehand as well. (One reason most chop-blocks are done on the backhand is it is assumed you can do more effective counter-attacks on the forehand, but that's not always true.)

A variation is the sidespin block, where the racket moves sideways (or sideways and down) to create a sidespin or sidespin-backspin block. This is also usually done on the backhand, with the racket usually moving right to left (for a righty), but can be done in both directions and on the forehand as well.

One word of caution—you should rarely chop-block twice in a row. The first one throws off an opponent's timing and catches him out of position (too far off table). The second one doesn't change the timing and the previous one already brought him in. So normally follow up your chop-blocks with aggressive blocks or counter-attacks. Players with long pips and hardbat often chop-block over and over, but their surfaces are deader than inverted, and so they can really deaden the ball and keep it short. With inverted, it's tougher to do this over and over, and so it's usually best to use it as a variation, not the normal block.

Playing Blockers

The first rule about playing blockers is don't try to be quicker than they are. That is their strength. But you can beat them many other ways.

A primary weakness of a blocker is often his own quickness. To take the ball so quickly he must stand right at the table. He has little time to decide what shot to use, and so even if you make a weak shot, he will often just block it. This is why a blocker needs to anticipate weak balls so as to be ready to kill them. A blocker will also make a lot of mistakes by his own attempts to be quick, thereby rushing himself into mistakes.

Some blockers are very strong in the middle but weak to the corners where they have to move their racket farther. Others are the reverse, weak in the middle since they have to decide which side to block with. Find out early in a match which type you are playing.

Like hitters, a blocker usually doesn't have a very strong loop (especially if they use pips, as many blockers do) and so is vulnerable against long serves. Test him out and find which ones work best. Especially effective are fast, dead serves to the middle and wide backhand, and breaking serves to the backhand. Experiment with long serves to the forehand, which some blockers attack well, while others have great difficulty. Short side-top serves aren't usually too effective as the blocker quick-hits them, thereby rushing you (which is his game), but short backspin and no-spin serves are highly effective in setting up your own attack, since the blocker has little time to react to the spin/no spin. However, a blocker may rush and angle you if you serve short, so mostly serve long if the blocker can't attack it effectively.

Since a blocker wins mostly by your mistakes, he wants to rush you as much as possible. You are most vulnerable when slightly off balance after making a strong loop, so if that loop is blocked back effectively, don't try to force another strong loop—focus on consistency, depth, and placement, and look for a better chance.

Blockers often like to play against loopers. If you can also hit the ball flat, either forehand or backhand, then throw that in there as well, forcing the blocker to block against both heavy topspin and flatter drives.

Most blockers are stronger on the backhand. If so, go after their forehand side relentlessly. They may be strong in the middle since they often cover this with their backhands. But this may just mean their middle is more toward their forehand side, so try going after that spot.

When a blocker attacks, focus on steady, deep returns. A blocker's own quickness over the table makes it difficult for him to continue to attack, and he'll end up blocking again.

As noted earlier, there are basically three types of blockers: aggressive blockers, steady blockers, and change-of-pace blockers.

Table Tennis Tactics for Thinkers

Aggressive ones want to block the ball hard and quick, forcing you away from the table and into mistakes. If he succeeds in forcing you away from the table, he has extra time to watch your incoming shot and so he becomes quicker. Worse, it gives him time to smash.

What you want to do against an aggressive blocker is to attack aggressively with enough spin, depth, and variation that he makes mistakes trying to block aggressively, or is forced to slow down his blocks so he can keep his own shots on the table. Once he has slowed down his blocks you have time to really go on the attack.

A consistent blocker tries to keep the ball in play until you make a mistake. He can be like a brick wall, getting everything back until you almost drop from exhaustion. His shots are usually pretty passive but they are quick enough so as to prevent you from teeing off on them. And when you do, they often keep coming back!

His weakness is his own passiveness. He is putting so much effort into getting everything back that he can't do much else. You can slow down your own shots, giving yourself more time to set up for the next shot. Take your time, look for the right shot, and then end the point with a winner to the wide corners or middle.

Don't make the mistake of letting a consistent blocker get into a rhythm by always attacking at the same pace. Surprisingly, a blocker usually has more trouble blocking slow, spinny loops than faster ones that he can get to. The spin on a slow loop grabs the racket more, and jumps out more. The blocker will often pop them up or block them off. The slowness of your own shot makes his shot slower, and the slowness of both shots (especially if you keep the ball deep) gives you more time to get into position for your own more aggressive follow-ups. A fast loop just comes back faster, and should be used with discretion until you can put it past him.

Change-of-pace blockers are in between, constantly changing the pace, blocking one ball hard, one ball soft, often with misdirection. The key to playing them is knowing that their own constant variation means they are not as consistent as they could be, and they will probably give you more weak balls than other types of blockers. So consistency is important as you wait for the right ball to go after or for them to make a mistake. Don't overplay against seemingly soft blocks unless you are set for the shot; change-of-pace blockers thrive on opponents mistaking a soft block for a weak block when they aren't actually ready to make a strong attack.

Many blockers like to push to your wide backhand over and over, waiting for you to step around with your forehand. Then they give you a quick block to the wide forehand. (It is basically a style on its own, a pusher/blocker style.) You have five ways of combating this.

1. You can attack with your backhand, and not go out of position at all. A backhand loop is ideal for this, especially if you vary the placement.
2. You can loop the push itself for a winner. You have to judge whether you can do this consistently enough.
3. You can loop with the forehand from the backhand side, and be quick enough to get to the likely block to your wide forehand. The key here is balance; if you are off-balance after you loop the forehand, you won't be able to get a quick start to cover the forehand side. If you stay balanced throughout the shot, and you have even average foot speed, you'll be surprised at how quickly you can cover that wide forehand. If you are in decent shape, proper technique is more important than how fast you are. If your loop is strong enough, most often you'll either win the point outright or force a weak ball you can attack again with your forehand.
4. You can use your forehand but loop slow and deep. The very slowness of your shot gives you time to get back into position, and the depth keeps the blocker from contacting it too soon and rushing you. Again, balance is key to getting that quick start to cover the wide forehand, and the slowness of your own shot means even a slower player can cover it.
5. If the blocker has a passive forehand, you can push to his forehand to take away the angle into your backhand, and attack his return. Or push to the middle, which also takes away most of the angle.

Counter-drivers

A counter-driver likes to stand in the middle of the table and aggressively stroke back whatever you hit at him. He often takes everything at the top of the bounce or just before, and smashes given the first opportunity, especially on the forehand side. He can seemingly counter your best shots and go on all day doing so. If you loop, they mostly block, though they will also sometimes hit. It is a simple game, with placement, consistency, and speed of drives the most important elements.

A counter-driver's basic strategy is to drive balls mostly to the opponent's weaker side. If the weaker side is the backhand, then the goal is to keep pounding that side until the opponent misses. If the weaker side is the forehand, then the goal is to hit the ball hard enough to the forehand so that opponent cannot smash the return. (Normally you can't play into the forehand over and over or even an opponent with a weaker forehand will smash, so the counter-driver will move the ball around against this type of player, going to the forehand aggressively as much as he can get away with.)

Table Tennis Tactics for Thinkers

If an opponent tees off on his shots, the counter-driver has to pick up the speed of his own shots. If he starts missing, he should slow down; he has to find a balance. He should always be on the lookout for balls to smash, but doesn't need to force it.

Often a counter-driver's best tactic is to force backhand-to-backhand exchanges, which is usually their best type of rally—few will beat them at this, especially if the counter-driver moves the ball around to keep the opponent guessing. If the opponent tries to break this up by going to the forehand, the counter-driver is in position and ready to smash.

The weakness of a counter-driver is that his shots are generally not especially quick, fast, or spinny. Just as he can drive back whatever you throw at him, you should be able to do the same to him. It usually comes down to whether your attack is more consistent than his counter-hitting. If you loop, you can turn a counter-driver into a blocker, where he might not be as comfortable.

Just as he does to you, you should concentrate your attack at his weaker side, and even more to his middle. While most counter-drivers are strong from the corners, they are usually weaker on one side, and almost always have trouble in the middle. Take your time attacking. Pick your shots, and make sure that the winners that you go for are the right ones to go for. It takes sharp judgment, but you must avoid trying to force winners, a temptation when playing counter-drivers. Remember—just as when playing blockers, if he can't put the ball past you, you are under no pressure to force the attack.

On the other hand, don't take too long. A counter-driver is going to be more consistent than you at his own game, and if you rally with him too long, you're going to make too many mistakes, or he'll find a ball to smash. However, you might counter just long enough until you see a chance to smash or loop, either forehand or backhand.

Another way to play the counter-driver is to end the point before he gets a chance to counter-drive, usually by looping. The key here is good serves and a good loop, usually winning the point with your first two or three loops. Against a more aggressive player, it is dangerous to over-anticipate a third ball loop kill too often—a good receive catches you off guard. But since a counter-driver is usually less of a threat on the attack, you can play a flexible attack. If you're a hitter, then you can end the point better than the counter-driver, so you can aggressively but patiently rally while you look for balls to smash. If you are a looper, look for every chance to loop, especially to the middle.

CHAPTER FIFTEEN
Choppers

*2012 U.S. Open Men's Singles Semifinalist Wang Qing Liang ("Leon"), the #1 chopper in the U.S. Photo courtesy of **JOOLA USA***

Choppers are defensive players who win mostly on your mistakes. They go far off the table and return each of your aggressive topspin shots with backspin, making it difficult to attack effectively.

There aren't that many choppers around anymore, but there are always a few. An entire book could be written on chopping tactics—both for and against—but the audience for that is relatively small. Still, chopping tactics are important to those who chop regularly, to those who chop occasionally, and most commonly, for those who play choppers. If you play tournaments or leagues, you will no doubt face a chopper sooner or later.

Like other styles, there are many types of choppers, from purely defensive ones to ones who are almost as aggressive as attackers. Most have long pips on the backhand, inverted on the forehand. A "classic" chopper basically chops and pick hits when he sees a chance, often with the backhand (either with long pips, or sometimes flipping to attack with the inverted side). A "modern" chopper mostly chops on the backhand, but mostly loops and counterloops on the forehand, chopping on that side only when forced to. Since the tactics of attacking are covered extensively elsewhere, let's focus on defensive chopping tactics, both for and against.

A chopper's goal is to make you miss. It's as simple as that. There's a myth that choppers do not want to play power players who rip every ball. Nothing can be further from the truth—a chopper *wants* an opponent who tries to rip every ball, because that's the type of player who is more likely to miss! What a chopper *doesn't* want to play is someone who plays very patiently and tactically until he gets the right shot, and *then* rips it. There's nothing scarier for a chopper than a big, strong guy with a brain.

Table Tennis Tactics for Thinkers

A chopper has many ways of getting—or tricking—an opponent into missing. How does he do this? Here are a number of ways—and if you are a chopper, you should focus on learning as many of these as possible.

5. **Steadiness**. If a chopper keeps getting the ball back, the opponent is eventually going to miss. A chopper who is not super steady is pretty much lost.
6. **Low**. The lower the ball, the less margin for error the opponent has, and the more mistakes he will make.
7. **Depth**. A ball that goes deep on the table is more difficult to attack than one that lands in the middle (depth-wise) of the table. (Don't confuse this with short pushes, which would bounce twice on the table, given the chance. A chop that lands in the middle of the table would normally go off the end after the first bounce, and is relatively easy to put away.)
8. **Heavy**. It's tricky lifting heavy backspin, and a truly stiff chop can cause all sorts of mistakes.
9. **Variable spin**. After chopping heavy a number of times, a sudden light backspin or no-spin can cause an opponent to go off the end. A light backspin or no-spin to the middle of the table is especially effective, as it gives the opponent less table to aim for—he can't go corner to corner, the longest part of the table—and so is more likely to lift the ball off the end.
10. **Placement**. Chopping side to side forces the opponent to move, which can cause mistakes. Some players have more trouble looping from one spot than another. For example, a slower player may have trouble getting around his backhand to loop a forehand. And some players have more power when they loop forehands from the backhand side, since the table isn't in their way.
11. **Off-surface**. Most choppers have an off-surface on one side, usually long pips, but sometimes antispin, hardbat, or short pips. Many players have difficulty playing these surfaces, and a chopper should find the ways to use the off-surface most effectively. Often opponents have trouble with the relatively no-spin push returns of the off-surface, or with the heavy backspin returns made against a loop with an off-surface that returns spin, in particular long pips.
12. **Flipping**. If a chopper has two different surfaces, he should find chances to flip the racket, catching the opponent off guard. For example, a chopper with long pips might flip and push a shot with inverted on the backhand side, which can throw an opponent off with its heavier backspin.

13. **Attacking**. A chopper who just chops is at a huge disadvantage. The best choppers can attack as well, especially when serving. So a chopper should look to attack whenever possible. At minimum they should be ready to end the point quickly if the opponent makes a weak shot.

If you are a chopper, you have to decide which of the above tactics will work best against whoever you are playing. If the player is mistake prone or not very powerful, concentrate on keeping the ball in play until he misses. Change the spins only when you see an easy chance to. If he has trouble with heavy chop, give it to him. If he has trouble reading spin, change the spin over and over, even if it means popping up a few balls.

A chopper should put pressure on his opponent by attacking whenever possible. Since you pick which shots you will attack instead of attacking over and over like a normal attacker (called "pick hitting" or "pick looping") you should make most of them. Usually go for immediate winners when you do attack—if you were as effective attacking for several shots in a row you'd likely be an attacker, not a chopper.

The backhand chop of
Viktoria Pavlovich
of Belarus
Photo by Diego Schaaf

Some players are emotionally incapable of playing a steady chopper. Even if he has the shots to win, a chopper can beat this type of player by playing on his impatience. They mostly just keep the ball in play and watch him swat shots all over the court. (Of course, a few nice changes of spin, or just heavy backspin, help here, especially if the chops are deep.)

Playing Choppers

There is nothing more infuriating than losing to a patient chopper who lets you beat yourself with your own errors. Losing to a chopper is like four-putting in golf; you may have made some good drives to get to the green, but all you remember are the misses at the end. Rather than four-putting forever, let's learn how to beat the chopper.

A chopper does not simply get the ball back. Chopping is perhaps the most tactical of styles simply because to win a point, a chopper must trick his opponent into making a mistake in some way. This can be done with all the ways listed earlier.

A chopper is weakest in the middle and you should focus your attack there. However, you have more table (and so more margin for error)

Table Tennis Tactics for Thinkers

by going diagonally to a corner. Going for a winner down the line often catches the chopper by surprise. A chopper who is not particularly fast is vulnerable at the corners, especially if you aim one way and go the other. A chopper with inverted on both sides is more vulnerable in the middle. (You have to chop more into the ball with inverted, with less margin for error, so a player with long pips on the backhand can more easily cover the middle with the long pips than an inverted chopper.)

The natural weakness of a chopper is that he must rely on your mistakes. He can pick hit when he sees the chance, but basically he must score most of his points on your making a careless mistake. In theory, you should be able to dominate against a chopper—after all, if you can't attack a given ball, you can push it and attack the next one instead. Any time you are not sure of the spin you can do this. So how does a chopper win?

From an attacker's point of view, he is in control of the rallies when he attacks. But from the chopper's point of view, the chopper is in control. Against a low chop or push, an attacker can only attack so hard and still be consistent. If the chopper can chop that shot back effectively, he is in control.

In general, if a chopper can return your best attack back without giving you a high ball, he is going to win. But there are ways to make your attacks more effective.

As noted earlier, a common misconception about playing choppers is that you have to overpower them. That only works if you are a much stronger player. If you can beat a chopper on pure power, then you would beat him even worse by choosing your shots carefully.

After a chopper has made one return of a strong loop or drive, he will probably return the same shot over and over again. A chopper can adjust to just about anything if he sees it enough. What does give a chopper trouble is change. Changing the spin, speed, direction, depth or even the arc of the ball can cause havoc to his timing and lead to misses and weak returns.

A chopper is strongest at the corners unless you can force him out of position and ace him to a wide angle, or if you can use misdirection so he moves the wrong way. He is weakest in the middle where he must not only decide whether to chop with the forehand or the backhand but also must get his body out of the way so he can make a proper stroke. More than anything else you should punish a chopper by relentlessly attacking his middle over and over.

Tactically, when playing a chopper, constantly change depth and direction. Loop or hit one deep, then short and soft (perhaps with extra spin to the inverted side, if he has one, where he's more vulnerable to spin). Draw him in close to the table and then attack hard before he can respond to it. Choppers are vulnerable to in-and-out movement, which causes havoc to their timing against arcing topspins and to their control since the

Joo Se Hyuk chops another one back. Photo by Diego Schaaf

distance to their target—your side of the table—constantly varies. So focus on moving them in and out more than side to side, which choppers can seemingly do forever.

Have patience, but when the shot is there, take it—you must be patient yet decisive. If you have trouble reading the spin, push it or attack it soft. Don't attack hard to the corners too much—concentrate on his weaker middle. Put as much pressure on him as you can and he will make mistakes. Often the mistakes he makes are not obvious. An outright miss or a high ball are obvious mistakes, but he might also chop too short. A chop that lands midway between the net and the end line (i.e. not too long, not too short) is usually easier to loop kill or smash, even if it is low. Take advantage of all his mistakes, limit yours, and you will probably win.

Another way to play a chopper is to push with him very patiently, looking for a good ball to attack. Push ten balls, then *wham!* He won't know when you are going to attack and might get stuck too close to the table to return your shot. You can even push until the expedite rule takes effect and then you will have an advantage, since an aggressive player can win the point quickly under expedite better than most choppers can. (More on that shortly.) The problem here is that a chopper is usually better at pushing and can do so forever. He can also catch the attacker off guard by attacking when he sees the chance, while the attacker can't do the same since the chopper is expecting it. Choppers are used to pushing over and over and picking their attack shots, so it's difficult to beat them at their own game.

One common mistake against choppers is to go for too many drop shots, as opposed to regular pushes. A drop shot is an excellent way to win a point if you can catch your opponent too far from the table, but it is risky. There are three reasons for this. First, a drop shot is a very delicate shot and it is easy to miss. Second, it is very easy to pop a drop shot up, giving the chopper an easy ball to pick hit. Third, it is very difficult to do a good drop shot against a very deep chop, and if the ball lands any shorter it should be easy to attack and so you shouldn't want to drop shot. (Unless, of course, it lands so short that it would bounce twice.) Another mistake is to drop shot when you aren't sure of the spin. The worse thing you can do when you don't read the spin is to drop shot since you will invariable either put the ball in the net or pop it up. Choppers are notoriously good at swatting in high drop shots, even on the run. If you aren't sure of the spin, just use a normal push or attack softly. If you are sure of the spin, and the chopper is far from the table, then by all means drop shot.

A long push to the off-surface (such as long pips) often sets you up since the long pips cannot create much on the push return. So when a

Table Tennis Tactics for Thinkers

chopper is off the table, sometimes go for a quick, aggressive push to that side, and attack the next ball.

A no-spin serve, short or long, is often effective against a chopper since it will tend to cut down on how much backspin he can put on the ball. In general, mix your serves up to mess up the chopper's control. If he has an off-surface such as long pips (as most choppers do), serve lots of no-spin to the long pips (thereby getting no-spin returns) or spin to the inverted side (where he's more vulnerable to spin).

You should always get one "free" shot against a chopper, assuming he's willing to chop your deep serves back. Serve long, watch their return carefully, and loop it at wide angles or the middle, and go on from there. If the chopper backs up too quickly after your serve, perhaps fake a loop and drop shot, and then attack—or drop shot again!

Playing the Chopper-Attacker

One of the more infuriating styles to play for many is the opponent who both chops and attacks, the so-called "modern" chopper. The first thing to understand is that since the opponent has developed both of these games, he has many tactical advantages. It's your job to nullify them. Since the game tends to be dominated by attack, you should take advantage of this.

If he serves and attacks, play him like any other attacker when he serves. See the appropriate section or chapter in this book—is he a looper or a hitter? Once you get past his attack, he'll probably fall back on defense, and that's when you apply the tactics for playing a chopper. If he attacks with the forehand but chops on the backhand, perhaps go to the forehand and come back to the backhand.

If he attacks out of the rally, things get trickier. Usually a chopper does this on one side, usually the forehand. If so, look to attack strongly to his attacking side, since you don't want to attack weakly there, where he'll counter-attack. If he steps around to attack his forehand out of the backhand side, then he's probably leaving his forehand side open, so look for chances to go there. If you go to the wide forehand and he attacks, you can probably block back to the wide backhand and get him back to chopping, but be ready to attack that ball, or to quick-push to the backhand again so you can attack the next ball.

Four Specific Ways to Play a Chopper

When playing a chopper, you need a plan. Here are four specific plans you can use for beating a chopper. (The first two require at least intermediate skills.) They basically condense the more theoretical discussions from this chapter into specific tactical plans. You don't have to follow them religiously; use your own variations, or combine them in various ways. Informally, these styles are called European style, Asian style, Pick-Hitting Style, and Chiseling. (However, plenty of Europeans use Asian style, and vice versa.)

1) European Style

The goal here is to bring the chopper in close to the table, and then attack hard, especially at the chopper's middle. The chopper is too close to the table to make the return, and so misses. When using this technique, you should mostly serve short to bring the chopper in, and try to follow with a strong attack. Sometimes, however, fake the attack, and instead push short again—the chopper, in his haste to back up for the expected attack, will have trouble with this ball, and will often have to make a last-second lunge to return it. Even if he makes the return (often a weak one), he will be left jammed over the table and vulnerable to the next ball, which you can promptly loop for a winner. If the chopper stays closer to the table to guard against this drop shot, then you attack while he's too close to the table to respond. The chopper has absolutely no way of answering this . . . in theory.

During a rally, if the chopper makes a good return from away from the table, push short again, and start over. The object in a rally is to catch the chopper too far away from the table or moving backward so that you can drop the ball short, force him to rush in, and attack when he's jammed up against the table. If he's off the table, he's ready for your attack, and so you shouldn't attack unless you have an easy ball. Alternatively, you can push a few balls, keeping the chopper close to the table, and then attack when you think he's not expecting it.

2) Asian Style

The goal here is to control the spin and pace of the rally. This method is especially good against a chopper with an "off" surface that can't create much backspin on its own, either long pips (which most choppers use), short pips, antispin, or hardbat. It takes regular practice against a chopper to learn to do it effectively. Pips-out players are especially good at this style, but many good inverted players often play this way against choppers, including me. This style doesn't work well against an all-inverted chopper who chops very heavy. Let's assume you are playing a chopper with long pips.

Here the aim is to get the chopper off the table, and then attack relatively softly over and over, into the long pips side, but not with full spin. The chopper can only return whatever spin you give him because of the long pips, and so their returns are not particularly heavy, making your continuous soft attack easy. After topspinning a few balls, you find one you like and loop or smash a winner. (A chopper with short pips or hardbat can add some backspin to their returns, but not that much compared to an inverted chopper.)

Table Tennis Tactics for Thinkers

Depending on what you are more comfortable with, you can topspin many balls in a row before going for a winner, or only a few—be unpredictable. Some players just topspin over and over, not going for a winner unless they get a very easy one. You might sometimes vary your spin, sometimes looping very dead, sometimes spinny. However, beware of varying spin returns when you vary your own spin. For example, when you give heavy topspin, expect heavy chop, and so either lift the ball more on the next shot, or push and start over. Don't fall into the trap of spinning heavy over and over—a chopper loves it, and all you'll get are heavy chop returns, which can be very difficult to loop consistently. You might just topspin every ball the same, to maximize your own consistency, and win points both on this consistency and sudden winners. By giving the same topspin over and over, you'll get pretty much the same backspin over and over, which greatly helps your timing both for consistency and going for winners.

You should also mix in pushing, but too much pushing will throw your own timing off. By topspinning over and over to the long pips side (but not with full spin), you can build up a rhythm that a chopper will have difficulty breaking. Try to get down to almost eye level with the ball by bending your knees. This will help your consistency by making the lifting easier and will get your eyes closer to the ball so you see it better.

3) Pick-Hitting Style

The goal here is to pick your shots against the chopper's push, and if you can't easily put away the return, push and patiently look for another ball to attack. Unless you have a put-away shot, you rarely attack two balls in a row. Instead it's push a few balls, attack, push a few balls, attack, push a few balls, attack, etc., until you get a putaway shot or the chopper misses. Most of the attacks should go to the chopper's weakest spot, usually the middle, sometimes the forehand. (The backhand chop, often with long pips, is usually a chopper's most consistent shot, but not always.) Most players attack by forehand looping, but you can also drive or smash, forehand or backhand.

You need to vary your pushes to find a ball to attack. For example, a quick, off-the-bounce push to a chopper's long pips often forces a weak return, and any push with long pips has little spin, which you may be able to attack. A sudden push to the forehand can set up your own forehand attack. After a series of heavier pushes, a sudden no-spin or light backspin push can set up a higher return to attack.

The advantage of this style is you don't have to deal with varying chop returns, which are where attackers make most of their mistakes. The disadvantage—besides the obvious patience needed and long rallies that you'll sometimes play—is that the chopper may start attacking. You have to find a balance. The more the chopper attacks effectively, the more you'll need to attack to stop that.

4) Chiseling

I am generally not fond of this style. This basically means pushing with the chopper until the chopper either misses, pops up an easy one, or gets impatient and attacks too much. At the higher levels, chiseling is rare, but at the lower and medium levels, it is more common. Since I'm a strong believer that the game has to be FUN (it is a game!), I don't like this way of winning. Unless you're a chopper yourself (in which case *someone's* got to push, and it might as well be you), I'd rather see a player lose by attacking in some way, thereby practicing their attack and thereby developing their game strategically. You may lose now, but you'll learn how to play a chopper better in future matches. (The exception would be in a really important match, such as a national or state championship, or whatever you consider important.)

On the other hand, if you do push with a chopper, he may start attacking, and as long as someone's attacking, the game is fun.

However, if you do chisel with a chopper, you have to be extremely patient. The points will be long (and boring) unless the chopper decides to attack. Since a chopper generally doesn't have a strong attack—or he'd be an attacker—push mostly to his weaker side. Focus on steadiness, and changing placement and spin to force misses or pop-ups.

One reason to chisel with a chopper is to play for expedite.

Expedite Rule

Choppers and those playing choppers should be aware of the expedite rule. Before the expedite rule, there were matches between two passive choppers that would last for hours. One point at the 1936 World Table Tennis Championships lasted over two hours.

If any game is not complete after ten minutes (not including official breaks), the expedite rule comes into play for the rest of the match. Under expedite, players alternate serves. If the receiver makes thirteen consecutive returns in the rally, he wins the point. This means that whoever serves has thirteen shots (including the serve) to win the point. If a chopper is in a match that is approaching expedite, he should attack more and try to end the game before expedite takes over.

In an umpired match, the umpire counts the shots out loud, which can be distracting. This lets both players know how close they are to the thirteenth shot. If the receiver makes a thirteenth return, the point ends and the receiver wins the point. Players should prepare themselves mentally for playing with an umpire calling out the strokes—it can be disconcerting the first time it happens.

Some players will push with a chopper for ten minutes to get to

Table Tennis Tactics for Thinkers

expedite, since an attacker has an advantage under that system. To end a game before the ten-minute time limit, a chopper might have to attack, even if it risks losing that game, since once called, expedite continues for the rest of the match. (Some choppers wear a watch for this very reason, to keep track of time, or they simply ask the umpire regularly how much time is left. Normally you'd need an umpire timing the match for it to go expedite.)

Keep in mind that you don't have to rush the attack, even in expedite. Very few rallies actually go thirteen shots, and so pick your shots carefully. It is better to hit a winner on the twelfth shot then to miss a panicky attack early on. If two defensive-minded players play, they may request that the match be played under expedite from the beginning or at any time during the match—see rule 2.15.01.

Once under expedite, the server who normally attacks should probably play exactly as he normally does, until he approaches that thirteenth shot. At that point, he does need to get a bit more aggressive. A server who normally plays defense might have to start his attack sooner since he's not used to ending the point quickly.

Under expedite, it would seem logical for the receiver to play steady and try to return thirteen shots. Against a passive opponent, this might work. However, if you change your normal style of play too much, your own level will go down, and you'll probably lose far more points from that then you'll win by returning thirteen shots.

There is one time when a receiver might attack more—as he approaches thirteen returns! This may seem contrary to common sense, but the idea is that it keeps the server from attacking. If you push the twelfth ball, the server can try to end the point. If you instead attack and force the server to block, you have an easy thirteenth return and the point.

THE EXPEDITE SYSTEM

2.15.01 Except as provided in 2.15.2, the expedite system shall come into operation after 10 minutes' play in a game or at any time requested by both players or pairs.

2.15.02 The expedite system shall not be introduced in a game if at least 18 points have been scored.

2.15.03 If the ball is in play when the time limit is reached and the expedite system is due to come into operation, play shall be interrupted by the umpire and shall resume with service by the player who served in the rally that was interrupted; If the ball is not in play when the expedite system comes into operation, play shall resume with service by the player who received in the immediately preceding rally.

2.15.04 Thereafter, each player shall serve for 1 point in turn until the end of the game, and if the receiving player or pair makes 13 correct returns in a rally the receiver shall score a point.

2.15.05 Introduction of the expedite system shall not alter the order of serving and receiving in the match, as defined in 2.13.6.

2.15.06 Once introduced, the expedite system shall remain in operation until the end of the match.

Larry Hodges

Table Tennis Tactics for Thinkers

CHAPTER SIXTEEN
Fishers and Lobbers

*Dragutin Surbek of Yugoslavia, one of the great lobbers from the past, leaps for one against Kjell Johansson of Sweden. (*Most* lobs don't involve leaping.)*
Photo by Mal Anderson

Normally fishing and lobbing isn't a style on its own, but there are players where these shots are central to their game. It's not always the most effective way to play, since you are essentially letting your opponent smash or power loop, but it might be the funnest style to play. And it is an effective way to stay in points that others would have already lost.

Make sure you understand the difference between fishing and lobbing. A fisher returns the ball anywhere from a few inches over the net to perhaps head-high, while lobbers put the ball much higher, often up to the ceiling. Both put topspin on the ball; at the higher levels, fishing and lobbing are basically defensive loops.

Most players use the lob only as a variation or desperation shot. But some players use it over and over, and if they find you have trouble with it, they will use it even more.

The keys to effective fishing and lobbing are consistency, depth, placement, and spin. If you can't fish or lob a smash back consistently from off the table, then you either need to work on it or find some other style. Assuming you can do this, you are ready to drive your opponent nuts.

Keeping the ball deep is probably the most important thing you can do when fishing and lobbing. As long as you do that, you can stay in the point. (In fact, against a good fisher or lobber, the main tactic isn't to smash a winner on one shot; it's to force a shorter ball that *can* be smashed for a winner.) You want the ball to hit deep on the table and bounce out, forcing the opponent to hit the ball from well behind the table. This makes his shot more difficult (more mistakes) and gives you more time to respond to his shots (so you make fewer mistakes). A short lob can especially be smashed at such a wide angle that there is nothing you can do to get it back.

Topspin and sidespin are important to force mistakes. You want topspin to make the ball jump off the opponent's side of the table, and sidespin to make it jump sideways, both of which force mistakes. Topspin is more important and should be on every fish or lob; sidespin is more for variation and surprise, especially on the forehand side, where many fishers and lobbers generate both topspin and sidespin.

Placement is also important. Place the ball side to side (especially when fishing, where the opponent has less time to move to each shot), and make the opponent move to the wide forehand, wide backhand, wide forehand, wide backhand, and so on. The more he moves—normally to play forehands—the more likely he'll miss.

Mostly lob crosscourt to a wide corner, since that gives you more table to aim for. Another reason to lob crosscourt to the wide corner is that it cuts off part of the table. It's tricky smashing a lob down the line (less table, awkward angle, and so more misses), and so most lobs to a wide corner are predictably smashed right back to the opposite corner, which makes things easier for the lobber, who has less ground to cover.

You should also put the ball more often opposite your stronger side, since most smashes will be crosscourt right back at your stronger side. For example, many lobbers like to fish or lob over and over to the opponent's wide forehand, which often results in a crosscourt smash back to the forehand, where the fisher/lobber is often stronger (bigger hitting zone and more reach), and can put more spin on the return and counter-attack more easily. So a lobber sometimes lobs down-the-line with his backhand to get to the opponent's forehand side. But if the lobber's opponent is smart, he won't fall for it; he'll smash mostly to the backhand or middle.

A key to lobbing is how to get out of the lobbing rally—and you do this primarily by counter-attacking, either with a counter-smash or a loop. It's generally easier to do this on the forehand side, where you have a bigger hitting zone and more natural power, so look for every chance to counter-attack on that side (or on the backhand, if that's your strong side). When

Table Tennis Tactics for Thinkers

counter-attacking a smash to the forehand with a loop, a lobber should normally sidespin loop to the wide forehand so as to cut off the often open backhand side.

If the opponent's loop or smash is weak, you might chop it back to get back into the point. Or switch from lobbing to fishing, which is slightly less defensive.

One nice strategy used by lobbers is to lob to the wide backhand, perhaps with sidespin breaking it even wider. It's extremely difficult to smash this ball down the line, and so it is almost always smashed crosscourt. As the opponent moves way over to smash his forehand from the wide backhand side, the lobber anticipates the crosscourt smash, and at the last instant he also steps way over to his backhand side, and looks to counter-smash or loop with his forehand. (After which he better rush back to the table in case the opponent blocks the ball back!)

Playing Lobbers

There are generally two ways to smash a lob. A smother kill, where you take the ball right off the bounce, is most effective if it hits, least effective if it misses. Generally it's better to take the ball later, normally just above your head or so. (However, you can make this shot more effective by adding right-to-left sidespin, so that it breaks to the right for a right-hander.) You have to judge for yourself. Some players smother kill all lobs, others never do it. A good balance is to smother kill only against lobs that land short on the table, close to your target, since it's very difficult to smother kill a deep lob.

Regardless of how you hit the lob you should follow one fundamental rule when playing most lobbers, and that is to smash mostly to the backhand and middle. (Of course, somewhere out there is the exception to this rule and you will no doubt play him in your next match.) The forehand lob is usually spinnier, and it is far easier to counter-attack with the forehand than the backhand. So just smash to the backhand and middle over and over until you force either a miss or a weak return. When the weak ball comes (usually one that lands short) go to the forehand only if you can smash an ace or at least force a leaping return. Why take chances? When in doubt, go to the backhand or middle. If the opponent threatens to counter-attack with the forehand from the middle, go to the wide backhand or (if he's leaving it open to cover the middle) go after the forehand side.

When the ball lands short, end the point. You can angle the ball to either side, and unless your opponent can anticipate (or guess) which side you are going to, you should be able to put it past him. Ideally, don't decide which side to go to until your opponent has committed himself to one side. If he doesn't commit himself, he should be open on both wings. (And with both sides being equal, you should usually go to the backhand, just in case, unless you have a good angle into the forehand side.)

You should rarely drop shot against the lob. If the ball is deep, an effective drop shot is nearly impossible, and if the ball is short you should be able to put it away. Normally you should only drop shot if you are completely caught off guard by the shot. All a drop shot usually does against a lobber is let him back into the point. One exception to this rule is if your opponent has gotten into such a rhythm that you cannot smash past him in the rally, or if you simply do not have great power in your smash. A drop shot might be effective just to throw off his timing, and by bringing him in, he might not be able to respond to your next shot.

Playing Fishers

The fisherman (or fisherwoman?) is the scourge of many. He is the player who backs up and softly and defensively topspins everything back a few feet over the net. His shots are not quite lobbing, not quite looping, and not quite counter-hitting. It can take a lot of work to race around the table attacking his shots with your forehand—not easy when the fisher puts the ball side to side, deep on the table, with both topspin and sidespin so the balls jumps as it hits your side of the table. How does one play this style?

First off, you have to decide how physical you can play. If you have the foot speed, stamina, and a strong enough forehand (looping or smashing) to attack each of these shots with your forehand, then by all means do so, though (as explained below) the occasional change-of-pace may be important, depending on how steady the fisher is. The key is how you attack them.

If you don't have the foot speed, stamina, or a strong enough forehand to keep attacking, then you will have to mix in blocks, especially with your backhand. (Of course, if you have a far more powerful backhand than forehand—rare, but sometimes the case—then attack with the backhand. But it's difficult attacking a high, arcing ball with the backhand.) Don't feel as if this is a major weakness; more players lose to fishers by over-attacking than by ones who change the pace by mixing in blocks along with their attacks.

Here are the keys to playing a fisher.

Placement: Never attack the middle forehand or middle backhand—those are the easiest shots for the fisher to return. (This, of course, is a general rule for just about all opponents.) Instead, focus on the wide backhand and middle (elbow area), and the wide forehand when you think you have a clean winner, or if the fisher happens to be weak on that side. Since a fisher needs to anticipate where your attacks are going in order to respond to them, if you can aim one way and go another, he'll struggle.

Table Tennis Tactics for Thinkers

- On the **forehand side**, the fisher has a bigger hitting zone, more range, can more easily create both topspin and sidespin, and can more easily counter-attack, usually with a counterloop. Normally avoid this side until you have an extreme angle or can hit a clean winner.
- On the **backhand side**, the fisher is more cramped, and normally has less range, less spin, and less potential for a counter-attack. Go after this side with a vengeance, along with the middle. Most attacks to the wide backhand side will come back to your backhand side, allowing you to continue your attack into the wide backhand, where you have more table than if you go down the line or to the middle. The catch is to do so, you have to step all the way around your backhand side if you want to use your forehand.
- In the **middle**, the fisher has to make a split-second decision on whether to go forehand or backhand, plus it's usually easier to run a ball down in the corners then to get out of the way of a ball in the middle. Focus on attacking the middle slightly on the backhand side to force an awkward backhand return. This is often a good spot to end the point on. However, there's more table when you go after the corners, so if you attack the middle over and over you are more liable to make more mistakes. Some fishers seem to get every ball back on the backhand side, but that's because all the attacks are going right to the backhand side; mix in attacks to the middle and sometimes to the forehand, and the fisher will begin to crumble.

Change of Pace: Once a good fisher gets his timing down, he can often seemingly return shot after shot even as you smash or power-loop over and over. How do you break out of this pattern? Try changing the pace. Attack one ball softer than normal, or perhaps block one. The fisher is consistent off your strong attacks only because he is anticipating them, and so his timing and positioning are set for strong attacks. Change the pace, and you may mess up his timing and positioning. You might even try looping soft and spinny as a changeup, and watch the fisher struggle to adjust without missing or giving you an easy ball to put away.

Loop or Smash? You can do either against a fisher, or (often even more effectively) do both. Do whichever you are more comfortable with. If you have a powerful loop, the extra topspin of your loop will make it easier to keep your attacks on the table; at the higher levels, top players pretty much kill-loop over and over against a fisher. But if you have a good smash, use that, especially if you can be deceptive with it. An inside-out smash with sidespin to the wide backhand is especially effective and is the bread and butter shot for many players against both fishers and lobbers.

The Short Ball: As long as he keeps the ball deep on the table, a good fisher can run down almost anything you attack. The goal shouldn't be to end the point with each shot; the goal should be to put pressure on the fisher until he returns a ball that lands short. (Of course, in trying to force this, you'll get plenty of outright misses as well.) When you get that short ball, that's when you end the point. You can now attack the ball much closer to the table, at wide angles, and your opponent has less time to react. As long as you don't telegraph your shot, you should be able to rip this ball at a wide angle so that the opponent simply can't run it down, or to the middle where the opponent simply can't react. Or, if the fisher is way off the table, this is the one you can drop short for a winner, especially if you can double bounce it.

Table Tennis Tactics for Thinkers

CHAPTER SEVENTEEN
Non-Inverted Surfaces

One of the first problems you will face when you begin playing in tournaments will be combination rackets, often with inverted on one side, and either short pips or "junk rubber" on the other, either long pips or antispin. (There's also hardbat, covered in the next chapter.) Ironically, there was a time when sponge was the "junk." Until the fifties, nearly everyone used hard rubber with no sponge. When hard rubber players were first faced with the "weird" sponge surfaces, there was an outcry against it, since it dramatically changed the game, and in particular turned the balance in favor of attackers, while nearly killing off the defensive game.

Deng Yaping of China, only 4'11", blocked and hit with long pips on the backhand. She is considered by many the greatest woman player ever. Photo by John Oros

The term junk rubber is commonly used, but some find it derogatory, so I will use other terms the rest of the way. Other off-surfaces are short pips and hardbat. Most players use inverted on both sides, but some use inverted on one side, and an off-surface on the other. Some use off-surfaces on both sides.

These off-surfaces can be difficult to play against unless you regularly play opponents who use them. However, it must be noted that as hard as it can be to play well against them, it is also hard to learn to use them effectively.

Before the different color rule came into effect in 1983, many players used different surfaces, and by flipping their racket could make it difficult for an opponent to tell which side he was hitting with. This led to many unforced errors (due to the different playing characteristics of the different surfaces) and many cries of "foul." But with the color rule—one side must be black, the other bright red—you can always see what surface is being used and so there is no excuse for making mistakes against these off-surfaces. It's just a matter of learning to play each type. If you lose to a player because you can't handle his long pips, it's just as much a loss as if you lost to someone because you couldn't handle his inverted loop.

Make sure you know what surfaces your opponent is using before you start a match. The rules state, "Before the start of a match and whenever he or she changes his or her racket during a match a player shall show his or her opponent and the umpire the racket he or she is about to use and shall allow them to examine it." If the opponent is using something you aren't familiar with, try to hit a few shots against it while warming up for the match, if the opponent allows. (You have a two-minute warm-up period before a match begins, but many players with off-surfaces will avoid using that surface during the warm-up, often flipping their racket to use an inverted side for both forehand-to-forehand and backhand-to-backhand warm-up.) You might want to hit into the off-surface as much as possible early in a match to get used to it.

Beware the flipper! He likes to flip his racket, and so can often play either his off-surface or his (usually) inverted surface from either side. This can be awkward on both sides—for you if you don't see the flip, and for the flipper, who often is rushed while flipping, and is rarely as strong with both surfaces from both sides. If an opponent flips his racket, you should quickly attack the other side, where he's usually stuck with a side he's less comfortable with.

Against all off-surfaces, *keep the ball deep*. They are more used to playing your surface than you are playing their, so this gives you more time to react. Plus they can't loop, so deep balls give them trouble.

Since there is a rather large hardbat movement, and a number of hardbat tournaments, and because it is of special interest to me since I've won a lot of hardbat events, hardbat gets a chapter to itself, following this one. Another growing movement, sandpaper, also gets some coverage in that chapter, though sandpaper isn't legal except in special sandpaper events.

Many players with off-surfaces, especially long pips, are choppers. For more on that (including those with long pips), see the chapter on Choppers.

Short Pips

Short pips (also called pips-out) plays similar to inverted except that it gives less spin on each shot. Balls struck by short pips will have little spin but they will come out as expected—i.e., a topspin stroke produces predictable topspin and a chop stroke produces predictable backspin. The difficulty in playing it is that there is always less spin than the inverted sheets you are probably more used to playing, leading to many balls going into the net or off the end (not only because you misread the spin but also due to overcompensation). You will simply have to adjust to them.

Short pips is especially useful in attacking spin shots. But keep in mind that although pips-out players can handle spin shots well, they cannot produce as much spin as inverted and so you should take advantage of it.

Table Tennis Tactics for Thinkers

They cannot loop, push or serve with as much spin. They are highly vulnerable to an inverted player's heavy spins.

    Against short pips, use spin, depth, and consistency. Any deep ball with heavy topspin or backspin will normally give a pips-out player problems. (On the other hand, if it lands a bit short, they may smash it—those last six inches or so make a huge difference.) An inverted surface rebounds the ball out better, so you can probably keep the ball in play longer than a pips-out player, who has to stroke each shot more. Since the pips-out player can't loop with great spin, you can serve or push deep, even to his forehand, and if he attacks, you counter-attack. (If his attack is too strong for you, then perhaps your push wasn't strong enough—see chapter on Pushing.) If he doesn't attack your deep serve or push, you attack. By serving or pushing deep, the pips-out player cannot rush you or angle you, so you have plenty of time to wind up and loop, or do whatever you do best.

    Many players have difficulty in fast rallies against pips-out players and their quick, dead shots. There's a simple cure for this: play against pips-out players until you get used to it, and then rallying against it becomes easy.

Antispin

    Antispin rubber was first introduced in the early seventies. It is actually a variation of inverted sponge. The major characteristic of antispin is its slick surface. When the ball contacts it, it slides, and spin barely affects it. This makes it easy to handle spinny shots, such as spinny serves. Most antispin rubbers have a very dead sponge underneath which make it easy to return hard drives. With its slick surface and dead sponge, an antispin player can seemingly return anything!

    A ball hit with antispin has less spin than a ball hit with inverted or pips-out sponge. It somewhat deadens the spin, giving you relatively unspinny shots. Players often react as if there were more spin on the ball than there actually is. However, some players with antispin can return your spin, mostly by vigorously chopping into your topspin ball and thereby giving you all your spin back. If you play against antispin, you will learn to respond to its different characteristics.

    Some types of recent antispin rubbers are so frictionless that they return spin almost like long pips, in which case you should play them like long pips. Make sure you are familiar with this type of antispin, generally called frictionless antispin.

    The main weakness of antispin is that its returns are generally soft, spinless, and easy to attack. It is also very difficult to attack with it except against backspin or against balls that land short. This makes antispin a very limited surface unless used in conjunction with a different surface, usually a grippy inverted, and the racket is flipped so as to use whichever surface is wanted. The key thing to remember is that antispin rubber cannot generate spin, and it usually deadens what spin there is on the ball. Also, an antispin ball tends to land shorter on the table, since the sponge is usually slower.

Antispin is primarily used by two styles, choppers and blockers. Choppers use it to return loops consistently, sometimes winning by getting so many balls back the opponent tires and gets impatient. But the returns are easy to attack by a good player and there are fewer and fewer choppers using antispin these days—most use long pips instead, which returns more of a looper's spin. Those that do use antispin almost invariably have inverted on the other side, and most flip their racket to confuse their opponent.

Blockers sometimes use antispin to return serves and block loops and drives. The antispin makes it easy to push serves back short, stopping an attack, and its slick surface make spinny serves easy to return. It is also easy to block a loop with antispin, but the return is easy to attack if anticipated. Most blockers who use antispin use the Seemiller grip so as to be able to use either inverted or antispin on both sides at all times. They might push the serve back short with the antispin, flip back to inverted to play out the point, then flip back to antispin to block a ball short, often catching the opponent off guard, and then flip back to inverted.

Keep the ball deep to the antispin side, often with dead serves. Antispin gives the opponent control, but his returns will be soft and (especially against a dead serve) without much spin. You can also mess up some antispin players with deep, breaking serves (throwing off their control), and unlike long pips, you won't get much of your own spin back.

Long Pips

Note that there's a whole chapter on Choppers, and so choppers with long pips are primarily covered there. Also, as noted in the section above on antispin, remember that "frictionless antispin" should also be played as if it were long pips.

Long pips are a type of pips-out sponge with pips that are much longer and thinner than conventional pips. This lets the pips bend at contact with the ball, which creates an interesting effect. If the ball has spin on it, the spin continues to rotate in the same direction. But because the direction of the ball has changed, the spin has changed. A topspin ball continues to spin in the same way but since its orientation has changed (it is now going toward the original spinner), it is now backspin.

Imagine a topspin ball coming at you, with the top of it rotating towards you. If you hit it back without changing the rotation, the top will still be rotating towards you, or away from the opponent. This makes it a backspin return. Likewise, backspin can be returned as topspin, and sidespin as the reverse sidespin. This is called spin reversal. (Technically, it's

Table Tennis Tactics for Thinkers

not spin reversal, it's spin continuance, since the ball's spin doesn't reverse, it continues. But since the type of spin changes because of the change in direction the ball is going, it effectively is spin reversal, and that's what it is commonly called, though some disagree with the terminology.)

If you block a topspin ball with inverted, your return will have light topspin. The same block with long pips will have backspin. Even if you use a topspin stroke with long pips, against topspin you will return the ball with either a backspin or at most a no-spin ball. However, if you attack backspin you will get topspin since the ball is already rotating in that direction, but the topspin will be no more than the amount of backspin already on the ball.

If you chop a topspin with long pips, you will return all or most of the spin as backspin. Against a spinny loop you will give back all of the spin as a very spinny backspin. Against a light topspin, however, all you can return is a light backspin. And against backspin, a long pips push will either return a light topspin or at most a no-spin ball. (Weak players constantly hit this off the end, expecting backspin.)

Note that the longer and thinner the pips, and the more frictionless they are, the greater the long pips effect. No sponge or very thin sponge also dramatically increases it.

Basically, conventional surfaces put their own spin on the ball. Antispin mostly deadens the ball. But long pips reverses the spin, something many players are not used to. The amount of spin you receive from long pips depends more on the spin on your previous shot rather than on the long pips stroke itself. This is what makes long pips the hardest surface to play against for most. But don't despair. It is also one of the hardest to control.

Against a ball with no spin, a long pips user can only return no spin or at most (if there is sponge under the long pips) a very light spin. This makes it easy to attack against, at least for one shot. To keep attacking effectively, you must understand the way long pips returns different shots and be prepared for the spin reversal against your spin shots, and spinless returns against your no-spin shots, regardless of the stroke used by the user of the long pips. It can completely throw off your reflexes since the spins (or no-spins) of the returns are contrary to what you are used to. But they are predictable and you should be able to adjust to them with practice.

If you serve no-spin serves to long pips, you'll get no-spin returns to attack. You generally don't want to serve spin to them, though some long pips players are so used to getting no-spin serves that they have trouble with spin serves, so perhaps use them as a variation. If you serve backspin to long pips and they push it back, you get your own spin back as topspin or at most no-spin.

Long pips is difficult to attack with, except against backspin or short balls. Against backspin, it is easier to attack with but the effectiveness of the attack is mostly due to the weirdness of the playing characteristics of the surface. Most balls attacked with long pips with a topspin stroke will have less spin than expected (unless the attack is against heavy backspin) and so are often returned into the net. But once you have adjusted to the lack of spin of a long pips attack, it should give you less trouble.

The two features of long pips that make it attractive to choppers and blockers are the ease in returning loops and drives, and the heavy backspin spin reversal returns against loops.

Next to antispin (and perhaps a hardbat), long pips is the easiest surface to chop or block a loop back with because the spin doesn't take on it. And since the looper gets all his spin back, he will have great difficulty in continuing his attack. Thus long pips is especially effective when chopping or blocking against loops. The only problem is that if the looper pushes against a backspin return, the long pips player might have to push. If he does so with long pips, his return not only will have little spin (and often some topspin) and be easy to attack, but it will also be difficult to keep low. A backspin ball travels in a straighter line and so is easy to keep at just above net height, while still going deep. But a spinless (or light topspin) push with long pips arcs more and so is difficult to keep low, and if kept low, will tend to land short, making it easy to attack. Only a good touch and a lot of practice will enable a player to push effectively with long pips.

The better players with long pips often learn to quick-push aggressively against backspin, essentially a quick-block, usually done with the backhand. Opponents often read this as backspin and pop the ball up; instead they should treat it as any other topspin.

One solution is to have inverted sponge on one side and learn to flip. Even if the long pips player can't flip fast enough to always use the side he wants for every shot, at least his opponent can't get into a rhythm, expecting a weak return every time the long pips player pushes.

Against long pips, you don't want to spin too much, since you'll get your own spin back. Often loop soft with light topspin, looking for weak returns you can smash or loop for winners. Be patient and pick your shots.

Against a passive player with long pips, especially a blocker without sponge who dead blocks everything, play lots of spinless balls, since this takes away the long pips player's advantage in returning spin, and so you get lots of no-spin balls that you should be able to attack, often right off the bounce. Keep the ball deep so you'll have time to react to each shot—don't let him rush you.

Since most players with long pips have inverted on the other side, attack that side, since you are probably more comfortable there. But turn their long pips into a weakness by choosing when to go to that side (usually with spinless shots) and when to go to the inverted side (usually with spin).

Table Tennis Tactics for Thinkers

Long Pips Blockers

One of the trickiest styles to play is a long pips blocker (often called a "push-blocker"), especially if they play with no sponge under their long pips, and with the most frictionless pips they can use. This maximizes the long pips effect. It makes it easy to block against topspin and somewhat easy to quick-push or attack backspin.

But if you play this style, you will always (at least in theory) be at the mercy of your opponent. It can be difficult to push with since you cannot create backspin, and almost impossible to attack a topspin or no-spin, even a light one or one that is high. (Unless, of course, you have an attacking surface on the other side and know how to use it.) Yet some players have found success this way, often with the long pips on the backhand and an attacking forehand with inverted or short pips. They may flip to keep you off guard but basically rely on the long pips to keep the ball in play, moving the ball around until you make a mistake. With this style, the problem with pushing can be solved by staying close to the table, as blockers do, and pushing right off the bounce with a quick-blocking motion. This enables the blocker to be as close to his target as possible and therefore easier to keep the ball low while rushing and angling the opponent, even though the pushes are dead or with topspin. The ball comes out with a light topspin, which is hard for opponents to adjust to since it looks like a backspin shot. (Choppers with long pips normally can't do this as well since they can't stay close to the table since they need to back up to chop.)

The key to playing against this style is to play mostly without spin. Serve deep dead balls (or backspin balls if the opponent pushes them back and you are comfortable against these weird yet weak topspins), and continue to rally deep and with little spin, essentially just patting the ball back and forth until you see an easy ball to attack. You may feel like a beginner, but it's effective. You can give light topspin to control the ball, and if you move it around, eventually you'll get a weak ball you can pounce on to smash or loop kill.

However, the minute you really loop the ball with spin, if it comes back you'll get your spin back as backspin, and the long pips blocker is at home—so only loop aggressively when you can go for a winner or to set up a winner, and if you don't get a weak return, push or loop softly (in both cases without much spin) and start over. Give him dead ball after dead ball, move the ball around the table, and be patient and yet decisive when you see a shot to end the point.

Try to groove your attack against the many no-spin or light backspin returns you'll be getting. You should be able to loop or smash winners off many of them, especially if the ball doesn't land deep. Be patient and wait for the right one to end the point with.

Some long pips blockers try to essentially cover the whole table with their backhand blocks. Challenge them to see if they can do this by attacking the wide corners. A player like this might block well, but probably cannot attack much, and so you can play steady until you see the right shot to put away.

Since the blocker is close to the table, he is vulnerable to last-second changes of direction, so often aim one way, then go the other way. If the blocker uses both sides of his racket, he's probably weak in the middle so go there.

A long pips blocker is vulnerable when returning serves, if you know what to do and have a decent attack. He cannot put spin on your deep no-spin serves, he generally cannot attack them, and he can't rush you, since your serves are deep. So on your serve, you should often get one good shot against his return of your serve. (But watch out for last-second changes of directions, which is how a long pips blocker often stops an opponent's attack.) If you don't get a good ball to attack, or if the long pips blocker returns your attack effectively, be patient and start over. No-spin or light topspin shots, patience, and decisive putaways (to wide angles or the middle, as always) when the shot is there are the keys. Serve at wide angles (including to forehand), and fast to the middle (which may be toward the forehand side for backhand-oriented blockers).

Here's an example of how I beat a very strong long-pips blocker in a tournament a number of years ago. He had no sponge under his pips, and often covered the entire table with his backhand. I knew that I could play angled shots into his weak forehand or middle. If he tried to cover those shots with his backhand, he'd leave the wide backhand open, especially if I faked to his forehand side, then switched directions to the wide backhand. However, I figured there was only one way this player could beat me, and that was if I had trouble with the long pips. So rather than play into his weaknesses, I played right into his strength, mostly with light topspin or no-spin serves and rally shots deep to his steady backhand long-pips blocking, so I could get comfortable against the surface without having to worry about one shot being long pips, the next inverted. I'd get no-spin or light backspin returns, and when I got the right one, I'd rip it; otherwise I'd just patiently rally, waiting for the right shot. The first game was close, but near the end I went after his forehand and middle, and won. (In this case, his "middle" was actually well over on his forehand side.) In game two, I again went right into the long pips, again it was close, and again at the end I went after his forehand and middle, and again I won. In the third I went after his forehand and middle right from the start and won easily.

Table Tennis Tactics for Thinkers

Long Pips Blockers with Aggressive Forehands

A version of the long pips blocker is one who mostly blocks passively on the backhand side, but attacks on the forehand. Some will move around, attacking with the forehand from all parts of the table, which often means they are less weak in the middle, but their backhand blocking will be less consistent, since they are looking for balls to attack with their forehand. Others will mostly only attack against balls to the forehand, and are notoriously weak in the middle, plus when in trouble you can safely go to their backhand. And others sometimes will flip their racket and attack with their backhand, which leaves them vulnerable on the forehand (as well as middle), where they often aren't so good with the long pips.

Deng Yaping blocked and hit with her long pips backhand, but attacked all-out with her inverted forehand. She was World Women's Singles Champion three times and Olympic Women's Singles Gold Medalist twice.
Photo by John Oros

Against these types of players you are under tremendous pressure since if you play soft, spinless rallies, the opponent attacks. So you have to be more aggressive—but now you can attack their forehand side aggressively (as well as middle), and then go soft to the wide backhand when in trouble. (If they are very aggressive with the forehand, then play them like a one-winged looper or hitter.) Another weakness of this style is that it's difficult to block off the bounce over and over on the backhand and still be ready to attack with the forehand, so this type of player makes a lot of mistakes when he attacks—and when he does attack, he often has trouble switching back to effective blocks on the backhand side, so perhaps go to the forehand and back to the backhand or middle, and then tee off.

How to Play a Player Who Attacks With the Long Pips

One of the most difficult shots to handle is a ball attacked by a player with long pips. These players often have fast sponge under their long pips (usually on the backhand) and a fast racket. (There are also players who attack with antispin, but they are far fewer. Play them similarly to how you would play a long pips attacker.) You have little time to respond to an attacked ball, and so have to rely on your reflexes—except your reflexes usually aren't tuned to reacting to a ball attacked by long pips. So how do you handle this? Here are four ways.

1. Don't let them attack. Long pips can generally only attack against backspin, or sometimes against a short and weak topspin or no-spin ball. So keep the ball deep, and usually either put no spin on the ball (and so get a no-spin ball back) or give topspin (and so usually get a slower backspin ball return). Some players use medium-long pips so they can attack better, but then they lose much of the long pips effect as their rubber plays somewhat like short pips.
2. Take a step off the table, and return with a topspin drive of some sort. By backing off the table, you have time to respond. By putting topspin on the ball, the ball arcs onto the table, and stops the long-pipped player from attacking with the long pips again. You don't need to topspin too aggressively, just enough to force the long pips player to block, since it is very difficult to attack even a soft topspin ball with long pips.
3. Stay near the table, open your racket to counter hit, and be willing to lose a number of points as you get used to his shots. But don't try to be quicker than the long pips attacker—he's probably more used to your surface than you are to his, so you need more time to respond. Once you are used to the long pips, you should be able to out-rally them in any fast exchange.
4. Play against players who attack with long pips in practice as often as possible until you get used to it.

* * * * *

Here is a little poem I wrote that was published in USA Table Tennis Magazine many years ago. The gist of the poem was the tongue-in-cheek idea that "weird rubbers" will make you a better player. While there is some truth to this—in particular when you play someone who doesn't know how to play that surface—it works both ways. If your opponent is used to your "weird rubber" and knows how to play it, then his equipment gives him a tremendous advantage. After all, if these "weird rubbers" were an advantage, why isn't everyone using it? But there is no question that many matches are won and lost because someone doesn't know how to play or isn't used to playing against a particular surface. Don't let this happen to you!

Little Jack Ding-Dong
  By Larry Hodges
Little Jack Ding-Dong,
Was rotten at Ping-Pong,
But he could not figure why.
He tried some weird rubber,
And beat a top player,
And said, "What a good player am I!"

Table Tennis Tactics for Thinkers

CHAPTER EIGHTEEN
Hardbat Tactics

Why am I including a chapter on hardbat in a book on tactics, when all the best players in the world play with sponge? (Except when they occasionally play in a hardbat event, of course.) Because there are a lot of hardbat players, both old-timers and new ones who simply prefer the hardbat game, and there are hardbat events at some tournaments. Besides, it's a pet interest of mine. (No, I'm not from the hardbat era; I'm only 52 as of this writing.) Though I'm normally a sponge player, I often play in hardbat events at major tournaments where I'm primarily coaching. I've

The flamboyant and all-time hardbat great Marty Reisman.
Photo by Mal Anderson

been U.S. National and U.S. Open Hardbat Champion in singles (once each), and at those two tournaments have won Over 40 Hardbat four times and Hardbat Doubles 13 times. So I know a little about hardbat.

Hardbat is how the game was played during the "Classic Era," roughly the mid-1920s to 1950s, with pimpled rubber and no sponge. (Sponge was introduced in 1952.) Some players still favor that style of play over the modern sponge game of hyper-speed and spin. To learn more about hardbat, go to www.hardbat.com. Watch some of the videos, both of modern hardbat and hardbat from the classic age.

Hard rubber is basically pips-out sponge without the sponge. It is somewhat difficult to attack against heavy topspin with hard rubber though it's not that hard to smash against a normal topspin drive. It's rather easy to attack backspin, though the attacks aren't as overwhelming as a strong inverted loop. It is also very easy to chop or drive with hard rubber, and you can put a decent backspin on the ball with it by snapping your wrist into the ball at contact and just grazing the ball.

The most common question asked by newcomers to the hardbat game is, "How should I play different than with my sponge racket?" My recommendation is to take the best of both worlds—the best of the game as it was played in the classic age and the best of your own sponge game, including the advances made on the game from the sponge era.

Table tennis in the classic age was a different game than the modern sponge game, a different sport. Instead of the power, spin and short rallies of the modern game, there were longer rallies, a more equal emphasis on attack and defense, finesse and ball control, and rallies that were more understandable to a viewer than the hard-to-explain serve & rip (or miss) game often seen with sponge. Instead of bang-bang, end-the-point now rallies, there were duels between attacker and defender, often with both players taking their turn at attack and defense. There were also straight counter-hitting rallies, not much different than with sponge.

The modern sponge game has developed new techniques that were relatively unknown during the hardbat age, and some of these techniques work with hardbat as well. Specifically, modern hardbat players can develop deceptive and surprisingly spinny serves, and some, using modern looping techniques, have even learned to loop against backspin with more topspin than was probably seen in the classic age. Because of this, and because most modern hardbat players learned with sponge, the modern hardbat game is dominated by all-out attackers, just as the sponge game is. However, there are still a number of defensive players, and many of the all-out attackers do play chopping defense when they are in trouble, including myself. (With hardbat, I'm an all-out forehand attacker, but mostly chop on the backhand.)

You can't create as much spin with a hardbat as with sponge, but you can create enough to make the serve effective, especially if you disguise the spin by sudden changes of the paddle's direction around contact. Because you can't get as much spin with a hardbat, and because spin takes less on a hardbat than on a sponge bat (so opponents will return your spin more easily), hardbat serves are generally not as effective as sponge serves. The hardbat simply brings the serving game down to a less dominating level than in the sponge game—while still allowing you to use those "sponge serves" rather effectively with hardbat. You might not win as many points outright with these serves, but they will allow you to take the initiative in most rallies.

So how should one play differently with a hardbat than with a sponge bat? Use your normal (sponge) playing style as a starting point; sprinkle in a variety of classic and modern techniques; practice well; and soon you'll be transported back in time to the game as it was played at what many consider its peak—but with a few secret weapons!

Except where indicated, the following is for hardbat versus hardbat. However, much of it also applies to hardbat versus sponge, which has a section following. There's also a section on playing against hardbat, which sponge players should read, even if they skip the rest of this chapter.

Table Tennis Tactics for Thinkers

Hardbat Serving

During the hardbat era, serving was generally not a major weapon. Service technique simply had not been developed to the degree that it has in the sponge game. This makes sense, since you can't get as much spin with a hardbat, and so you are more limited in what you can do. However, in the sponge era, service techniques have reached an extremely high level, and these techniques have spread to the hardbat game.

First, a reality check. Unlike the sponge game, you aren't going to dominate with your serve against players your own level. However, you can use modern serve techniques to both take the initiative when serving against your peers, and to dominate against many weaker players, thereby avoiding upsets.

It's assumed that you know how to serve with spin (if not, go practice and perhaps see a coach), and have some knowledge of modern serve techniques. If you don't . . . well, you can always emulate the great hardbat masters, and serve just to get the ball in play. If you want to use your serve to take the initiative against your peers, and dominate against weaker players, learn some modern serving techniques, and then follow these tips.

Contact: With sponge, the key to spin is to just graze the ball with a grippy surface, accelerating the racket to maximum speed at contact, knowing that the surface will grab the ball no matter how fast the paddle is moving. If you use the same technique with a hardbat, the ball will slide some, and you'll get less spin. With a hardbat, you need to contact the ball with the racket moving somewhat slower—and then rapidly accelerate through the ball. (Since a hardbat is lighter than a sponge paddle, this is easy to do.) You want to lengthen the contact, which allows the pips to grab the ball rather than slide, so you can maximize the spin.

Spin vs. Deception: Since you can't get as much spin with a hardbat as with sponge, it is important to be deceptive. Right at contact, change directions, so the opponent has trouble figuring, for example, if you are serving light sidespin-backspin or light sidespin-topspin. Hardbat is a game of precision, and it only takes a little to throw the opponent off enough to force a slightly weak ball to attack and take the initiative.

Height: Hardbat is great for flipping short balls. Therefore, it is extremely important to serve low in hardbat. To do so, contact the ball low to the table. If you contact the ball too high, the ball will bounce high. Many players serve too high and don't realize it until they find their serve getting attacked in a tournament by a strong player.

Depth: Very short, low serves are very effective, both with spin and with no-spin, with a fake spin motion. Many players find fast & deep serves even more effective, especially if mixed in with short ones. Some players can hit against fast & deep serves, but many have trouble doing so with any speed and consistency. By serving deep, you have more time to see the incoming ball, more time to respond, and there will be less angle on the return. Plus, you don't have to worry about inverted loops! By serving fast, you rush the opponent, and force him to return with his weaker side if you choose. Be ready to follow a fast & deep serve with a strong drive or smash. Since there are players who are very good at hitting deep serves with a hardbat—I'm one of them!— be flexible with this tactic.

No-spin: Short, very low no-spin serves are very effective in hardbat, both singles and doubles. Surprisingly, they are often harder to attack aggressively than serves with spin, plus it is easier to keep them very low.

Look for Weaknesses: Throw all your serve variations at the opponent as early as possible to find which ones give him trouble. Most players have at least one type of serve that they aren't particularly comfortable returning, or that sets you up to attack, and it is your job to find it.

Choppers: Choppers often make the mistake of just serving to get the ball in play. That's throwing away an advantage. Instead, put pressure on your opponent by mixing in at least some tricky serves, and never let the opponent know if you are going to chop or attack. If you can't react or move fast enough to be able to choose between attacking or chopping depending on the return, decide before serving, and be decisive for that one shot. Then fall back and chop if you don't see an easy attack or putaway. (For more on chopping, see the chapter on Chopping.)

Hardbat Receive

The main differences between hardbat and sponge receive are 1) hardbatters don't usually loop deep serves, and when they do, it's not as spinny; 2) it's often easier to attack a short ball with hardbat; 3) hardbatters have more control; and 4) hardbatters cannot create as much backspin when pushing a serve back, though some can create a surprising amount.

You can almost divide hardbat players into two types of effective receivers—those who mostly attack the serve (that would be me), and those who use finesse. Most players can do both, but favor one or the other.

Since spin doesn't take much on a hardbat (and a hardbat serve doesn't have as much spin as a sponge serve), attacking the serve is not that hard if you have a good stroke. The key is to take the ball quick off the bounce with a sharp and well-placed stroke. Many players forget the "well-placed" part—make sure to attack at wide angles and at the opponent's middle. Since you have so much control with a hardbat (instead of a devastating sponge loop), it's easier to do last-second changes of direction.

Table Tennis Tactics for Thinkers

Aim one way, then go the other. Remember, your goal is to mess up your opponent.

Another way to mess up the opponent is with finesse. Very low, angled-off pushes, both short and long, taken right off the bounce to rush the opponent, can be highly effective in stopping a server's attack.

That's me smacking in a forehand in the Hardbat Doubles Final at the USA Nationals one year. Though I normally use sponge, I won Hardbat Doubles 13 times (at Open or Nationals), nine times with my partner here (Ty Hoff), and four times with Steve Berger (an opponent here, on left, wearing a "Hardbat Rules" shirt - I have one too). The other opponent seemingly looking on in rapt fascination at my smash is the illustrious Marty Reisman.
Photo by John Oros

Hardbat Rallying

Like sponge, there are a huge number of hardbat styles leading to a myriad number of rallying possibilities. There's no way of covering it with any type of comprehensiveness, so we'll just cover the general rallies. Use your tactical and strategic thinking skills to figure out what's best for you.

The four most common type of hardbat rallies are hitter versus chopper; hitter versus hitter; hitter versus blocker; and pushing. You should probably learn all of these strokes, but develop your own favorite shots. Contrary to popular belief, there aren't a lot of long pushing rallies in hardbat, but just as with sponge, pushing, done properly and at the right time, is effective.

Some players are mostly all-out hitters from both sides, while others are steady counter-drivers. Others hit mostly on one side, while chopping on the other. (That would be me!) Some favor blocking, though that's not too successful at the higher levels of hardbat play—too easy to hit through, though some hit on the forehand side, and block on the backhand. (Without sponge, it's difficult to block too aggressively, and so blocking is more effective with sponge than with hardbat.) Others favor chopping, either long-range chopping from way back or relatively close to the table chopping, pick-hitting when the chance comes up.

Just as with sponge, develop as many tactical weapons as you can, and learn to use them.

If you are a long-time sponge player, you can either adopt a hardbat style that roughly matches your sponge game (probably the most successful way, and usually means mostly attacking and counter-hitting), or you can learn to play a more classical style, perhaps mixing in more chopping than you'd do with sponge (probably the most fun way, and in the long run you might actually be better this way, since you'd be adding more weapons to your tactical toolbox). Ultimately, the most successful hardbat style for you is the style that is most successful for you, and the funnest hardbat style for you is the style that is most fun for you. Read that over a few times.

If you do become a hardbat attacker, as you play you'll learn the various nuances of attack. For example, I'm known for my forehand hitting, and yet few realize I have a regular smash, an inside-out smash, an off-the-bounce quick-hit, a top-of-the-bounce drive, an off-table counter-drive, a loop, and a roll when in trouble. Each has its place, and if you took any away, my game would suffer. I also use all sorts of misdirection, aiming one way, then going the other.

Learn to vary the spin when pushing and especially when chopping. A hardbat's control allows you to vary your spin somewhat easily, especially backspin when pushing or chopping. You do this with the wrist. If you do the vigorous wrist snap *after* contact, you get little spin even though it looks spinny, which will mess up your opponent. A favorite of choppers is a sudden no-spin or light chop to the middle. Opponents tend to lift too much, and by going to the middle, they don't have a long diagonal to go for, and so have less table—and so they go off the end.

Chopping is a relatively rare style in sponge play, where looping dominates. With hardbat, it's far more common. One of the advantages of this style is that it leads to long, physical rallies where the chopper has to cover a lot of ground to return shot after shot. This makes it an excellent aerobic exercise, as well as a lot of fun.

Choppers should often chop to the middle of the table, avoiding chopping too often to the corners. Chops to the corners gave the attacker a wide angle to attack into, and it's difficult to cover that angle and the sudden down-the-line shot as well. A chop to a corner gives the attacker a long diagonal to attack into, and with the extra table, it is easier to smash. Also remember that a chopper can't normally win an angling contest against an attacker—the attacker has a lot more time to cover the wide angles against your chops than you do against his attacks. Because hardbat attackers generally take the ball a lot quicker off the bounce than sponge players, these aspects are even more important in the hardbat game than the sponge game. The primary exception would be against a strong attack

Table Tennis Tactics for Thinkers

to a wide angle, where you most often would chop diagonally to the opposite corner just for safety, since it gives you the most table to aim for. Of course, this doesn't mean a chopper should go to the middle over and over—he should move the ball around, forcing the attacker to move, especially if he's chopping from close to the table.

The extra ball control from a hardbat makes drop shots much easier. Use them regularly, especially against choppers, but also when returning an attacker's short serve or against a push. The constant in-and-out will force the opponent into mistakes.

If you are an attacker, develop both a quick-hitting drive and a smash. A hardbat's control allows you to hit the ball quick off the bounce and to smash slightly high balls. Learn to attack to the wide angles and middle, just as sponge players do. You also need to handle an opponent's attack, and there are three ways. You can chop; you can block; or you can counter-hit.

One common misconception is that it is difficult to hit against backspin with a hardbat. This is because most inverted players only loop against backspin, and the drive against backspin is a dying art. It's actually a relatively easy shot with a hardbat, where you just stroke upward with a slightly open racket.

Hardbat versus Sponge

What about using a hardbat against sponge? I once played full-time hardbat for six months, including nine tournaments against sponge, and my level only dropped about 50 points in USATT ratings. Here are ten things I learned about how to play sponge players with a hardbat.

1. Remember the advantages of hardbat—primarily better control and better attack off short balls, plus the sponge player probably isn't used to playing against a hardbat. Use your control to play finesse shots such as short pushes and chop-blocks against the sponge player's attack. Attack short balls off the bounce to wide angles and opponent's middle, rushing him into mistakes. The quicker you play, the more problems the sponge player will have adjusting to your hardbat.
2. You'll be more successful if you focus on the extremes—either all-out attack or all-out defense. This doesn't mean you can't do both, but you should favor one, at least in any given rally (though you can switch in mid-rally), and whichever you do, go all-out. A tentative defense or tentative attack doesn't work very well against sponge. If playing defense, you can either chop or chop-block—both can be effective against sponge players.

3. If you attack all-out right from the start of the rally (including attacking the serve), you can mess up a sponge player. If you instead hit softer or use steady countering shots, you are playing into the sponge player's game, since he'll have time to adjust to your shot, and then his sponge advantage will take over as his sponge rebounds your shot back with topspin, and you'll quickly lose the initiative. So when you attack, be decisive. End the point quickly if you get the chance. This doesn't mean going for risky or dumb shots, it means taking the shot when it is there, and when it is not, hitting quick, aggressive and well-placed shots to set up the shot you can smash.
4. If you play defense, don't just chop the ball back. Change the spin. Hardbat gives you more control, and if you don't take advantage of this by mixing things up, you aren't taking advantage of the few advantages a hardbat has over sponge. As noted earlier, a favorite of choppers is a sudden no-spin or light chop to the middle. Opponents tend to lift too much, and by going to the middle, they don't have a long diagonal to go for, and so have less table—and so they go off the end.
5. Change the pace. A hardbat's control allows you to hit one ball, then dead-block the next. This will play havoc with a sponge player's timing. The key is that when you dead-block, really dead-block; don't just hit a softer drive that the sponge player can counter-attack easily. Against a loop, a quick, off-the bounce chop-block is one of the most effective shots, throwing off the timing of many loopers. Blocking isn't particularly effective hardbat to hardbat, but hardbat chop-blocks against inverted loopers can dominate a match.
6. Change the spin. As noted above in hardbat rallying, hardbat's control allows you to vary your spin, especially backspin when pushing or chopping. You do this with the wrist—you can get a surprising amount of backspin if you snap the wrist into the ball while grazing it. If you do the wrist snap vigorously *after* contact, you get little spin even though it looks spinny, which will mess up your opponent.
7. Learn to attack backspin decisively. While you can't loop against backspin as well as a sponge player, you can hit through it, or you can learn to loop it. (Yes, as noted earlier, you can loop against backspin with a hardbat.) Whether you hit or loop, you have to be aggressive when the sponge player pushes or serves backspin. If you just push it back, he gets to loop, usually his favorite weapon. (Exception—if you are a chopper, then you can mostly push, but push well and look for weak pushes to attack.)

Table Tennis Tactics for Thinkers

8. Attack decisively if the opponent gets soft. If you just keep the ball in play, the sponge player can topspin you to death or wait until he sees a ball to loop aggressively.
9. Learn to hit weak loops. It's not as hard as it seems, once you get the knack of it. The key is to choose which ones to hit—primarily slower loops that land short on the table, or weaker loops that aren't as spinny. Deep or spinny loops are much harder to hit.
10. Hardbat is very good against long pips and antispin, both of which are designed to return spin. They are both at their best against heavy spin, especially topspin, and so are better against inverted. A hardbat player doesn't give them as much spin to return, and so often dominates against long pips and antispin with steady drives and smashes.

Sponge versus hardbat

What about when a sponge player plays against a hardbat player? This is sort of like someone with a machine gun asking how to take on someone with a bow and arrow.

The hardbat player has three primary advantages over a sponge player. The big three are:

1. Pure ball control
2. Easy to hit with against anything except extreme spins
3. Sponge players usually are not used to playing against hardbat

The sponge player has numerous advantages over the hardbat player. The big five are:

1. Looping
2. Spinny serves
3. Counter-hitting
4. Heavy pushes
5. Fishing and lobbing

If your opponent chops with a hardbat, play him like any other chopper—see the chapter on Choppers.

If your opponent attacks with a hardbat, you can stop that attack simply by looping. A hardbat player can't effectively attack a strong loop, and will be forced to block or chop. Once on the defense, your loop should dominate, unless the hardbat player is simply better. A sponge player should use the natural advantages of sponge—speed and spin—and overpower the hardbat player. (But use tactics to set up your overpowering shots.) Above all, do not get soft, or most hardbat players will dominate with their hitting.

Use spinny serves to take the initiative. Here's where sponge players often mess up—they serve short, allowing the hardbat player to rush them with flips, short pushes, and quick angled pushes. These are things hardbat players excel at, so why give it to them? Instead, serve deep, and look to follow up the serve, hopefully by looping. This doesn't mean you always serve long; mix it up. Against some hardbat players, a short serve might be the most effective serve, especially if you keep it very low.

A hardbat player cannot normally compete in a counter-hitting duel with a sponge player. If he does, it's because he's simply better, or because the sponge player isn't used to the hardbat player's flatter counter-hits. If the latter, the sponge player needs to play into these rallies over and over until he gets used to them. He must win this type of rally since he's got the better weapon for it. A common mistake is to get soft and give the hardbat player easy balls to hit.

Heavy pushes give many hardbat players difficulty since most cannot loop them effectively. There are some hardbat players who can loop heavy backspin, and others are good at quick-hitting them, so beware of these players. Most will have difficulty with this, as long as the heavy push is low, deep, and angled. The same tactics from the chapter on Pushing apply here.

When all else fails against a hardbat attacker, fish and lob with topspin, if these are tactical weapons you have developed. While some hardbat players have no trouble with this, others have difficulty. They often cannot smash against topspin with the same consistency as a sponge player, and they don't have sponge to give them extra speed. Keep the ball deep with good topspin, and the hardbatter will have great difficulty. A weakness of fishing and lobbing against hardbat is that often a sponge player does this because he's not comfortable against hardbat, and gets defensive against even soft drives. Instead, get used to the surface and play defense only when necessary.

* * * * *

In closing, here's a poem I wrote about hardbat, which features three of the greatest hardbat champions of all time—Marty Reisman, Dick Miles, and Sol Schiff. It's not about tactics, but I'm going to include it anyway. (And no, I'm not ripping on sponge so much as I'm celebrating the hardbat game. Or at least that's my intent.) Enjoy!

Table Tennis Tactics for Thinkers

The Classic Game
By Larry Hodges

Reisman and Miles and Schiff, oh my!
On chopping and hitting and blocks they'd rely.
No sponges or gluing or carbon blades used,
Just classical ping-pong, before rules were abused.

'Twas a time of pure ping-pong, with rallies so pure,
Observers could watch and see the allure,
Of rallies of topspin and backspin so clear,
Beginners would join in with nary a fear.

But then came the sponges, soaking up life,
Leading the game into a great strife,
And soon a sport that had been really hip,
Became just short rallies of serve and then *rip!*

So always remember when you come by this page,
To remember that once, hardbat was the rage!
And so on these pages we keep lit the flame,
Of the pure and most classical form of the game!

Hardbat Superstars! L-R: Sol Schiff, Dick Miles, Lou Pagliaro, Dean Johnson, and Marty Reisman. Photo courtesy of Dean Johnson

Larry Hodges

Sandpaper

There's a growing sandpaper movement in the U.S. and the Philippines, sometimes called Liha table tennis. The Philippine players are currently the best in the world, and usually play under "Liha" rules, which you can learn about at www.hardbat.com. I've played some sandpaper, which tends to bring back "classic" table tennis, with more of an equal emphasis on attack and defense. (Modern hardbat tends to favor attack.) Suffice to say that with sandpaper, it's easy to attack backspin or to chop back attacks, but it's difficult to counter-attack. And so most rallies quickly become spectacular attack versus chop rallies. If you want to learn more about sandpaper table tennis, see the following:

Ty Hoff won numerous sponge titles, then numerous hardbat titles, and now is a sandpaper specialist, winning the Sandpaper event at the 2012 U.S. Open. He also runs the Federal Association of Sandpaper Table Tennis (see below).
Photo Courtesy of JOOLA USA

- **Federal Association of Sandpaper Table Tennis**: www.ttprotour.com
- **Table Tennis Nation**: www.tabletennisnation.com
- **U.S. Sandpaper Table Tennis Association**: www.floridatt.com/sandpapertt/news.php
- **The Untold Story of Liha**: www.carytta.net/sandpaperliha.htm

Colorful Liha buttons given to me by the Philippine Team at the 2012 U.S. Open.

Table Tennis Tactics for Thinkers

CHAPTER NINETEEN
Doubles Tactics

Tactics in doubles can be complex. It's like singles except now you have four styles to worry about instead of just two. The points are often shorter, and serve and receive become even more important. Placement also

China's Men's Coach Liu Guoliang coaches 2011 World Men's Doubles Champions Xu Xin and Ma Long between games.
Photo by Diego Schaaf

becomes more important as it is easy to win points by catching an opponent out of position. Generally, at the intermediate and advanced levels, the more aggressive team wins since one hot player can carry a team.

A lefty/righty combination has an inherent advantage, especially if each player favors the forehand. They can stand in their respective backhand corners, their natural ready position, without getting in each other's way. A lefty/righty combination can play mostly forehand shots, or at least stay in their natural ready positions, while two right-handers (or two left-handers) have to move quickly to keep up a forehand attack or to stay in position. (Doubles tends to favor forehand attackers over backhand players, since it's easier to hit forehands on the move, with a larger hitting zone than on the backhand.) However, though lefty/righty teams often dominate tournaments, many same-handed teams have become very good, including many world champion teams. It just takes good footwork and practice together.

Player Roles

It's often best to have one player focus on set-up and the other on attack. It's often the stronger player who plays set-up, as that is often more difficult than the attack itself.

The set-up player plays more control, looking to set up his partner to attack. He does this with placement and variation. For example, he might drop a ball short, catching an opponent off guard and forcing them to move in to push, often resulting in a long push or weak flip. Or the set-up player may go for a slow, spinny loop to set up his partner. However, while the set-up player doesn't usually go for risky attack shots, he has to be decisive in following up his partner's attacks, especially if he gets a putaway shot.

The attacker focuses on attack. Since he knows his partner is trying to set him up, he can simplify his game, looking to attack over and over. At the higher levels, this player's job is often to just loop everything.

Doubles Signals

The server in doubles should normally signal his partner with his hand under the table what the serve will be. There are several types of signals, but here are the ones that I believe are most common. It is assumed that all serves are short unless you start the signal by pointing at the opponents (under the table), which means a long serve. (At lower levels, where players mostly serve long and the opponents usually can't loop it, you might not need this.)

Kasumi Ishikawa of Japan signals her partner.
Photos by Diego Schaaf

You then point down with your index finger or up with your thumb to signal backspin or topspin. If the serve has sidespin, you then point with your index finger or thumb the direction of the sidespin. If it's a no-spin serve, you make a fist. Sometimes the stronger or more experienced player will signal the serve, even if his partner is serving. Or the players can have short consultations before serving.

Table Tennis Tactics for Thinkers

Doubles Serves

Because your opponent knows where you are serving (into his forehand side), deep serves are rarely used in doubles at higher levels except as a rare surprise. They are too easy to attack. Most teams favor short and very low backspin or no-spin serves (which will often set your partner up to attack, especially with a loop), with occasional short topspin-sidespin. The problem with short topspin-sidespin serves is that they can be flipped to a wide angle more easily, and if placed well, can cause the serving team to get in each other's way. Low backspin and no-spin serves are harder to flip aggressively.

Many players learn to serve in doubles with the backhand serve, which is often the easiest serve to serve very low. It also gives you a sidespin that breaks away from the receiver, which is effective against forehand receives, which is how most players return in doubles so they can more easily loop any serve that goes long. Even though my best serve is my forehand pendulum serve, I often switch to mostly backhand serving in doubles against righties who receive forehand. If they receive backhand, then I usually use more forehand pendulum serves. (If you are mostly serving backspin and no-spin serves, then just go with whichever serve motion that's lower and more deceptive.)

Most players are used to serving in singles, mostly from the backhand side, and so do not have good doubles serves, where you have to serve from the right-hand side crosscourt. Practice these serves if you want to be good at doubles. In particular learn to serve very low to the net and short, ideally so the second bounce would be near the end line.

It's often a good idea to serve toward the middle of the table, to cut off the wide angle and long diagonal if the receiver attacks. Such a crosscourt attack, especially with a flip against a short serve, are even more difficult to handle in doubles than in singles, since the server is often in his partner's way, and the partner may hesitate in moving to take the shot until the server steps back. (Woe be the server who steps to the right to get out of the way—and right to where the opponent has attacked the ball, thereby blocking his partner. He should always step *back*.) Serving toward the middle of the table also tends to put the receiver more in the way of his partner.

Remember that you are serving for your partner, not yourself, so make sure to discuss with him what type of serves he likes. You might have to find a compromise, as your best serves might not match what he wants. If necessary, go practice your serves so you can serve what needs to be served. At minimum, learn to serve low and short, with backspin and no-spin, and then you'll be ready for doubles.

Doubles Receive

Receivers should normally set up to receive with their strongest receiving side against serves. If they are stronger on the backhand or have a good banana flip, then they may receive backhand, even though the serve is going to the forehand corner. The main exception is if you have a lefty-righty team, where if the righty received backhand, he'd be in the lefty's way. (The lefty usually wants to stand near his right side of the table to favor his forehand. Even if he plays both sides more equally, his natural ready stance is on that side, since he'd want his playing elbow—midway between his forehand and backhand—near the center of the table.)

Xu Xin and Ma Long receiving serve. Who's receiving? Photo by Diego Schaaf

In the past, most players received forehand (and the majority still do), but these days many players are so much better receiving short serves with the backhand (often with banana flips) so as long as they can also loop the deep serve with the backhand, more and more are receiving backhand. However, if you are uncomfortable looping deep serves with your backhand, then you should probably receive forehand.

When receiving in doubles, be ready to attack any deep serve, mostly by looping. Vary the receive against short serves, but don't push deep too often or your partner may be faced with a strong attack. Mix in well-placed short and long pushes, and flips. It's often effective to attack the ball wide to the server's side so that he gets in the way of his partner. If the server's partner has a good loop, and the server is serving short backspin or no-spin, the ideal receive is often a short push. (If you have good touch, you may even drop short sidespin-topspin serves short.)

Short serves to the wide forehand give the receiver a wide angle to the opponents' wide forehand, which can cause havoc for the serving team, as noted in the section above on Doubles Serves.

Doubles Footwork

The simplest footwork method is for each player to take his shot, and then move backwards and *slightly* off to the side. This takes him out of the way of his opponent and keeps him in position for the next shot. If a

Table Tennis Tactics for Thinkers

player were to simply go off to the side, the opponents would quickly hit to that side before you are out of the way, and you would be in your partner's way. Even if he makes the shot, you would be way out of position for the next shot, which will undoubtedly be to the far side and out of reach, or else you'll be rushing so much to cover that shot that you'll leave the side you were on open. By tactically stepping backwards, your partner can move in front of you if necessary to cover the whole table.

While the above works for most cases, at the highest levels players learn to use circling footwork. (This assumes both are righties or both lefties, and both favor the forehand) After you take your shot, you back away from the table while your partner moves in from the backhand side, favoring his forehand. As your partner does this, you move off to the backhand side so that you can also approach the table from that side, also favoring your forehand. This takes lots of practice and teamwork to use effectively.

Roy Ke and Derek Nie. Doubles is for all ages. Photo by James Mu

Doubles Rallies

Doubles rallies are similar to singles rallies except that each player has to take into account his partner's playing style and abilities. For example, a defensive player might be perfectly at home letting the other team attack, but if his partner is an attacker, the partner might not be able to handle the opponent's attack.

In doubles, players are often slightly out of position and their partner is often in the way, so opponents are even more vulnerable to placement in doubles than in singles. Make sure to observe the player you are hitting toward. If he's not in position, punish him with placement. Often a player is still moving into position as you hit your shot; if you hit the ball behind him, he'll have great difficulty putting on the brakes and changing directions.

In and out movement is also highly effective in doubles since players are often stepping back to get out of the way of their partner. If you fake an attack and instead push or block the ball short, you may fake an opposing player out of his socks and out of the point.

Probably the most important rallying tactic in doubles is to hit the ball as wide as possible toward the opponent who hit the ball to you before he has a chance to get out of his partner's way. Ideally, hit wide to your opponents' weaker side, taking into account both players. Make them hit their weaker shots out of a two-person traffic jam. Remember, your tactical job is to mess up your opponents, and if that means causing a collision, great!

Done properly, loops are even more effective in doubles than in singles. This is because in doubles, you are constantly moving out of your partner's way, and then moving to get back to the table. It's generally easier to move and loop than to move and block. If the player you are hitting at is out of position, either loop to the open area or, since he will often be scrambling to cover that spot, aim behind him.

Serve or Receive?

In both singles and doubles, I usually advise players to choose to receive first, if they win the choice at the start of the match. This is the time when a player is most likely to miss easy shots—he may not yet be fully warmed up or he still may have early-match jitters—and it's better to blow a couple points receiving than on your serve, where you hope to win a majority of the points. (I wrote more about this near the end of the chapter on Conventional Tactics.)

Timothy Wang and Han Xiao, 2011 USA Men's Doubles Champions. Photo courtesy of JOOLA USA

In doubles, it's even more important to receive first. This allows you to set the order of play for the match. (Remember that in doubles, whichever team serves first has to choose which player serves first, and then the receiving pair gets to set the order for that game by choosing the receiver, with the order changing each game and when a team reaches five in the fifth.) You want to set an order that favors your team. How do you do this?

Suppose you have an order that favors your team, while the other team is favored with the other order. If you start the match with the bad order, then you will likely lose the first and third games, win the second and fourth, and start out the fifth by falling behind—but halfway through the fifth game, you'll switch sides and the order of play, and then you'll be in the good order in the second half of the fifth game, when the match is on the line. And if the two orders even out in that fifth game and you reach deuce, you'll have the good order at deuce, and probably win. So it is an advantage to start out a match with the bad order.

Table Tennis Tactics for Thinkers

However, you don't really change the order halfway through the fifth game; you do so when a team reaches five. Suppose your team starts the fifth game with the bad order. Suppose your team is down 4-5 when you switch sides in the fifth, and then the order changes to the better order, and now you outscore the other team 5-4. It's now 9-9, and you have the good order, both here and at deuce! Or suppose the order makes an even bigger difference, and you are down 3-5 at the switch, and then outscore them 5-3 with the good order. Then it's only 8-all, and you have the good order the rest of the way! So I recommend starting with the weaker order in the first game so that you'll have the strong order at the end of the fifth game.

It's actually more complicated than this, since about half the time you will only play two points when you reach deuce, and so the whole order of play—four different servers (and corresponding receivers) in a given game—is reduced to only two, and so the order that favors you overall might not favor you for those particular two. Few if anyone actually works it out that far, but it's something to consider in a big match.

The main reason to choose to serve first is if you or your partner needs to build up confidence, and so prefer to serve first. If you have a very nervous team (compared to your opponents), then you might consider this, though you might want to consult a sports psychologist later on.

Who on Your Team Should Serve First?

At the start of each game, the serving pair can choose which player serves first. When your team is serving, you should always start the game with your strongest combo of one serving the first two points, and the other receiving the next two. Why? Because after sixteen points have been played, all four players will have served four times, and you'll be back at the starting situation, which you'll have for the last four points.

In an unbalanced team, this often means having the weaker player serve first, so the stronger player can follow up his partner's serve twice and then receive twice. This maximizes how often the stronger player is in the rally while minimizing the weaker player's rally shots. If the stronger player serves first, he might be able to win points with his serve, but the weaker player will have to follow up the serve, and then will have to receive, while in both cases the stronger player will rally the least—in all four points, all three other players will hit the ball before the stronger player gets his first rally shot.

Hans, John, and Nathan Hsu - Doubles Champions at the 2012 Southern Open.

Doubles Serve Leads to Victory

At the Southern Open in 2012, John Hsu (a top USA 18-year-old, rated about 2250) and his dad (a recreational player, rated about 1300) played in Under 3600 Doubles. A few days before the tournament I saw them play a practice match, and realized they had a good chance—but only if they could avoid the same fate zillions of such lopsided teams had faced when playing together. A team like this would either be at its best or worst when the weaker player served, depending on how he served. If Hans could serve short and low, then they would dominate when he served. If his serves went long or popped up slightly, the opponents would attack, and things probably wouldn't turn out well. So Hans practiced that short serve extensively, and when they played, he kept it low and short. They won.

Did the short serve win them the event? No. What it did was give them the opportunity to win. In a different reality, where Hans didn't practice this serve, they likely would have lost, and never realize the opportunity they missed.

Team Roles

At the same Southern Open, Nathan Hsu (John's brother) teamed up with Yahao Zhang in Open Doubles as one of the lower seeds. The tactics changed match to match, but one thing remained constant. Yahao has a great attack, seemingly able to rip winners off anything long

Yahao Zhang and Nathan Hsu, 2012 Southern Open Doubles Champions.
Photo by Hans Hsu

from both sides. The key when playing with such a player is to focus on setting him up rather than trying to compete to see who can end the point first, a recipe for disaster. So I told Nathan to play control, with short pushes, deceptive flips, and steady loops. They won.

Table Tennis Tactics for Thinkers

CHAPTER TWENTY
Tournament Tactics

2009 Worlds Arena in Yokohama, Japan. Photo by Diego Schaaf

Now it's time to put it all together in a tournament. (When I say "tournament," this includes any important match, such as a league match.)

Ten-Point Plan to Tournament Success

1. **Put together a list of tips for yourself**
   For example, you might write down "Stay low" if you tend to stand up too straight. Or you might write down, "Relax and have fun." Or something tactical, such as "Serve short." You should refer to this list periodically throughout the tournament, and adjust as necessary.

2. **Decide what your mental frame of mind should be**
   Some players get too hyped up for their matches, and so don't play well. Others can't get up for their matches, and also don't play well. Decide where you stand in this spectrum, and either calm yourself down (as most need to do) or psyche yourself up before each match. Decide in advance what you need to do. You might prepare differently for each match, based on the opponent's playing style. If you anticipate that you will have to be more aggressive against one opponent, you might have to be more "psyched up" for that match. On the other hand, being hyped up might make you miss more. You have to decide what works for you.

3. **Work on specific strengths and weaknesses**
   Everyone has specific strengths and weaknesses that many of their matches are won or lost on. Decide what these shots are, and make sure to practice them both before and during the tournament. For example, if you have trouble with a specific serve, have someone serve it to you over and over—even if you have to pay someone to do it. Similarly, if you have a big strength, such as a forehand smash, make sure to get it going before the match begins, not when you've already dug yourself a hole by missing the first five attempts.

4. **Decide what your actual and working goals are**
   For most people, the actual goal is to win. This doesn't mean you aren't there to have fun, but ultimately, winning is your goal. However, if you go out to a match with this in mind, you might not play your best—this type of thinking will only make you more nervous. Instead, have an "acting goal," i.e. a goal that will maximize your chances of winning. Generally, make "playing your best" (which includes tactical play!) your active goal. If you play your best, your chances of winning are maximized, right? You may vary this, however; if you tend to play too passive, for example, your working goal might be to play aggressively. Or your goal might be to hustle like crazy, or to fight like a maniac. (My working goal in tournaments is always the same: "Push yourself!" I say this to myself over and over during matches, and it helps me to hustle, to play aggressively, and to focus.)

5. **Arrange a warm-up partner and practice routine in advance**
   The night before the tournament, arrange who you will warm up with and when. Pick someone who you are comfortable warming up with. This is not the time to practice against someone whose game gives you trouble, or plays what seems to you a "weird" style—that's what you should have been practicing against at the club in the weeks before the tournament. On the day of the tournament, you want someone who can help you groove your shots. Once your shots are warmed up, you can then adjust to the many wacky styles you may face, as well as more standard ones. Decide in advance what drills you want to do; don't just do forehand to forehand and backhand to backhand; make sure to do footwork drills and serve & receive drills. Make sure to either play out points or play some games before you go out for your tournament match—you don't want the first real points you play to be a tournament match! Make sure to arrive at least an hour or

Table Tennis Tactics for Thinkers

more before your first match—sometimes you may have trouble finding an open table to practice on, and if you don't allow enough time, you may get stuck playing without a sufficient warm-up.

6. **Bring food and beverages, and eat lightly**
   Good food and beverage services at tournament sites are rare. If you want something other than water, bring your own drinks (Gatorade or other sports drinks, for example), as well as snacks (such as fruit). Avoid eating a large meal during the tournament unless you have a couple of hours free afterwards. It's best to snack regularly on easily digested food (mostly carbohydrates), or you will be somewhat tired while you digest the larger meal.

7. **Prepare for slippery floors**
   One of the most common mistakes I see is not preparing for a slippery floor. Over half of tournaments are played on flooring that is not grippy enough for you to play your best. Many players don't even realize how much it is affecting them until they do something about it—and their playing level shoots up. What can you do? There are several options. First, make sure you have good, grippy table tennis shoes. I used to bring two pairs of shoes to tournaments—one normal pair, and one "extra grippy" for really slippery floors. Second, bring a small towel or paper towels to a tournament. If the floors are slippery, dampen the towel, and put it to the side of the table. Every few points, rub your feet on them. You'll find it makes a huge difference. (You can't always get paper towels at a tournament, since some bathrooms use air driers.)

8. **Practice your serves**
   The day of the tournament (and hopefully the day before), practice your serves. Tuning them up will pay off more for you, time-for-time, than just about any other practice that day. Yet most players don't warm up their serves before a match, and so don't have their best serves available. (This assumes the player has spent time developing effective serves. If not, then practicing ineffective serves isn't going to help much at this point.)

9. **Prepare physically**
   Prepare your muscles for combat. Before warming up, do some easy jogging to get them warm. Do a thorough stretching routine. Before each match, you might do some short but vigorous physical activity to get the muscles prepared. You might shadow practice, or

do a few sprints, but don't tire yourself out so much that you can't play the match. Somewhat related to this is getting enough sleep in the last few days before the tournament. (Studies have shown that it's actually more important getting enough sleep in the last few days before a sports activity than the actual night before—but both are important.)

10. **Do some meditation and mental visualization**
    You will play better if you take some time before a match to clear your mind and do some mental visualization. Go somewhere quiet, and blank your mind out. Then visualize yourself doing the shots you plan on doing. A few minutes of this is worth more than an equal amount of practice time on the table.

Table Tennis Tactics for Thinkers

CHAPTER TWENTY-ONE
Coaching Tournament Matches

Stellan Bengtsson coaching Teddy Tran.
Photo by Bruce Liu

While this book was written for both coaches and players, this section is written mostly for coaches. This is a book about table tennis tactics, and that is the primary purpose of coaching tournament matches, so we definitely need a section on it. Players should benefit as well, since they are the recipients of this coaching, and they need to maximize this benefit.

Many players either give or receive coaching at tournaments at some point. But what magic words of wisdom can a coach say between games that can transform a losing game into inspired victory?

If I had those words, I'd sell them for a lot of money.

Not having those words to give to you, here is the next best thing: what type of things you can say, as a coach, to get the most out of the short time you have between games with your player. It might not transform your player into a member of the National Team (or maybe it will), but it might turn a close loss into a victory, and might even make a lopsided match close.

Start by judging the player's emotional state. Is he too tense? Too lackadaisical? If the first, your first job is to calm him down. If the latter, you must wake him up.

If you are coaching an overly excitable player, make sure to be calm and relaxed when you speak to him. Speak slowly and clearly. Tell him to take his time and clear his mind. If he is angry with himself, you have to get him to put that aside, maybe even say a joke to get his mind off whatever is bothering him. You have to clear his mind.

If the player seems lackluster, this doesn't mean you do the reverse and talk fast and excitedly. (An interesting idea!) Tell him to *fight!* Use your own emotions to psych him up. Perhaps *be* a little excited. Let him know that his match is important, and perhaps he will start to think so as well. Note that a player often wants to win a match badly, and wants to try hard, but cannot get himself up for the match without help. You are that help.

Now that your player is properly psyched up and/or calm and relaxed, what do you tell him? The basic rule is: Not Too Much.

If you fill your player's mind with ten intricate tactics for winning, all you've accomplished is confusing your player's mind. He's not going to remember much of it, if any. It's best to decide the most important things, and forget the rest. Keep it simple. Remember KISS, which in this case can be for "Keep it Short and Simple."

Massimo Costantini coaching U.S. junior star Lily Zhang.
Photo by Bruce Liu

Remember the very start of chapter one? "Tactics isn't about finding complex strategies to defeat an opponent. Tactics is about sifting through all the zillions of possible tactics and finding a few simple ones that work." Remember this both when you play and when you coach.

A good breakdown of advice between games would be, at most, two or three things about serving, one or two things about receiving, and one or two things about rallying. But remember that less is often more—you don't want to come up with the maximum number of items for each of these three areas. Sometimes you might only do perhaps one thing about serve, one about receive, and one about rallying. Or perhaps some other combination of two or three things.

During a rally a player can't stop and think about each shot. The only time he can do that is when he is serving. Therefore, service tactics are the most useful ones that can be given, and the most easily followed.

Service tactics can be broken down into the same two types as they were in the chapter on Service Tactics: set-up serves and trick serves. Set-up serves are those that the player should use most often, i.e. perhaps serve short backspin to the forehand and follow with a loop, or maybe serve fast and deep and following up by hitting. Trick serves are those that a player can use to get a "free" point, but can only be used occasionally, such as a fast down-the-line serve to the forehand, or a fast no-spin to the middle. A good coach can figure out which of these types of serves will be most effective.

Receive tactics are often very specific. Should the player loop the deep serve? Against short serves, should the player mostly flip, push short, or push long? Should he return serves to the forehand or backhand side?

Table Tennis Tactics for Thinkers

But remember to remind the player to vary the receive. Often a player, in following the coach's advice, becomes predictable.

Rallying tactics are the hardest for most players to follow—they can't stop and think over what to do, and usually they're busy getting back into position, rather than being in a ready position as when receiving. Give simple and more general strategy, such as "Stay close to the table," or "Look for chances to attack his middle." Or the generic, "Play aggressive!"

Service tactics should often be combined with how the serve should be followed up, since that's normally the whole purpose of the serve. For example, you may tell a player to do a certain serve mostly short to the forehand and follow with a loop mostly to the opponent's elbow.

One thing that often comes up: when coaching kids, don't talk down to them. Literally. Squat down to their level. Deep down, it's psychologically intimidating to have to crane your neck to look up at a coach, who is looking down at you while spewing his words of wisdom.

USA Men's Coach Stefan Feth coaching Michael Landers at the Worlds. Photo by Diego Schaaf

Also be careful about being preachy when coaching. Make it a two-way thing—there's no crime in asking the player what his tactics are, and then expanding on what he's already doing. Before a match, before I say anything tactical, I sometimes ask the player I'm coaching, "What's your game plan?" If he has a good one, then all I do is expand on it.

Stay upbeat and positive. If you're not happy with what the player is doing, there's a temptation to be negative or start lecturing in a preachy fashion. This doesn't help. Instead, stay positive as you coach. Always remember that what may seem simple from the sidelines isn't always so simple at the table.

Never bring up the opponent's rating. If the opponent is higher, it might intimidate your player, while if it's lower, it puts pressure on them to win against this "weaker" opponent. Never mention how important the match is or anything else that might bring unneeded pressure to the match. In fact, do the opposite to remove pressure. I often tell players to imagine it's just another match at the club.

Make sure you are familiar with a player's game and skills if you are coaching him. The last thing you want to do is tell him to do something he isn't able to do at a proficient level, or isn't comfortable with. You might want to ask the player to let you know if there's anything you are saying that he's not comfortable with—otherwise you may never find out, and your coaching may be counterproductive.

Li Zhenshi coaching Jim Butler at the 1995 World Team Cup.
Photo by Michael Wetzel

Except occasionally at the beginning levels, between games is not the time to talk about technique. It's too late; techniques have to be ingrained in advance. Occasionally a coach can spot a basic technique flaw that was causing the player to miss, but it's rare that the player can make an adjustment on the fly in the middle of a match. However, there are exceptions.

Sometimes a coach doesn't even have to coach much; sometimes all a player needs is someone he can explain his tactics to, to help him clarify his own thinking, though you should speak up if you have something to add. A good coach should be a good listener before and after matches, and even during a match, within the constraints of the short amount of time he has between games and in time-outs (one minute in each case).

A coach might also want to call a **time-out** at a key point in a match. See the section on this in the chapter on Conventional Tactics. Remember that the final decision on whether to take a time-out is the player's, so I always tell my players in advance that if I call a time-out, but they feel they are focused and know what to do, they should turn it down and save the time-out for later when they may better need it.

Now for the clincher. If you are a player and don't have a coach when you play, you can follow the above and coach yourself between games. Break things down as shown above, and pretty soon you'll be your favorite, most reliable coach.

AFTERWORD
Tactical and Strategic Thinking Revisited

Throughout this book I've talked about tactical and strategic thinking, both theoretical and in practice. I didn't want to put together a mindless checklist for every possible style playing against every other possible style—as noted earlier, that just isn't possible, and it wasn't what I was aiming for. Instead, the primary goal was to develop the *habit* of thinking tactically and strategically, as well as a fundamental tactical understanding of the various playing styles. So I'll finish this book with the question I asked in the Introduction, and whose answer will determine whether this book was successful.

Did I make you think?

Larry Hodges

Great tactics can lead to smashing success!
Photo of Peter Pradit by Mal Anderson

Table Tennis Tactics for Thinkers

GLOSSARY

American grip—See Seemiller grip.

Antispin—An inverted rubber sheet that is very slick so that spin does not take on it. It usually has a very dead sponge underneath. It is mostly used for defensive shots. Also known as "anti."

Backhand—A shot normally done with the racket to the left of the elbow for a right-hander, to the right for a left-hander.

Backspin—A type of spin used mostly on defensive shots. When you chop the ball, you produce backspin. The bottom of the ball will move away from you. The backspin pulls the ball up, while gravity pulls it down, so the ball tends to travel in a line. It is also called underspin or chop.

Banana flip (or flick)—A wristy backhand return of a short ball that's sort of a mini-loop, with topspin and sidespin, with racket moving from right to left (for a righty). Against a sidespin serve, you would mostly do this when you can go with the spin, i.e. against a forehand sidespin-type serve between two righties. The path the racket goes through is roughly like a banana.

Blade—The racket without covering.

Block—A quick, off the bounce return of an aggressive drive done by holding the racket in the ball's path.

Blocker—A style of play where blocking is the primary shot.

Chop—A defensive return of a drive with backspin, usually done from well away from the table. It is also sometimes used as another name for backspin.

Chop-block—A block against topspin where the racket is chopped down at contact to create backspin.

Chopper—A style of play where chopping is the primary shot. (See Chop.)

Closed racket—If the racket's hitting surface is aimed downward, with the top edge leaning away from you, it is closed.

Conventional penhold backhand—The way most penholders used to hit their backhands, using the same side of the racket as their forehands, and mostly blocking. This means less weakness in the middle and a better block, but limits the backhand attack.

Corkscrewspin—a type of spin that makes the ball jump sideways when it hits the table, most often done off a high-toss serve.

Counter-drive—A drive made against a drive. Some players specialize in counter-driving. Also known as counter-hitting.

Counter-hitter—See counter-drive.

Counter-loop—To loop against a loop.

Counter-smash—To smash against a smash.

Crosscourt—A ball that is hit diagonally from corner to corner.

Crossover—A style of footwork that require you to cross your feet. It is used to cover the wide forehand.

Dead—A ball with no spin.

Deep—A ball that will not bounce twice on the opponent's side of the table if given the chance.

Default—Getting disqualified from a match.

Double bounce—A ball that hits the same side of the table twice. The person on that side loses the point.

Down-the-line—A ball that is hit along the side of the table, parallel to the sidelines.

Drive—An aggressive topspin shot done forehand or backhand, but without as much topspin as a loop. Some players call an aggressive loop a "loop drive."

Drop shot—Putting the ball so short that the opponent has trouble reaching the ball. It is usually done when the opponent is away from the table. Given the chance, the ball would normally bounce twice on the table.

Fishing—A defensive topspin return from off the table, with the ball often returned a few feet or more above the net, but not as high as a lob.

Flat drive—A drive where the ball hits the racket almost straight on, putting little topspin on the ball.

Flick—See Flip.

Flip—An aggressive topspin attack of a short ball. In Europe it is called a flick.

Forehand—A shot normally done with the racket to the right of the elbow for a right-hander, to the left for a left-hander.

Free hand—The hand not holding the racket.

Half-long serve—A serve where, given the chance, the second bounce would be near the end line, making it difficult to loop. There are varying definitions for this. Some say the second bounce of a half-long serve always goes just off the end, so the end line gets in the way if the opponent tries to loop. Others say that the second bounce should always be just short of the end, so the serve is as deep as possible while still being short enough that it can't normally be looped. Others say that these are both half-long as long as the second bounce is near the end line. It is also called a "tweeny serve."

Handicap events—An event in a tournament where points are spotted to make the match even.

Hard rubber—A type of racket covering with pips out rubber but no sponge underneath. It was the most common covering for many years until the development of sponge rubber. Also called pimpled rubber.

Hardbat—A racket covered with hard rubber. Hardbat was the primary rackets used from the 1930s until the 1950s.

Heavy—A ball with a lot of spin, usually backspin.

Heavy no-spin—A no-spin shot, usually the serve, with a lot of motion to fake spin.

High-toss serve—A serve where the ball is thrown high into the air. This increases both spin and deception but is hard to control.

Hitter—A style of play where hitting is the primary shot.

Hook loop—a sidespin loop where a forehand loop breaks left (for a righty), or (less common) a righty's backhand loop breaks right (also for a righty).

Hyperbolic serve—An extremely fast serve with extreme topspin, often done with a forehand motion, but with contact made with the backhand side of the racket (by aiming the forehand side up) with an extremely fast topspin motion. It's a relatively new serve, though there are reports of players doing this long ago. It's the fastest serve in table tennis.

Inside-out loop—a sidespin loop where a forehand loop breaks right (for a righty), or (less common) a righty's backhand loop breaks left (also for a righty).

Table Tennis Tactics for Thinkers

Inverted sponge—The most common racket covering. It consists of a sheet of pimpled rubber on top of a layer of sponge. The pips point inward, so the surface is smooth. This is the opposite of pips-out sponge, where the pips point outward.

ITTF—International Table Tennis Federation. The governing body for table tennis in the world. See www.ittf.com.

Kill shot—See smash.

Let—If play is interrupted for any reason during a rally, a let is called and the point does not count.

Loaded—A ball with a great deal of spin.

Lob—A high defensive return of a smash, usually done with topspin or sidespin.

Long—See Deep.

Long pips—A type of pips-out rubber where the pips are long and thin and bend on contact with the ball. It returns the ball with whatever spin was on it, and is very difficult to play against if you are not used to it.

Loop—A heavy topspin shot, done forehand or backhand, and the dominant shot at the higher levels. Most players either specialize in looping or in handling the opponent's loop.

Looper—A style of play where the primary shot is the loop.

Match—Usually best three out of five games to 11. Sometimes matches are best two out of three (rarely in tournaments) or best four out of seven games, also to 11.

Middle (deep balls)—On deep balls, a ball to the middle goes to the opponent's crossover point between forehand and backhand, usually around the elbow.

Middle (short balls)—On short balls, a ball to the middle of the table, near the doubles line.

Neutral racket—The racket is neither open nor closed, and so is perpendicular to the floor.

Open racket—If the hitting surface of the racket is aimed upwards, with the top edge leaning towards you, it is open.

Pendulum serve—The most common serve at higher levels. The serve is done on the forehand side, with the racket tip down, and the racket moving from right to left (for a right-hander). (See also Reverse Pendulum serve.)

Penholder—A type of grip used mostly by Asians. It generally gives a strong forehand but sometimes a more awkward backhand if done conventionally instead of with a reverse penhold backhand.

Pips—The small conical bits of pimpled rubber that cover a sheet of table tennis rubber.

Pips-out—A type of racket covering. It consists of a sheet of pips-out rubber on top of a layer of sponge. The pips point outward, the opposite of inverted. Also called short pips.

Playing surface—The top of the table, including the edges.

Push—A backspin return of backspin.

Pushblocker—A player who returns nearly everything with quick, dead blocks, even against backspin, usually with long pips (often without sponge), sometimes with hardbat or antispin.

Racket—The blade plus covering.

Racket hand—The hand that holds the racket.

Rally—The hitting of the ball back and forth, commencing with the serve and ending when a point is won.

Rating—A number that is assigned to all tournament players after their first tournament. The better the player the higher the rating should be. The range is from just above 0 to nearly 3000. See USATT ratings.

Rating events—An event in a tournament where to be eligible you must be rated under a specified number.

Receive—The return of a serve.

Reverse pendulum serve—Like a pendulum serve, except the racket moves from left to right (for a right-hander), creating the reverse type of spin. This is one of the most popular serves at the higher levels. (See also Pendulum serve.)

Reverse penhold backhand—A backhand by a penhold player where he hits with the opposite side of the racket rather than using the same side for forehand and backhand (i.e. a conventional penhold backhand). Most top penholders now play their backhands this way as it gives a stronger backhand attack, though it leaves the player weaker in the middle and often isn't as good for blocking.

Rubber—The racket covering. Sometimes refers only to the rubber on top of a sponge base.

Rubber cleaner—Used to keep the surface of inverted rubber clean.

Sandwich rubber—A sponge base covered by a sheet of rubber with pips, with the pips pointing either in or out. If pointed in, it is inverted sponge. If pointed out, it is pips-out sponge.

Seemiller grip—A grip that is often used in the United States. Named after five-times U.S. National Champion Dan Seemiller, who first developed it. Most coaches consider it an inferior grip, and outside the U.S. it is almost unheard of. Also called the American Grip.

Serve—The first shot in a rally, done by the server. It begins with the ball being thrown up from the palm of the hand and struck by the racket.

Shakehands grip—The most popular grip. It gives the best balance of forehand and backhand.

Short—A ball that would bounce twice on the opponent's side of the table if given the chance.

Short pips—See pips-out.

Shovel serve—A forehand serve where the racket is almost parallel to the floor. By pointing the racket tip slightly up or down the server can create serves with sidespin in either direction.

Sidespin—a type of spin that makes the ball jump sideways when it hits the opponent's racket.

Sidespin block—A block with sidespin.

Smash—A putaway shot. Ball is hit with enough speed so opponent cannot make a return.

Smother kill—To smash right off the bounce. Usually done against a lob.

Spin—The rotation of the ball.

Sponge—The bouncy rubber material used in sandwich rubber. It is used under a sheet of rubber with pips. It revolutionized the game and ended the hard rubber age in the 1950's. Inverted sponge dominates the game, especially at the higher levels.

Strategic thinking—Finding a way to improve your game so you win more in the future.

Table Tennis Tactics for Thinkers

Strawberry flip (or flick)—A wristy backhand return of a short ball that's sort of a mini-loop, with topspin and sidespin, with racket moving from left to right (for a righty). Against a sidespin serve, you would mostly do this when you can go with the spin, i.e. against a backhand sidespin-type serve between two righties. This is a relatively rare and difficult shot, meaning the surprise factor if you learn it is high. Most players and coaches probably haven't even heard of this shot. (Why is it called a Strawberry flip? Because it's the opposite of a Banana Flip, and another fruit name was needed! It was named this by Stefan Feth.)

Stroke—Any shot used in the game, including the serve.

Tactical thinking—Finding a way to win a given match.

Time-out—During a match, each player is allowed a single one-minute time-out. This allows the player to rest, clear his mind, think about tactics, or talk to a coach.

Topspin—A type of spin used on most aggressive shots, with an extreme amount being used in the loop shot. When you topspin the ball, the top of the ball moves away from you. Topspin pulls the ball down.

Tomahawk serve—A forehand serve with the racket tip up, and the racket moving from left to right (for a right-hander).

Tweeny serve—Another name for a half-long serve.

Two-step footwork—A popular style of footwork.

Umpire—The official who keeps score and enforces rules during a match.

Underspin—See backspin.

USATT—USA Table Tennis. The governing body for table tennis in the United States. Until the 1990s it was the United States Table Tennis Association (USTTA). See www.usatt.org.

USATT Ratings—A rating system run by USA Table Tennis. Beginners start off somewhere under 1000. An average club player is around 1500, an average tournament player around 1800, a "master" player is 2000 or perhaps 2200, U.S. team members are in the 2500-2750 range, and the best players in the world approach 2900. Roughly speaking, a player will upset a player rated 100 points higher about one out of six times.

U.S. Table Tennis Hall of Fame—Each year the U.S. Table Tennis Hall of Fame Committee inducts players and contributors into the U.S. Table Tennis Hall of Fame, with 138 members as of January, 2013. See http://usatt-halloffame.org

Volley—To hit the ball before it bounces on your side of the table. It results in an immediate loss of the point.

APPENDIX
Recommended Reading

The following is a list of coaching-related table tennis books that I can recommend. For a complete listing of my table tennis book collection—211 books at this writing—see: www.larrytt.com/ttbooks.html

General Table Tennis Coaching Books
- **Breaking 2000,** by Alex Polyakov, 2012
- **Table Tennis: Tips from a World Champion**, by Werner Schlager and Bernd-Ulrich Gross, 2011
- **Professional Table Tennis Coaches Handbook**, by Larry Hodges, 2010
- **PATT Notes: Volume One**, by Donn Olsen with Kyongsook Kim, 2010
- **PATT: A Principles Approach to Table Tennis**, by Donn Olsen with Kyongsook Kim, 2009
- **Advanced Coaching Manual**, by ITTF, 2009
- **Table Tennis: Steps to Success** (new version), by Richard McAfee, 2009
- **Table Tennis: Steps to Success** (original version), by Larry Hodges, 1993, updated in 2007; New version titled **Table Tennis Success** coming out in 2013
- **Table Tennis: Level 1 Coaching Manual**, by Glenn Tepper & ITTF, 2003
- **J-O Waldner: When the Feeling Decides**, by Jens Fellke, 2003
- **Table Tennis 2000: Technique with Vladimir Samsonov**, by Radivoj Hudetz, 2000
- **Table Tennis From A to Z**, by Dimosthenis E. Messinis, 2000
- **Instructor's Guide to Table Tennis**, by Larry Hodges, 1989, updated by Dan Seemiller and Mark Nordby in 2000
- **Learn Table Tennis in a Weekend**, by Andrzej Grubba, 1998
- **Train to Win**, by Michel Gadal, 1997
- **Winning Table Tennis**, by Dan Seemiller & Mark Holowchak, 1996

Books on Sports Psychology
- **Get Your Game Face On! Table Tennis**, by Dora Kurimay and Kathy Toon, 2012
- **With Winning in Mind**, by Lanny Bassham, updated in 2011
- **Finding Your Zone**, by Michael Lardon, M.D., 2008
- **The Inner Game of Tennis**, by W. Timothy Gallwey, 1997
- **Winning Ugly**, by Brad Gilbert, 1994

Table Tennis Tactics for Thinkers

ABOUT THE AUTHOR

USA Table Tennis Hall of Famer Larry Hodges has spent most of the past two decades coaching at the Maryland Table Tennis Center in Gaithersburg, MD, along with co-coaches Cheng Yinghua and Jack Huang. He is certified as a National Coach, the highest level of coaching certification in USA Table Tennis. He was also one of the initial two ITTF certified coaches from the U.S. in 2010. He maintains the coaching site TableTennisCoaching.com, with numerous coaching articles, videos, and his daily table tennis blog.

He's a former chair of the USATT's Coaching committee. In 2002 he was named Developmental Coach of the Year for Table Tennis by USATT, and in 2014 was named the Doc Counsilman Coach of the Year. He has been the match coach for over 200 Junior Olympic and Junior National gold medallists, more than any other USA table tennis coach. He has worked with many of the best players in the country, both in Maryland and as manager and later a director and coach at the Olympic Training Center from 1985-1989. For many years he coached the U.S. National Junior Team at major tournaments in the U.S. and around the world. He has taught table tennis in colleges, schools, and clubs all over the United States.

Photo by John Oros

As of January, 2015, he was the author of over 1500 published articles in over 140 different publications, including over 1300 on table tennis, over half of them coaching articles. He has six other books on table tennis: *Table Tennis Steps to Success* (28,000 copies sold, in six languages); *Table Tennis Tales & Techniques*; *Instructor's Guide to Table Tennis*; *Professional Table Tennis Coaches Handbook*, and *Table Tennis Tips*. (They are on sale at LarryHodgesBooks.com.) He was editor of *USA Table Tennis Magazine* (cir. 8000) for 12 years and 71 issues.

Larry began playing table tennis in 1976 at age 16. He has been ranked among the top 20 players in the U.S. and has won state championships in Maryland, Colorado and North Carolina. He was U.S. National Collegiate Doubles and two-time Team Champion for University of Maryland, where he received a bachelor's degree in Math and a master's degree in Journalism. Although he normally uses sponge, he also has 22 national titles in hardbat table tennis, including U.S. National and U.S. Open Singles Champion, 13-times National or Open Doubles Champion, and 4-time Over 40 Champion.

When he's not coaching, playing, or writing about table tennis, Larry enjoys reading and writing science fiction & fantasy—he's a member of Science Fiction Writers of American, with over 60 short story sales. See his science fiction & fantasy page at www.larryhodges.org.

Other Table Tennis Books by Larry Hodges

For ordering and other info, see **larryhodgesbooks.com**

Table Tennis: Steps to Success
(New version may arrive in 2015 as Table Tennis Fundamentals)

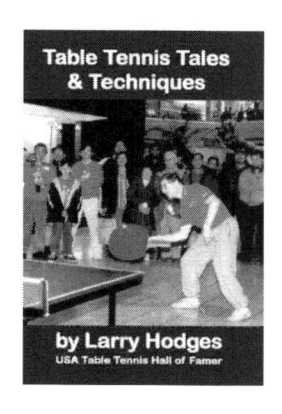

Table Tennis Tales & Techniques

Table Tennis Tips

Professional Table Tennis Coaches Handbook

Instructor's Guide to Table Tennis
(new version may arrive in 2015)

And don't forget to check out **TableTennisCoaching.com** and read Larry's daily Table Tennis Blog!

Table Tennis Tactics for Thinkers

NAME INDEX

Adam Hugh 120
Ai Fukuhara 142
Amaresh Sahu... 73
Andy Li... 73
Ariel Hsing.. 110
Bobby Fischer 3
Brian Masters.. 140
Chen Qi 153
Cheng Yinghua................. 16, 21, 144, 238
Crystal Wang.. 24
Dan Seemiller 67, 68, 78, 79, 106, 140, 146
Daniel Habesohn....................................... 124
Dave Sakai...34, 94
David Zhuang 139, 146, 160
Dean Johnson.. 213
Dell Sweeris 3
Deng Yaping.................................... 193, 201
Derek Nie...................................74, 78, 219
Dick Miles 212, 213
Dimitrij Ovtcharovby 90
Ding Ning 88
Doru Gheorghe 72
Dragutin Surbek...................................... 187
Eric Boggan 79, 140
Gao Jun 72, 145, 168
Guo Yan 84
Guo Yuehua 171
Han Xiao 21, 144, 220
Hans Hsu 222
Hiroshi Takahashi.................................... 139
Ilija Lupulesku....................................... 146
Jack Huang.........................21, 24, 238
Jan-Ove Waldner 8, 46, 83, 91
Jeffrey Zeng Xun 21
Jim Butler 230
John Hsu 52, 222
John Tannehill... 3
Jonathan Ou 6
Joo Se Hyuk 42
Kalinikos Kreanga 125

Kasume Ishikawa.................................... 216
Kjell Johansson 187
Li Zhenshi.. 230
Lily Zhang... 228
Liu Guoliang.. 215
Lou Pagliaro... 213
Ma Long 153, 170, 215, 218
Marty Reisman 203, 207, 212, 213
Maryland Table Tennis Center 4, 17, 79, 144, 238
Massimo Costantini................................ 228
Michael Landers........................... 118, 229
Mikael Appelgren..................................... 77
Nathan Hsu 81, 222
Peter Pradit 231
Rick Seemiller 140
Roy Ke 219
Ryu Seung Min 59
Scott Boggan... 77
Sol Schiff 212, 213
Stefan Feth 122, 229
Stellan Bengtsson................................... 227
Steve Berger.. 207
Teddy Tran 227
Timo Boll 15, 115
Timothy Wang 147, 220
Todd Sweeris 80
Tong Tong Gong................6, 21, 81, 142
Ty Hoff 207, 214
USA Table Tennis 4, 5, 7, 11, 17, 79, 202, 209, 236, 238, 239
Viktor Barna 162
Viktoria Pavlovich 179
Wang Hao 85, 139
Wang Liqin.. 149
Wang Qing Liang.................................... 177
Werner Schlager................9, 27, 38, 237
Xu Xin 138, 215, 218
Yahao Zhang 222
Zhang Jike 86, 121

Printed in Great Britain
by Amazon.co.uk, Ltd.,
Marston Gate.